PACIFICATION IN ALGERIA

1956–1958

David Galula

New Foreword by Bruce Hoffman

This research is supported by the Advanced Research Projects Agency under Contract No. SD-79. Any views or conclusions contained in this Memorandum should not be interpreted as representing the official opinion or policy of ARPA. *Pacification in Algeria, 1956–1958* was originally published by the RAND Corporation in 1963. This new RAND edition includes the original text and a new foreword.

Library of Congress Cataloging-in-Publication Data

Galula, David, 1919–1967.
    Pacification in Algeria, 1956–1958 / David Galula.
      p. cm.
    Originally published in 1963.
    "MG-478-1."
    Includes bibliographical references.
    ISBN 0-8330-3920-2 (pbk. : alk. paper)
    1. Galula, David, 1919–1967. 2. Algeria—History—Revolution, 1954–1962—
Personal narratives, French.
    3. Counterinsurgency—Algeria. I. Title.

DT295.3.G378A3 2006
965'.04642092—dc22

                                                  2006004404

The RAND Corporation is a nonprofit research organization providing objective analysis and effective solutions that address the challenges facing the public and private sectors around the world. RAND's publications do not necessarily reflect the opinions of its research clients and sponsors.

RAND® is a registered trademark.

Cover design by Eileen Delson La Russo

© Copyright 2006 RAND Corporation

All rights reserved. No part of this book may be reproduced in any form by any electronic or mechanical means (including photocopying, recording, or information storage and retrieval) without permission in writing from RAND.

Published 2006 by the RAND Corporation
1776 Main Street, P.O. Box 2138, Santa Monica, CA 90407-2138
1200 South Hayes Street, Arlington, VA 22202-5050
4570 Fifth Avenue, Suite 600, Pittsburgh, PA 15213-2665
RAND URL: http://www.rand.org/
To order RAND documents or to obtain additional information, contact
Distribution Services: Telephone: (310) 451-7002;
Fax: (310) 451-6915; Email: order@rand.org

Foreword to the New Edition

> I felt I had learned enough about insurgencies, and I wanted to test certain theories I had formed on counterinsurgency warfare. For all these reasons I volunteered for duty in Algeria as soon as I reached France.

Thus begins Lt Col David Galula's account of his two years commanding a company of French troops in the Kabylia district, east of Algiers, at the height of the 1954–62 Algerian War of Independence. That uprising against French rule is remembered, if at all, as the last of the immediate post–World War II nationalist struggles waged by a colonized population against its European masters. For that reason, perhaps, France's experiences in Algeria were mostly ignored by other countries, including the United States, which later found itself fighting remarkably similar insurgencies in Southeast Asia and Latin America, and today in Southwest Asia (e.g., Iraq).

This inability to absorb and apply, much less even study, the lessons learned in previous counterinsurgency campaigns is a problem that has long afflicted the world's governments and militaries when they are confronted with insurgencies. Guerrilla groups and terrorist organizations, on the other hand, learn lessons very well. They not only study their own mistakes, but also the successful operations of their enemies, and they adapt nimbly. Insurgent and terrorist movements as diverse as al Fatah, the African National Congress, the Provisional Irish Republican Army, and the Tamil Tigers, for example, have cited the Algerian struggle's influence on the strategies and tactics that they later adopted. Among the officer corps of most countries' standing armies, however, counterinsurgency—at least until very recently—was disdained as a "lesser included contingency" unworthy of contemplation, much less serious study.

David Galula was different—even if his background and the army in which he served conformed to this same historical stereotype. A 1940 graduate of Saint-Cyr, France's equivalent of West Point, Galula's early career path seemed to follow the typical trajectory of a French infantry officer of his generation. Blooded in battle during the campaigns to liberate North Africa and France, Galula participated in the invasion and subsequent occupation of Germany. In 1945, he was posted to the French Embassy in Beijing, eventually becoming the assistant military attaché. China at that time was in the grip of one of modern history's greatest upheavals: the mass insurgency cum peoples' revolution led by Mao Tse-tung. Between 1945 and 1948, Galula witnessed first-hand the Chinese civil war and became thoroughly acquainted with the principles and implementation of guerrilla strategy and tactics.

Later, as a military observer with the United Nations Special Commission on the Balkans, Galula was able to build upon and hone his knowledge of this distinctive mode of warfare during Greece's insurgent-driven civil war. His next assignment was as French military attaché to Hong Kong, a key posting that afforded Galula still further opportunities to refine his expertise in insurgent warfare. He arrived just as insurgencies were either raging or gathering momentum in French Indochina, Britain's imperial possessions on the Malay peninsula, and America's former colony, the Philippines. Given Hong Kong's close proximity to all three places, Galula had a unique vantage point from which he was able to maintain close personal contacts with his fellow officers serving in Indochina and their British counterparts in Malaya. He rounded off this self-directed study of insurgency and counterinsurgency with visits to the Philippines. There, Galula saw the results of the successful campaign against the Huk guerrillas.

In February 1956, Galula returned to France and immediately requested assignment to Algeria. On August 1, 1956, then-Captain Galula reported for duty with the 45th B.I.C. (Colonial Infantry Battalion) in Kabylia, a region of intense insurgent activity where French pacification efforts had proven to be both frustrating and problematical. His recollections, mostly as a company commander but also as deputy battalion commander during the last four months of his tour, still have a remarkable, almost timeless resonance nearly half a century later. The parallels with America's own recent experiences in Iraq are striking. A few examples follow:

- **The absence of counterinsurgency doctrine:** "In my zone, as everywhere in Algeria, the order was to 'pacify.' But exactly how? The sad truth was that, in spite of all our past experience, we had no single, official doctrine for counterinsurgency warfare."
- **The perils of failure to recognize the signs of a budding insurgency:** "'Ordinary banditry,' said a high-ranking government official in Algiers . . . By the time the insurrection was finally recognized for what it was, only drastic political and military action would have reversed the tide, and slowly in any case."
- **The insurgents' urban terrorist strategy:** "The rebels realized that they could achieve the greatest psychological effect on the French and on world opinion at the cheapest price by stepping up terrorism in the main cities, notably in Algiers, which served as headquarters to most French and foreign correspondents and thus acted as a natural amplifier. A grenade or a bomb in a café there would produce far more noise than an obscure ambush against French soldiers in the Ouarsenis Mountains."
- **The imperative of separating the population from the insurgents:** "Our forces were vastly superior to the rebels. Then why couldn't we finish with them quickly? Because they managed to mobilize the population through terror and persuasion . . . It was therefore imperative that we isolate the rebels from the population and that we gain the support of the population. This implied that under no circumstances could we afford to antagonize the population even if we had to take risks for ourselves in sparing it."
- **The concomitant imperative of not inadvertently alienating the indigenous population:** "If we distinguish between people and rebels, then we have a chance. One cannot catch a fly with vinegar. My rules are this: outwardly treat every civilian as a friend; inwardly you must consider him as a rebel ally until you have positive proof to the contrary."

- **Promoting women's rights to counteract support for the insurgents:** "Reflecting on who might be our potential allies in the population, I thought that the Kabyle women, given their subjugated condition, would naturally be on our side if we emancipated them."
- **The emphasis on policing rather than military tactics in countering an insurgency:** "While the insurgent does not hesitate to use terror, the counterinsurgent has to engage in police work . . . The police work was not to my liking, but it was vital and therefore I accepted it."
- **The fallacy of a decapitation strategy to defeat an insurgency:** "Then, five top leaders of the rebellion, including Ben Bella, had been neatly caught during a flight from Rabat to Tunis. Their capture, I admit, had little effect on the direction of the rebellion, because the movement was too loosely organized to crumble under such a blow."
- **The critical importance in a counterinsurgency of an effective information operations campaign:** "If there was a field in which we were definitely and infinitely more stupid than our opponents, it was propaganda."
- **The importance of sealing off the borders:** "The borders with Morocco and Tunisia would easily have required 100,000 men to control with reasonable effectiveness, given their length and the local terrain. In order to save personnel, it was decided to build an artificial fence, a project which was completed along both borders by the spring of 1958."
- **The importance of according humane treatment to captured insurgents:** "Throughout the war our prisoner camps were open for unannounced inspection by the International Red Cross, the reports of which were made public . . . In the best camps, efforts were made to sift the tough prisoners from the soft; where it was not done, the camps became schools for rebel cadres."

Although many, if not all, of these seminal insights into the dynamics of insurgency and counterinsurgency can be found in Galula's well-known treatise on the subject, *Counterinsurgency Warfare: Theory and Practice,*[1] they in fact come from a recently rediscovered, vastly more comprehensive account of his experiences in Algeria, written for the RAND Corporation in 1963. Galula was one of the expert practitioners of counterinsurgency and guerrilla warfare invited to a symposium convened by RAND in 1962.[2] He so distinguished himself at the forum that its chairman, Dr. Stephen T. Hosmer, invited Galula to write a detailed, in-depth study of counterinsurgency for RAND. The resulting publication, *Pacification in Algeria, 1956–1958,* follows. In keeping with the perennial amnesia that has long surrounded the study of insurgency and counterinsurgency, it too was generally forgotten until a chance conversation at a social event between Fred C. Iklé, a head of RAND's Social Sciences Department during the 1960s, and *Washington Post* reporter Tom Ricks set in motion the chain of events that led Michael Rich, RAND's executive vice president, to decide to reissue it now.

"I am not writing all this," Galula says near the end of *Pacification in Algeria,* "to show what a genius I was, but to point out how difficult it is to convince people, especially the military, to change traditional ways and adapt themselves to new conditions." His words, written over forty years ago, have a continuing, undeniable relevance, given the challenges that today confront the United States in Iraq—as well as with insurgencies elsewhere that we will likely face in the future.

Galula died in 1967 at a relatively young age, thus tragically depriving America of his wisdom and guidance at a time when we were becoming more deeply involved in Vietnam. The current republication of *Pacification in Algeria, 1956–1958,* is especially timely. It again affords us an opportunity to learn from one of history's incomparable authorities the fundamental principles of successfully countering insurgency.

Bruce Hoffman
January 2006

---

[1] First published by Frederick A. Praeger (New York) in 1964 and as a reprint in 2005.

[2] S.T. Hosmer and S.O. Crane, *Counterinsurgency: A Symposium April 16–20,* 1962 (Santa Monica, CA: RAND Corporation, November 1962, R-412-ARPA).

Preface

David Galula, the author of this Memorandum and a consultant to RAND's Social Science Department, has had an extensive military career that includes experience in several theaters of revolutionary warfare. A graduate of Saint-Cyr, he served with the French Army in North Africa, France, and Germany during World War II. In the post-war years, he was able to observe at first hand the strategy and tactics of communist guerrillas, first in China, while serving as his country's assistant military attaché, and later in Greece, as military observer with the U.N. Special Commission on the Balkans. In his subsequent post as French military attaché in Hong Kong, Mr. Galula maintained close personal contact with many of his fellow officers then serving in Indochina.

In 1956 Mr. Galula, then a captain, volunteered for active duty in Algeria, at the height of the rebellion. For most of the next two years, he had command of a company assigned to the district of Greater Kabylia, east of Algiers, a center of intensive FLN operations. Drawing on his earlier experiences and observations, he succeeded during his tour in clearing the district and restoring it to government control.

Mr. Galula spent the better part of the next four years at national defense headquarters in Paris, working on various aspects of unconventional warfare and, in particular, the war in Algeria—an assignment he interrupted for six months to attend the Armed Forces Staff College at Norfolk, Virginia. In the spring of 1962 Mr. Galula, then a lieutenant colonel, came to the United States to accept a year's appointment as research associate at the Center for International Affairs at Harvard University.

In the present Memorandum, Mr. Galula has reconstructed from memory in considerable detail the story of his highly successful command in Kabylia, and has laid down his theories of counterinsurgency

Note: This is a reprint of the original Preface to *Pacification in Algeria, 1956–1958,* RM-3878-ARPA, published December 1963 by the RAND Corporation.

and pacification, which he believes to be valid for most counterinsurgent situations today.

This highly personal memoir of a field officer makes no pretense of dealing systematically and analytically with the larger political aspects of the Algerian war, or of judging the merits of the issues and the manner in which they were solved in Algiers and in Paris. Mr. Galula rarely leaves his own vantage point, which was that of a commander in a single sector in a period of the war when the French government and its army were committed to the military defeat of the rebels. The problems he faced, the methods he used to meet them, the behavior of officers and men toward the local populace and toward the rebels and their sympathizers which he describes, were not necessarily those of the other commands. Indeed, it is precisely because Mr. Galula's approach to pacification was individual and imaginative, as well as singularly effective, that his account is valuable to us.

Though he does not argue the major political questions, Mr. Galula does, of course, allude to them to the extent that they bore on the military and psychological situations he encountered. He observes that in many instances the instability of the central government seriously complicated the tasks of counterinsurgency and pacification. He points out, too, that the earlier, vacillating policies of the French in Indochina, Tunisia, and Morocco cast serious doubts on the dependability of their promises to loyal Algerians, and kept alive the FLN's hopes of victory even at a time when the French, through preponderant strength and increasingly sophisticated methods, had almost defeated the rebels in the field. Given the military success of the French effort, the ultimate outcome of the Algerian war appears to the author proof of his belief that, in the long run, the political factors were decisive. If this thesis is correct, his account of pacification in Kabylia becomes the more interesting, for it reveals the extent to which an intelligent and imaginative program for controlling and winning the population in difficult areas could succeed in spite of political uncertainties.

The very form and style of this narrative are evidence that the Memorandum sets forth only the experiences, observations, analysis— and inevitably the bias—of the author. No attempt has been made to editorialize or otherwise to force on the Memorandum a comprehensiveness and balance that its author does not claim. Rather, RAND has chosen to present this memoir as it was written, in the belief that this informed and sensitive personal account makes an important contribution to our knowledge of the operational testing of theories and principles of counterinsurgency.

RM-3878-ARPA is one of several studies on problems and techniques of counterinsurgency that the Social Science Department has prepared for the Advanced Research Projects Agency's Project AGILE.

Contents

Figures

Summary

In this Memorandum, the author has reconstructed and evaluated his unique experience as participant and eyewitness in a critical period of the Algerian war. During the two years of his service in that theater, the Algerian rebels, having come within sight of victory, saw their hopes thwarted by a sudden increase in the French military effort, and both sides fought intensively for the allegiance and support of the population. The emphasis on "pacification," rather than military operations, in the present study reflects the writer's special concern with that aspect of counterinsurgent warfare.

The author's field experience was confined to two military sectors of Kabylia, the rugged, densely populated mountain region east of Algiers. From August 1956 until April 1958, the then Captain Galula commanded the 3d Company of the 45th Colonial Infantry Battalion in the Tigzirt sector; in the four months following his promotion to major, he served as deputy battalion commander in Bordj Menaiel.

I.

In the section entitled "The Stage," the author analyzes the main political, psychological, and military factors that were operative at the outset of the war, and goes on to describe the situation at the various levels of the French command at the time of his arrival in Algeria.

When the Algerian insurgents launched their rebellion in November 1954, the political and military situation augured well for their success. A succession of weak governments in Metropolitan France had failed to cope with the rise of nationalism in the French empire. Indochina had been lost after a long and costly war. Tunisia and Morocco were close to gaining independence after a show of terrorism and guerrilla warfare. Most of the French Army was in the process of being shipped home from Indochina or was tied down in Tunisia and Morocco. The French public was tired of colonial wars. Both Arab and communist countries actively favored rebellion in Algeria. The rest of the world was not unsympathetic to the nationalist strivings of colonial countries. Among the nine million Muslims of Algeria, living side by side with one million Europeans who dominated the political and economic life, a large majority could be expected to join a war of independence. Even those satisfied with French rule (and their number was not small) had lost confidence in the effectiveness of the French authorities. The French administration in Algeria was inadequate; it was virtually nonexistent at the grassroots. Police strength was under fifty thousand, and military forces even fewer, in a large and difficult territory with a widely dispersed, predominately rural population.

The insurgents' strategy was to begin with a wave of "blind terrorism," designed to attract publicity for the movement and to spread fear and insecurity, and to go on to a campaign of "selective terrorism" through which to acquire control of the population in a very short time. Once the rebels had secured the willing or forced complicity of the people (a goal they achieved early in the Algerian war), they were ready to launch guerrilla warfare. From there, they were prepared to go on to larger-scale engagements if necessary.

French reaction to the rapidly expanding insurgency was slowed and haphazard. As successive cabinets tossed ideas, money, and men piecemeal into the fray, hoping to reach an acceptable settlement with the rebels, they came close to losing the war in its initial phase.

Early in 1956, however, the rioting in Algiers of European settlers who had considerable support in France forced a change in governmental policy. That spring, newly drafted soldiers and reservists recalled to active duty poured into Algeria, allowing the French to pass from a desultory defensive to the offensive, and to launch full-scale military operations against insurgent bands that had grown rapidly in size as the rebellion seemed to be gaining ground.

The French forces—infantry, with a minimum of support and service units—were divided into static and mobile units. The former (the "grid") were spread throughout the territory, each responsible for pacifying its own area; the mobile units acted as a striking force whenever needed, and fought any large-scale infiltrations from across the borders. At the same time, the French began their costly but highly successful effort to seal off the Tunisian and Moroccan borders so as to prevent such massive infiltrations.

As a result of this heavy French investment of men, money, and matériel, the insurgents were unable to develop an effective military apparatus and to acquire bases within Algeria. As time went on, they had increasingly to content themselves with harassing action and minor guerrilla forays. However, although militarily their situation was deteriorating, the rebels were counting on the fatigue and disenchantment of the French to help turn the tide if the war lasted long enough. They recognized that their chief problem in the meantime was to solidify their hold over the Algerian populace—their main source of strength—and to that end they resorted once again to the terrorist tactics of the earlier period.

The French for their part realized that military action by itself could not put a permanent end to the insurgency. If a rebel band was destroyed, the rebels' political organization, strongly entrenched in the masses of the people, would create another. Ultimate victory, therefore, depended on the ability of the French to win over the population. But, while the central authorities acknowledged the principle of a systematic pacification effort and instructed their officers in the field accordingly, they lacked agreement on method. Despite their experience in Indochina and other insurgent theaters, they had yet to formulate a concrete counterinsurgent doctrine applicable to the realities of the Algerian situation. The order to "pacify," therefore, was variously interpreted by the officers in the field, among whom the company commanders, in particular, bore the burden of its execution. There were the "warriors," who believed in the efficacy of military conquest and intimidation, and the "psychologists," who put their faith in persuasion and other psychological means without show of force. But the large majority of commanders were not committed to either extreme; they were faced with a multitude of concrete problems to which each improvised his own answers. The broad high-level directives, sound though they were, failed to meet the urgent need for precise instructions at the bottom.

II.

"The Struggle for Control of the Population" is the author's detailed account of his theory and practice in what he regards as the mandatory first phase of any counterinsurgent effort. His company's *sous-quartier* in the rebel-infested Aissa Mimoun range of Kabylia proved to be a perfect testing ground for the ideas on counterinsurgency and pacification that he had developed through experience and observation in China and Greece.

He started from the premise that support from the population—the main objective of both insurgent and counterinsurgent—meant more than sympathy or idle approval; it required the people's active participation in the struggle. Such support, however, would not be spontaneous, especially after the rebels had effectively terrorized the population into silence, nor could it be forced. The author believed that it could come about only through an organization developed within the population. As a starting point, therefore, he sought to identify those Moslems, however few they might be, who were pro-French. They, in turn, would not only furnish valuable intelligence but could be relied on gradually to influence and rally the neutral Moslems, until eventually a majority of the population could be enlisted in the elimination of the rebels and their militant supporters.

The author's first act was to break up his company, which had been stationed as one unit in an isolated farm, and to distribute its elements near the two villages and several hamlets of his territory; one platoon was actually installed in the main village. Then, while actively tracking the armed rebels and setting large numbers of ambushes to prevent their ruling the area by night, he began working on the population.

His initial contact with the Algerian villagers of his area demonstrated to the author their reluctance to co-operate with the French authorities, for they feared the punishments of the French far less than the reprisals of the rebels, whose cells were keeping them under constant surveillance. Not until these cells were destroyed, therefore, could the French hope to break through that barrier of silence.

As a first step in the process of imposing control on a village and physically isolating its inhabitants from the armed rebels outside, the author conducted a thorough census and instituted a system by which all movement of persons in and out of the village was rigidly checked. Simultaneously, he committed villagers to the French struggle by requisitioning their labor and paying them for their work. And even in this early phase of pacification, he embarked on the kind of civic action he believed to be the most persuasive in the long run. He established a medical dispensary, opened a school, and initiated a program of information.

Aided by a fortuitous circumstance that provided him with a list of the rebel cell members and their most active supporters, the author successfully "purged" the first of a series of villages, developing there the virtually foolproof method he was to use again and again as the area of his *sous-quartier* was enlarged. He proceeded from the knowledge that, willing or not, every villager participated in the rebellion at least to the extent of making his monthly contribution of money, and was therefore bound to know the identity of some or all of the local cell members. To persuade them to part with this knowledge, the author would arrest villagers for relatively minor offenses in groups of no fewer than four and interrogate them singly for several days. In almost every case, one or more of the men, protected by the fact that any one of them might have been the informer, would divulge the names of rebel cell members in the village, thereby permitting a chain of arrests that would eventually, and sometimes very quickly, lead to the destruction of the entire cell.

These purge tactics became the more effective as the author demonstrated his policy toward the arrested cell members: those who proved their repentance by fully disclosing their past activities and links to the top were instantly released; those who did not were turned over to the legal authorities.

To prevent the armed bands outside from creating new political cells, as they invariably tried to do, the author stationed a small detachment of fifteen to twenty soldiers in every village that had been purged, and the method proved successful in nearly every case. As a result, his company was ultimately dispersed over a number of posts that covered the entire southern slope of the Aissa Mimoun range as well as a large area in the valley. Higher command objected on military grounds to this fragmentation of forces, but the author was able to prove that the risks of such dispersal were smaller than the dangers of losing political control of the population; so successful were the purge of his area and his methods of safeguarding its results that the rebels' higher echelons abandoned the Aissa Mimoun range as a lost cause.

III.

"The Struggle for the Support of the Population" concerns the next step in the process of regaining the initiative and solidifying counter-insurgent control. Here again, the 3d Company's *sous-quartier* supplies the case history of a workable pragmatic approach to the problem.

After a village had been cleaned and the French forces were visibly in control, the author observed a dramatic change in the villagers' behavior; once eager to avoid all contact with the French, they now became openly friendly toward them and showed their lessened fear of the rebels by defiance of the insurgents' rule of conduct. This was the moment for the French to lay the groundwork for a trustworthy local self-government and to launch an intensive program of social and economic improvement.

Though it would have been tempting simply to appoint as village leaders those who already had proved their loyalty to the French, the author preferred to run the risks inherent in holding local elections. Almost invariably, he found, the populace elected the kind of men he himself would have put forward.

Once these new local leaders were in office, their reliability and efficiency were tested by the willingness and success with which they met two basic tasks: the management of village affairs, and the enlistment of the populace in an active counterinsurgent effort. In most instances, the elected officials took the desired initiative in the social and economic betterment of the village, and in recruiting volunteers and organizing them into an auxiliary defense force.

With peace restored to a village, the author's plans for much-needed civic improvements met with enthusiastic response and support from the population. The greatest effort was directed toward the children, as the key to the country's future. The 3d Company's *sous-quartier* ultimately operated six schools, in which French soldiers taught about 1,400 children, including girls, which was a radical innovation. Village dispensaries and the battalion doctor's weekly visit provided medical care. Villagers received government funds with which to build roads, schools, wells, and reservoirs. They were persuaded to clean and whitewash their houses. The writer even went so far as to initiate the emancipation of the Moslem women, who theretofore had been kept in semislavery, and he was struck by the readiness of their response.

As they recognized the difference between their prospering environment and those surrounding areas still in the grip of hostilities, villagers were easily convinced of the need to preserve their peace by helping to prevent rebel infiltration. They co-operated in the thorough checking of visitors from the outside and in the general policing of their area. They were aware, on the other hand, that their co-operation with the French authorities rendered them conspicuous, and that their future security hinged on the continued presence and firmness of the French. Hence, every cabinet crisis in Paris that put the Algerian policy in question had an adverse psychological effect on them, just as it gave heart to the insurgents even in the face of many setbacks. This continual uncertainty of the Moslems set definite limits to what a local pacification effort could achieve.

The author's methods soon became standard procedure throughout his battalion, and their results received much publicity and favorable comment at high levels of command. Yet not until 1959 did the theater command, in the well-known "Plan Challe," issue an overall blueprint for pacification incorporating the ideas and methods that had proved so strikingly successful wherever they were tried. Until then, Algeria remained a checkerboard of areas in various states of pacification, depending on the initiative and conviction of individual commanders.

The author never had the opportunity to realize the final step in his program, which was to organize active supporters, once they had been so identified and tested, in a large political party capable of effective resistance to the Algeria-wide political front of the insurgents. Having failed to convince the top civilian echelons in Algeria of the wisdom of such a policy, he had to limit the effort to his own small area of jurisdiction. He had just begun to put the idea into practice by grouping local Kabyles into a small political machine, when he was promoted and reassigned.

IV.

In the section "War and the Bordj Menaiel Sector," the author describes the situation he faced in his next command post, which was radically different from the "island of peace" of Aissa Mimoun, despite the fact that terrain and populace were much the same in both areas. In Bordj Menaiel he found a full-scale war; an increasingly hostile population; rebel bands operating at company strength undeterred by enormous losses; and French units ineffectually stationed in "commanding" positions on mountain ridges. He attributes this disastrous situation and the rebels' irreversible gains to the previous commanders' distrust of pacification and their failure—for different reasons—to seek the support of the population. One of his two predecessors had believed that vigorous military operations alone could break the back of the insurgency; the other had refrained from pacification efforts out of concern for the people, because he was convinced that the French government would ultimately abandon the country and with it any Algerians who had demonstrated their loyalty to France. Both attitudes were common among French officers and helped explain the variations in approach from one command to another.

Even in this heavily rebel-infested sector, however, Moslems voted overwhelmingly in favor of the French constitution in September 1958, a reflection, the author believes, of the change in atmosphere brought on by the May revolution in Algiers. As he sees it, that even had persuaded Moslems throughout Algeria that the French Army was in control and French policy toward the rebellion therefore would thenceforth be firm and consistent, and this assurance had emboldened them to declare their loyalty without fear of recrimination from the rebels.

V.

In his "Conclusions," the author has singled out as most important and generally valid five principles of counterinsurgent warfare that he found confirmed in his Algerian experience. (1) The objective is the population. (2) The support of the population is not spontaneous; it must be acquired and organized. It is obtained, essentially, through the efforts of the minority that actively favors the counterinsurgent. (3) This minority will emerge, and will be followed by the majority, only if the counterinsurgent is recognized as the ultimate victor. (4) The counterinsurgent, unlike the insurgent, needs much to achieve little, and he therefore must concentrate his efforts on one area at a time. (5) In time, the issue of war and peace becomes the central one in any insurgency, making the relative merit and popularity of the contending causes a matter of secondary moment.

The French Organization in Algeria and the Location of Greater Kabylia

Legend:
- Greater Kabylia
- Igamie boundary
- Department boundary

Scale (km): 0   50   100

Mediterranean Sea

Barrage

KABYLIA

CONSTANTINE

NEMENCHA MOUNTAINS

AURES MOUNTAINS

Setif

Algiers

Boufarik

Blida

Bone

ALGIERS

ORAN

SAHARA

MOROCCO

Aflou

Tiaret

Geryville

Mostaganem

Thiersville

Saida

Oran

La Senia Air Field

Sidi-Bel-Abbes

Tiemcen

El Aricha

Barrage

Mecheria

Interdiction Zone

Ain Sefra

Introduction

I left Hong Kong in February 1956 after a five-year assignment as military attaché. I had been away from troop duty for eleven years, having specialized in Chinese affairs since the end of World War II. I was saturated with intelligence work, I had missed the war in Indochina, I felt I had learned enough about insurgencies, and I wanted to test certain theories I had formed on counterinsurgency warfare. For all these reasons I volunteered for duty in Algeria as soon as I reached France. When my four-month leave was over, I was assigned to the 45th B.I.C. (Colonial Infantry Battalion) to which I reported on August 1, 1956. I was to spend two years in Algeria, first as a company commander until April 1, 1958, then as a deputy battalion commander until August 1, 1958.

Looking back today at the history of the Algerian War, I can distinguish four broad stages:

(1) **November 1954–April 1956.** The insurgency expands from almost zero to near-victory.
(2) **May 1956–May 1958.** The counterinsurgent means and efforts having suddenly increased, the FLN victory hopes are thwarted, and a long battle for the population ensues.
(3) **May 1958–January 1960.** The balance swings sharply to our side.
(4) **January 1960–February 1962.** Although our success is consolidated in the military field, the progressive deterioration in the political field, accelerated in June 1961 by the beginning of our negotiations with the FLN at Melun, leads eventually to the FLN's final victory.

This is an account of my personal experience during my two years in Algeria. The events I have described belong to the second stage as identified above. Due allowance must be made for this fact when drawing general conclusions from my experience.

I am relying on my memory, since I kept no diary. The various figures quoted in Part One, Sections I and II, are taken from Michael Clark's *Algeria in Turmoil*,[1] the most factual book I know on the Algerian War.

I will follow the chronological sequence, digressing occasionally in order to correlate certain aspects of the operations. I shall also describe the general background of the events when it is necessary to do so for an understanding of the situation at my level.

Names marked with an asterisk (e.g., "Colonel Lemoine*") are fictitious.

---

[1]   Frederick A. Praeger, Inc., New York, 1959.

PART ONE

The Stage

I. The Background

The war in Algeria offers most of the usual characteristics of a revolutionary war.

On the insurgent side, a small group of leaders aim at overthrowing the existing order. Their initial physical strength is almost nil. They have, however, two chief assets: (1) a cause by which they can attract supporters, and (2) freedom from any responsibility, and hence the possibility of using any means toward their ends, including terrorism to coerce neutrals and to cow enemies. They choose the population as their major strategic objective, because their assets then become immediately exploitable, and thus they balance the odds against them. Gradually growing in strength, they methodically conduct a protracted struggle, step by step, in order to achieve specific intermediate objectives leading finally to the defeat of their opponent.

On the counterinsurgent side, a government endowed with vastly superior strength, but ideologically handicapped and burdened with the responsibility of maintaining law and order, reacts to stay in power.

Experience shows that in this sort of war the political factors are just as important as the military ones, if not more so. This was particularly true in Algeria, where, especially after 1956, there was practically no military contest in the conventional sense owing to the superiority of the French armed forces in size, equipment, training, and command.

Politics dominated strategically the outbreak, the development, the fluctuations, and finally the outcome of the war. Politics had tactical effects, too. I remember, for example, Robert Kleiman, *U.S. News and World Report* correspondent in Paris, visiting my area in the early spring of 1958. I took him one morning to the Préfecture at Tizi Ouzou so that he might get a briefing on the general situation in Kabylia. A member of the *préfet's* staff was showing him various charts, one indicating the ups and downs of FLN strength, another the rising number of Kabyle auxiliaries in our forces, another the number of deserters.

"This graph," said the official, "shows the FLN activity in Kabylia since the start of the rebellion in November 1954. We have counted here every one of their actions, ambushes, murders, and acts of sabotage, whether directed against our own forces or against the civilian population."

"What are these regularly spaced peaks in the curve?" asked Kleiman.

"You mean those in November–December 1957, 1956, 1955? It's what we call here the 'United Nations fever.' Every year at about the time the General Assembly in New York discusses the Algerian problem, the rebels increase their activity here."

This anecdote explains why I have to sketch in broadly the background of the Algerian War, not as an historian but from the point of view of an officer of the counterinsurgent forces in the field who felt in his work, in his area, the direct impact of events as remote and as varied as the Suez campaign or the fall of Mollet's cabinet.

On the international front, the situation was favorable to the insurgents from the beginning. While France had no ally, the rebels benefited from the material, financial, diplomatic, propaganda, and moral support of communist bloc and Arab countries, and particularly from the sanctuary they found in Tunisia and Morocco. They also had the more or less open and active sympathy of the rest of the world. Even in neutral Switzerland, rebel agents could operate with total impunity, not only as propagandists but as organizers of sabotage and terrorist action, without even bothering to camouflage their activity. As a result, hope for their final success could always be kept alive for the rebels in Algeria even when they were desperately pressed.

On the national front, I must start with the statement, sounding somewhat like General de Gaulle in his TV addresses to the nation, that instability and paralysis of the government had been the dominant feature of political life in France, at least since the end of World War II. Parliament had become the real source of power. There, a cluster of small democratic parties, united against the Communists on the far left and against the Gaullists on the right, sometimes combined but more often competed for the privilege of running the government. A parliamentary majority could always be found for any problem, but when the problem changed, the majority changed with it, so that long-term, coherent policy was impossible to formulate—much less to implement.

Short-lived cabinets built on precarious coalitions succeeded each other, often after a long crisis, and fell apart at the first serious hurdle.

If the consequences were, after all, not too tragic for Metropolitan France because a strong, centralized, competent bureaucracy actually ran the country almost out of habit and in spite of the political circus at the top, and also because of France's natural wealth and the consensus of its population, the effects were bound to produce disaster in the overseas territories. The postwar rise of nationalism demanded bold decisions, which the governments were invariably too weak to make in time.

Thus Indochina was lost after a nine-year war because the government, unable to force a victory or to disengage itself by a timely agreement, had followed the easiest policy, which was to let events take their course. Having first proclaimed that we were there to stay, we left Indochina after a spectacular military defeat at Dien Bien Phu.

History repeated itself in Tunisia and Morocco, the only difference being the speed of the process. When trouble started there in 1952, the French government flatly announced that independence was out of the question. The Tunisian nationalists, already a well-organized party, mobilized the population, made a little show of guerrilla warfare, and received their autonomy in 1955. The Moroccan nationalists, not so well organized as a party initially, and lacking broad popular support, had to use terrorism to a large extent in order to mobilize the masses; having done this, they had just initiated guerrilla warfare when the Sultan was brought back from exile and Morocco became independent. The slaughter of French civilians at Oued Zem near Casablanca, including women, children, hospital patients, and even cats and dogs, made a lasting impression on the European population in Algeria.

The formal agreement signed with M. Bourguiba, and the statements of the Sultan of Morocco at the time of independence, sounded very reasonable. They provided for the protection of French persons and properties, and for the continuation of strong French economic, military, and cultural influence. "Internal sovereignty" was the formula used by M. Mendès-France, then Premier, referring to the agreement with Tunisia. The next Premier, M. Edgar Faure, qualified the agreement with Morocco as "*l'independance dans l'interdependance.*" Within months, however, the Tunisian document became a mere scrap of paper, and the Moroccan moderation gave way to open, active support of the FLN. The *"pieds-noirs"* (literally "black-feet," the self-assumed nickname of the European settlers in Algeria) did not fail to notice it and to draw their conclusions.

When a sudden outbreak of terrorism occurred in Algeria on November 1, 1954, M. Mendès-France swore the usual "Never!":

> It is inconceivable that Algeria should secede from Metropolitan France. This should be clear forever to all, in Algeria, in Metropolitan France, and abroad. France will never, no Parliament, no Government will ever, yield on this basic principle. Algeria is France, and not a foreign country under our protection [such as Tunisia and Morocco].

Notwithstanding the legal niceties and the forcefulness of his statement, the nationalist wind was blowing strong in Algeria. Independence was a powerful slogan appealing to the passions of many among the millions of Moslems, a passionate race if ever there was one, prompt to assess where the real power lies. They constitute a nine-to-one majority of the Algerian population. As soon as the outbreak of violence focused attention on the insurgent movement, the FLN ranks began to swell with a first layer of convinced supporters.

M. Mendès-France's cabinet fell shortly thereafter for reasons only partly related to the Algerian crisis. Free from the responsibility of power, the former Premier started at once to campaign in favor of "immediate peace in Algeria through negotiations with the FLN." Hence the popular reasoning among the Algerian Moslems: "If a French Premier says NO now, maybe the next one will say YES."

The French police in Algeria obviously suspected what was brewing. Intelligence reports from Cairo were not lacking. But the warnings were dismissed. The first terrorist rash, which had been ineffectual on the whole but had attracted huge headlines (which was precisely its purpose), was regarded as a minor affair, the more so since almost nothing followed it. "Ordinary banditry," said a high-ranking government official in Algiers, when reports came that men and weapons from Tunisia were converging on the Aurès Mountains. Ordinary banditry did indeed exist in those remote mountains as well as in some parts of Kabylia, but this was something else again. The delay in appreciating the situation and the true extent of the threat resulted in an insufficient answer to the challenge, and the fire ignited in the rugged Aurès Mountains easily survived the first French reaction. The rebellion had thus passed its first test, perhaps the most critical one, and its spreading became inevitable.

Eventually the worsening of the situation had to be faced. But what to do? Negotiation was tempting, but what was to be negotiated? with whom? The rebels' attitude and methods clearly indicated that they were in no mood for settlement or compromise, and that they cared for nothing short of complete independence—independence not granted to them but won by force. "Bourguibism," the clever mixture of force and negotiation by which Tunisian nationalists had achieved their aims, was anathema to them. Yet it would have been political suicide for the French government not to take into account the fate of the European settlers, one million of them, who had long been rooted in Algeria, considered it their home, and had their own representatives in the Parliament and a sizable body of supporters in Metropolitan France. Moreover, the leaders of the rebellion were political nonentities: Ben Bella, a former noncommissioned officer in the French Army condemned for a post-office robbery reminiscent of Stalin's coup in Tiflis under the Czar; Krim Belkacem, a former corporal who had killed a rural policeman because he had been preferred to him for the job. None of the educated Algerians, none of the bourgeois, none of the known nationalist figures had participated in the movement. Not only had they been deliberately left out, but Ben Bella had ordered the liquidation of any possible "*interlocuteurs valables.*" So there remained only one possible course of action, to fight the rebellion.

By the time the insurrection was finally recognized for what it was, only drastic political and military action would have reversed the tide, and slowly in any case. Politically, in spite of all evidence to the contrary, the government kept behaving as if a settlement were possible after all, as if hastily devised economic and social reforms could stem the rebellion. These reforms only encouraged the rebels, convincing them that they had been right when they chose the path of revolution rather than evolution. As for the Moslem masses, their main problem was one of security, and the FLN threats and assassinations had greater effect on them than had better educational opportunities and land reform. Latin Americans today see the United States giving them more aid than they ever received until Castro appeared. Why should they help suppress the bogeyman? The Moslems in Algeria reacted in the same way. Under FLN pressure, the French government was granting them in a hurry more than they had dreamed of, and often clamored for, in peaceful circumstances.

From a military point of view, the rebels had chosen their time well. The best part of the French Army was still in Indochina, slowly to be shipped home. Most of our available forces this side of the Suez Canal were kept busy by troubles in Morocco and Tunisia, where we had, respectively, 100,000 and 40,000 men. In France there remained only training units of raw draftees, suffering from a serious shortage of officers since the professional cadres were away. Transferring to Algeria our NATO-committed divisions stationed in France and Germany would have caused an uproar. In Algeria itself, our total strength at the outset of the rebellion, including security forces (Gendarmes Mobiles and Compagnies Républicaines de Sécurité), did not exceed 50,000 men. Recalling reservists was the only logical answer, but this would have meant the instant fall of the government, for public opinion at home was just as divided at the time as the Parliament.

The majority of the French people, satisfied that peace in Indochina had ended at last the drain on French resources, hated to contemplate the prospect of another long, drawn-out war, in Algeria or anywhere else. Although the situation of state finances was precarious, the Marshall Plan and hard work on the part of the French people had brought full recovery within sight; signs of mass prosperity were already apparent. The theory that colonies were more a liability than an asset was gaining ground (witness the prosperity of Switzerland and Germany, which had no colonies, and of The Netherlands in spite of the loss of the Dutch East Indies). Had it not been for the attitude of the FLN leaders, who did not facilitate the solution of the problem, and for the existence of the European settlers, the Algerian crisis would soon have been solved along the Morocco or Tunisia pattern. On the other hand, the majority in France recognized that Frenchmen across the Mediterranean Sea could not be abandoned and left at the mercy of terrorists, forced to choose between "the coffin and the suitcase," as the FLN put it to them.

It was once more a case of too little too late. The government adopted the easiest course, increasing slowly, almost painlessly for the French economy, the means devoted to the struggle. Professional units repatriated from Indochina were directed to Algeria as they arrived, the length of conscription was gradually extended from eighteen months in 1954 to twenty-eight months in 1956, French NATO divisions were eventually moved to Algeria. As it turned out, of course, France was always several steps behind the demands of the situation on the military front, with the result that the race between an expanding insurgency and a growing counterinsurgency was won by the FLN.

The following table gives an idea of the race.

Needless to say, the size of the FLN's regular forces in October 1955 does not convey a true picture of the rebels' real strength.

Date	French forces in Algeria	Spread of the rebellion
Nov '54	50,000	Aurès Mountains (FLN regular forces, 400–500).
Feb '55	84,000	Nementcha Mountains, Kabylia.
May '55	100,000	North Constantine region.
Jul '55	115,000	
Sep '55	140,000	Rebels in North Constantine region make junction with those of South Constantine. FLN front now extends continuously though diffusely from Tunisia to Kabylia.
Oct '55	About 200,000, forces having been augmented by 3 NATO divisions. (France at this time recalls 75,000 reservists, and keeps 100,000 servicemen beyond release date.)	New front established in Oran region on Moroccan border. (At this time, FLN regular forces in all of Algeria totaled approximately 5,000, including 3,100 in Constantine, 500 in Kabylia, and 360 in Oran.)
Nov '55	230,000, forces having been augmented by 2 more NATO divisions.	

●▼●▼●

By the end of 1955, the *pieds-noirs* were exasperated both by the constant FLN terrorist action and by the lack of firmness on the part of
the French government. Thirty-seven French civilians, including ten
children, had been savagely murdered at El Halia, a pyrite mine near
Philippeville; mayors, councilmen, *caids* (local chieftains), postmen,
schoolteachers (both French and Moslems) were assassinated daily as
homemade bombs and grenades exploded at random; farms and crops
were burned and destroyed. Why weren't death sentences on terrorists
executed? What did the government do to protect the Moslems, and they
were many, who still believed in France? The support openly given the
FLN by the highly organized French Communist Party and its fellow
travelers was to be expected, but what about the Christian Progressists
and various other left-wing movements? The French press fanned the
settlers' anger, particularly *Le Monde, L'Express* (a Mendèsist weekly),
the crypto-communist *France-Observateur, Témoignage Chrétien* (a
weekly with strong leanings toward the Christian Progressists, a communist front organization), and even *France-Soir.* These papers ignored
the bad side of the FLN, amplified and gave credence to the rebels'
propaganda, and acted on the *pieds-noirs* like a red cape on a fighting bull. Was it not treason? asked the French settlers, who blamed
the government for its failure to take positive action. The "sell-out" in
Tunisia and Morocco raised their anxiety and their fury to the critical point. They had every reason to believe that their turn would come
next, and soon.

    Late in 1955, the Parliament was dissolved in the wake of a crisis
of which Algeria was again but an element. Elections brought back the
same divided House with the new, strong Poujadist Party on the right
wing. A minority party, the Socialists, which had made no secret of its
intention to end the war by negotiation, organized the new cabinet presided over by Guy Mollet with Mendès-France as Vice-Premier.

    One of Mollet's first tasks was to appoint a new Governor General
to replace Jacques Soustelle in Algiers. He chose General Catroux, a
retired general strongly suspected of "decolonizing" tendencies, who
had indeed played a major role in bringing back the Sultan of Morocco

from his exile in Madagascar. Algiers erupted at once. The new Premier flew there to assess the situation and to appease the Europeans. He was greeted with ripe tomatoes, rotten eggs, and riots. Algeria, it must be noted, had long been integrated into the French political system, and since the Second World War had been considered something of a Socialist preserve; nearly every Governor General since 1945 had been appointed by the Socialist Party even when the party was not in power. Whatever the decisive factor, whether it was domestic policy or the sudden realization that the *pieds-noirs* were on the verge of open revolt (the Army had remained perfectly loyal and disciplined so far, but who could predict what its attitude would be if drifting was allowed to continue?), Mollet decided there and then to alter his policy radically. Another Governor General, M. Robert Lacoste, was appointed with full cabinet rank. In April 1956, 160,000 reservists were recalled for a six-month period and sent to Algeria. By July 1956, the total strength of the French forces had reached 360,000 including the Navy and Air Force; by August, 400,000.

Premier Mollet's cabinet lasted more than a year, longer than any other in the Fourth Republic. It was able to carry out for the first time a relatively coherent policy in Algeria. The *tour de force* was achieved by appeasing the right with a tough stand on the rebellion, and the left with more social reforms in France. But the financial bill was paid by inflation, and, when the right felt unable to stomach any longer the cost of social reforms, the cabinet fell.

Lest this government be taken as a model of firmness and determination, I must add that it was still attracted by the lure of a quick negotiated end to the war. It had every right, of course, to sound out the other side, but the French political system was such as to rule out any possibility of secrecy. The news that secret talks had been conducted spread rapidly all over Algeria and contributed to making the Moslems still more reluctant to commit themselves on our side.

II. Insurgency and Counterinsurgency in Algeria

According to the orthodox pattern recommended by the Chinese Communists[2] for insurgencies in "colonial and semicolonial" countries, the insurgent must:

(1) create and develop a strong, tested revolutionary party;
(2) gather around it as large as possible a popular front;
(3) then, and only then, proceed to open violence and initiate guerrilla warfare;
(4) when bases have been acquired, organize a regular army and wage a war of movement;
(5) having achieved overall superiority over the opponent, launch a final annihilation campaign.

The first two steps in this process obviously require much time, patience, organizational effort, and plain luck. The insurgent leaders in Algeria were in a hurry; they chose another pattern already tried to a certain extent in Morocco, which constitutes in essence a shortcut and is better adapted to the Arab mind and temper.

Nationalist parties were not lacking in Algeria. There were the MTLD (Movement for the Triumph of Democratic Liberties) with Messali Hadj; the UDMA (Democratic Union for the Algerian Manifesto) with Ferhat Abbas; the Ulemas Association; and the PCA (Algerian Communist Party). But while playing, on the whole, the legal political game and preparing for an insurrection, they had been unable to agree on a common program, and they were rent with dissension in the classic Arab fashion. Their very existence, however, was proof that the raw material for insurgency—a body of militant believers—was largely available. Only the right spark was needed.

In the spring of 1954, a "Revolutionary Committee for Unity and Action" (CRUA) was formed in Cairo, with the full support of Nasser,

---

[2] Cf. the address by Liu Shao-chi at the Trade Union Conference of Asian and Australasian Countries, Peking, November 1949.

by Ben Bella, Boudiaf, Kbider, and a few others who had fled to the Egyptian capital to avoid arrest. They were a minority, a splinter group of the MTLD. They wanted to develop their movement rapidly, outside and at the expense of the existing parties. The only solution, they rightly decided, was direct action. They would start it and see what happened. The CRUA held a war council in Switzerland in July 1954, after which six of the participants returned to Algeria to prepare the explosion. They divided the territory among themselves into six *wilayas* (regions), recruited some followers, and planned for D-Day, which was finally set for November 1, 1954.

How much of a gamble it was can be seen from the statement made recently to *Le Monde* by Mohamed Boudiaf (see Appendix 1).[3] The FLN leaders did not plan much beyond the first step, and they improvised as they went along. Their strategy, as it can be reconstructed now, was shaped along the following lines:

1. A brief period of *blind terrorism,* designed primarily to attract publicity both for the cause of Algerian independence and for the movement (and thus to attract supporters) and, secondarily, to spread insecurity. It took the form of noisy attacks against isolated small French military garrisons, sabotage, bomb throwing, and random assassinations. Thus seventy separate actions took place simultaneously on D-Day (November 1, 1954): in the Aurès Mountains, near Constantine, in and around Algiers, in Kabylia, and in and around Oran.

2. *Selective terrorism,* which followed and lasted throughout the war. Its essential purpose was to control the population and thus to win what has been termed "the battle for silence," a prerequisite for successful guerrilla operations. To this effect the rebels proceeded to:

(a) terrorize or eliminate Moslems working for the French administration or suspected of being pro-French (*caids*, elected town and village officials, policemen, postmen, tax collectors, school teachers, veterans, etc.);

---

[3] Boudiaf broke with Ben Bella in the postwar struggle for power. He naturally plays up his part and plays down Ben Bella's. His statement must be taken with a grain of salt in some parts, but seems factually accurate on the whole.

(b) split Europeans and Moslems by destroying trust and mutual confidence (ordering a boycott against work for the Europeans; murdering isolated farmers with the forced complicity of their Moslem farmhands; ambushing French doctors on their way to false calls; throwing bombs at French schoolchildren so as to bring on blind reprisals against Moslems, etc.);

(c) forcibly involve the Moslem population vis-à-vis the authorities in such a way as to bring repression down on their heads (forcing villagers to burn schools, to destroy public properties, to dig holes in the roads, to cut telephone lines, etc.);

(d) raise the political consciousness of the Moslems and force them to participate, if only passively, in the struggle (exacting financial contributions to the cause from every Moslem; enforcing a widespread tobacco boycott by cutting off the noses of a few offenders, ordering rigid observance of the Islamic rites, etc.); and

(e) organize the population under local committees, the cadres being selected on the basis of their efficiency in collecting monetary contributions.

Not all terrorist actions were so well calculated with a precise goal in mind, but since disorder automatically helps the insurgent, incoherent terror served its purpose merely by promoting instability. With such a simple program the rebels could afford to operate with the crudest organization.

At this point the FLN pattern meets the Chinese one, at least in theory, for in fact the Algerian rebels were never able to expand beyond a low level of guerrilla warfare.

They did not, of course, stick rigidly to the line and wait for the population to be well under control in order to start guerrilla activity. In the Aurès Mountains, for instance, where French authority was practically nonexistent and the terrain favorable, they plunged into guerrilla warfare right away.

All this was accompanied by intensive propaganda, supported from the outside by broadcasts from Morocco, Tunisia, Egypt, Iraq, Albania, Hungary, and Soviet Russia, the total of which exceeded by five to one the output in Arabic of the French stations in Algeria and Metropolitan France. It was impossible to jam effectively all this volume.

If the rebels' slogan directed at the Europeans ("the suitcase or the coffin") was rather crude and ineffective, they had more telling points for the Moslems. "The French," they said, "swore they would never leave Indochina; they left. They swore they would never leave Tunisia; they left. They swore they would never leave Morocco; they left. Now they swear they will never leave Algeria . . ." Those Moslems who entertained any doubt on the outcome of the insurgency had to make a prompt decision which side to lean to, the FLN or the French. The choice was easy considering the past performance of the French government, and remembering the fate of those who bet on the wrong horse in Tunisia and Morocco.[4] French decadence was another powerful theme, as rebel propaganda pointed with great effect to the remarkably strong FLN organization in Metropolitan France itself (where the only way we could protect friendly Moslems was to keep them in jail) or to the weakness of French justice. To the Moslems who wondered how they could go to work in France after independence, or how Algeria could survive without French money, the rebels just pointed to the example of Morocco and Tunisia: workers from there still went to France; French money was still pouring into the two countries.

Taking advantage of the credulity of the rural population, FLN agents circulated fantastic rumors: "Nasser's planes have killed thousands of French soldiers at such and such place"; "Russian (or Chinese) volunteers are already in Tunisia"; "The French put poison in the milk they give our boys in schools so as to make them impotent."

Propaganda and persuasion, however, were not sufficient by themselves to boost the strength of the rebel movement. Terrorism was and remained the main force. Statistics reveal that eight Moslems

---

[4] "Glaoui" became a common name in Algeria. "I don't want to be "glaouised," Moslems used to reply when pressed to commit themselves on our side. Glaoui was the Pacha of Marrakech in South Morocco. He opposed the Sultan and remained faithful to the French until the bitter end. He died shortly after Morocco became independent. All his properties were seized, his family was thrown in jail, and several of his aides were lynched on the main square of the town by being doused with gasoline and burned alive.

were killed by the FLN for every European all through the war. At no time were the rebels able to stir up a general uprising. Not even at the darkest period for us, in late 1955 to early 1956, did they succeed in disrupting greatly the economic life of Algeria. The insurgency did not spread at once all over Algeria; it did so slowly, area by area, very often jumping over territory in between as if insurgent cadres had been injected from the outside.

Because of the size of Algeria, the difficult terrain, the scattered rural Moslem population, the deficiency of French bureaucracy at grassroot level (where it counts most), the weakness of the French forces available initially, and their slow build-up, it took few insurgents to infect an area and eventually to control its population. In the Aurès Mountains there were no more than 300; in Kabylia, in November 1955, Krim Belkacem had only 800 rifles against 12,000 French soldiers.

One may wonder then why it took so long, more than a year, for the insurgency to spread all over the territory. The fact may be attributed to the incompetence and inexperience of the leaders; to the Arabs' notorious inability to organize (I sound no doubt terribly colonialist, but it's a fact, as witness the small Israeli Army and the huge Arab manpower all around it); to their tendency to bicker among themselves; to the FLN's ignorance of insurgent warfare except in its crudest form; to the rebels' vanity, which led them to refuse expert communist advice. "Thank God we are not dealing with Viets here!" was the most common remark heard among French soldiers who had fought in Indochina. It may be also, as I already mentioned, that the rebels had not carefully planned their insurgency, that they had prepared nothing beyond the immediate step. They clearly counted on an early victory. When the French collapse failed to materialize, they were obliged to organize and to improvise as they went along. Nevertheless, in their crude fashion, they eventually succeeded in attaining a strong grip over the Moslem masses throughout the country. By early 1956, when it seemed that the French government was about to give in, their control of the Moslems was almost absolute.

Their territorial organization covered all Algeria, although a large gap always existed between the theoretical structure and the reality in the field. The *wilaya* covering Sahara, for instance, existed only on paper. The six *wilayas*, each ultimately commanded by a colonel, were divided into *mintakas* (zones) under a major or a captain. The next-lower echelon was the *nahia* (sector) under a lieutenant; it was divided, finally, into *kasmas* (districts), each under a senior NCO.

The rebels' military setup had not yet developed beyond the level of bands, some large, some small, but all loosely organized and equipped. Formal units such as platoons, *katibas* (companies), or *fer-kahs* (battalions) did not exist even on paper; this would have to wait until late 1956 or early 1957. The best that can be said of the insurgents' system at this stage is that it comprised *moujahidines* (regulars), commonly called *fellaghas*, and *mousseblines* (auxiliaries), the former full-time, the latter part-time fighters. Their strength in March 1956 was estimated as follows:

Areas of operation	Regulars	Auxiliaries	Total
Oran	1,250	3,000	4,250
Greater and Lesser Kabylia and Mitidja Plain (around Algiers)	2,000	6,000	8,000
North Constantine	1,700	5,000	6,700
East Constantine	1,300	4,000	5,300
South Constantine	1,800	3,000	4,800
Totals	8,050	21,000	29,050
Armaments:	Machine guns	4	
	Machine rifles	72	
	Submachine guns	530	
	Army rifles	3,200	
	Shotguns	18,000	

Shortage of weapons was obviously the only obstacle to the expansion of their forces.

Parallel to the military structure, and under the same chiefs, was the vitally important "Political and Administrative Organization" (OPA), whose task it was to control the population, to mobilize its support for the rebel forces, and to supplant the French administration. At the lowest level—i.e., the *douar* (village or tribe)—the OPA consisted usually of a three-man cell, one member charged with military affairs (support to the regulars, intelligence, and counterintelligence), another with administration and justice, the last with tax collection. This third man was generally the most efficient.

◗◖◗◖◗

A look now at the counterinsurgent camp.

Technically part of France, Algeria was administered like any French Metropolitan area. The territory was divided into three *départements* (Algiers, Oran, Constantine), each headed by a *préfet*. There were, however, some differences in the administrative setup. A Governor General in Algiers stood between the *préfets* and the Minister of the Interior in Paris. In addition to the Algerian representatives in the French Parliament, there was a territorial legislative body, l'Assemblée Algérienne, whose members were elected in two separate ballots, one for the Europeans and for those Moslems who had chosen the full French citizen status, and one for the majority of Moslems who had kept their local status. There also existed two types of *communes* (townships), one self-administered, with elected mayor and councilmen, exactly as in France, and another in some of the rural areas—the *communes mixtes*—predominantly Moslem and under a French civil servant. Algeria had its own budget and its own tax system under which the Europeans, one-tenth of the population, carried half the tax burden.

Algeria formed the 10th Military Region, which was under a lieutenant- or major-general with headquarters in Algiers. It was divided into three territorial divisions corresponding to the *départements*, each under a major- or brigadier-general. The next level was the subdivision under a colonel aided by a small staff. In some cases the subdivision was organized into *cercles*. Algiers was also the seat of the 5th Air Region covering all of French North Africa. A Navy command was established at Mers-el-Kebir near Oran.

Three major problems arose when the rebellion began. How to adapt the legal system to the situation? How to reorganize the administration which was notoriously deficient in the rural Moslem-populated areas? How to fight the rebels?

In the existing legal framework, proclamation of martial law was the only provision in case of disturbances endangering the security of the state. It would have entailed handing over all powers to the military authority and suspending private and public liberties. Government and Parliament considered this step too extreme. Hence they devised a new contingency, the so-called "state of emergency," which was declared for the first time for the Constantine area and for Kabylia in April 1955, and was extended to all Algeria in August 1955. Parliament voted a Special Powers Act (with the support of the Communists!), which gave the government a free hand for conducting its policy in Algeria by decree, notably in matters pertaining to economic development, economic and social reforms, territorial reorganization, public order, security of persons and property, and protection of the integrity of the territory. These special powers were vested in the existing government and would lapse with the end of its incumbency; the succeeding government would have to request an extension from the Parliament.

The government in turn gave authority to the Minister-Resident (who by then had replaced the Governor General in Algiers) to regulate movements of persons and goods, assign places of residence, create forbidden zones, order searches, ban meetings, control the press, dissolve associations, collect reparations for willful damage and for aid given to the rebels, suspend or transfer civil servants, deprive elected representatives of their seats, postpone by-elections, and delegate certain civil powers to the military. Travel between France and Algeria was made subject to strict control (at least in theory).

While these powers satisfied most of the practical needs of the counterinsurgents in Algeria, a crucial problem remained unsolved throughout the war: little or nothing was done to adapt the judicial machinery to the situation. A terrorist caught *flagrante delicto* could immediately be brought before a military court. But he had the right to appeal, and, if unsuccessful, his lawyer could still bring the case to the Cour de Cassation (a supreme court that judged not on substance but on form). If he was condemned to death, he would ask for a commutation of the penalty to life imprisonment, which the President of the Republic alone had the power to grant—and granted in most cases. Literally years passed between a crime and a final sentence.

When the crime was relatively minor and the case therefore was handled by an ordinary civil court, such was the backlog that it took just as long to pass a sentence, and the tendency was to dismiss most cases because legal proof of guilt could not be furnished or because no witness was produced by the prosecution. Who indeed would be foolish enough to serve as a witness and then be left exposed to FLN vengeance? Thus it was not rare to see an OPA member arrested on denunciation, confessing to the police, retracting at his trial, and returning free to his village, there to confront those who had informed on him. The results were disastrous, for either the local official in charge, civilian and military, would decide to take matters into his own hands— and make a mockery of the legal process—or he would do nothing and become useless as far as pacification was concerned.

The main defect of the administrative structure in Algeria resulted from the simple fact that it covered too large a territory with too few people, even under ordinary, peaceful conditions. For example, the total police force in Algeria, including municipal police and rural gendarmerie, was less than 40,000, i.e., slightly more than the normal police strength in Paris. Yet Algeria has 10 million inhabitants and 115,000 square miles.[5] Particularly dangerous was the gap between the *administrateur de commune mixte* and the bulk of the Moslem population. I will cover the subject in more detail when describing my own area. Meanwhile, here is an example concerning La Meskiana, a *commune mixte* in the South Constantine area: the French administration there consisted of the administrateur, one assistant, and five gendarmes for a mountainous territory of 853 square miles with 35,000 inhabit-

---

[5] This does not include the Sahara. I am leaving this territory out of the picture because the rebels never managed to make any headway in the desert in spite of all their efforts—except, of course, at the very last minute, in February 1962, when the local population realized finally that the Sahara was being handed over to new masters.

ants. In short, Algeria was grossly underadministered. The fact explains much of what happened.

The administrative reform of June 1956 led to the creation of nine new *départements*, bringing the total to twelve. *Super-préfets* in Algiers, Oran, and Constantine were given jurisdiction over areas corresponding to the three original *départements*. The new *départements* were divided into *arrondissements*, a total of 37 for Algeria, each under a *sous-préfet*. *Communes mixtes* were suppressed, and, to fill the vacuum between the *sous-préfet* and the population, six hundred SAS (Specialized Administrative Sections) were eventually created, with Army officers from the new Corps of Algerian Affairs Officers. The latter was organized on the model of the Corps of Native Affairs, which had proved so successful in Morocco until 1936, when its role was greatly decreased and its jurisdiction handed over to civil bureaucracy.

French military strategy, from the start of the rebellion until mid-1956, was dictated by the weakness of our establishment. All we could do was to react as best we could, rushing troops here and there whenever the rebels lighted a new fire.

Our tactics, however, underwent several conceptual changes. The first idea was to apply military pressure against the rebels. A revolt in Algeria in April 1945 had thus been quickly suppressed by military action. But this time we faced not a revolt but an insurgency. Instead of a mass uprising with large and loosely organized bands attacking European centers head-on, we had to cope with small groups of rebels who avoided encounters with our forces, operated in too diffuse a manner, and concentrated their efforts on mobilizing the population through persuasion and terrorism. There was no enemy that could be identified, to whom we could give battle, except in the Aurès Mountains. This is where our units first went to work. But what with the apocalyptic terrain, its rocks, its caves, its abrupt changes of altitude, we vainly played hide-and-seek with the guerrillas. We encircled, we combed, we raided, with little result.

It soon became obvious that military operations alone could not defeat the rebels. The population had to be protected, controlled, won over, and thus isolated from the rebels. Work in depth was necessary. This is how we had pacified Morocco in the 1920s and early 1930s.

Accordingly, a team of Native Affairs Officers from Morocco and Sahara was dispatched to the Aurès in May 1955. The area was carved into pacification zones corresponding roughly to the tribal divisions. The officer-in-charge would build a *bordj*, a combination of fort and administrative building, to serve as an anchor and as a center of attraction to the population. While the Army kept tracking the rebel bands, he would give immediate protection to the population with his *goum* (a company of 180 native auxiliaries), provide various administrative facilities, collect intelligence, undertake a program of civic action, and progressively arm the population for its own defense. By the end of 1955, rebels had lost so much ground in the Aurès that their organization soon lapsed into anarchy.

The Aurès experiment showed us that we had the beginnings of an answer to the problem; it was the origin of the new concept of *quadrillage* (framework, grid). The principle consisted in dividing our forces into two types:

(1) the static forces, permanently assigned to an area, where they would deploy in a grid, track the rebels in their own area, and work on the population in liaison with the SAS;
(2) the mobile reserves, operating along more conventional lines, either to reinforce static troops temporarily or to act independently in areas empty of static troops and along the Algerian borders.

There were, unfortunately, two catches in the process. Doing this kind of work on the population in depth with an elite of Native Affairs Officers who had done nothing else during their entire career was one thing. But six hundred new SAS officers could not become experts overnight. Their action would have to be closely supervised.

SAS officers, besides, could not operate unless a reasonable degree of security was provided by the Army. There are approximately one thousand *douars* in Algeria with an average of ten hamlets each. Allowing one platoon for every hamlet, 400,000 men would have been required for the static forces. Fifty thousand were needed for the mobile reserves, taking into account the threat posed by the borders. Seventy thousand were required to protect the six or seven thousand vulnerable points. The total bill came to 520,000 men, not counting the support services and the Navy and Air Force. Not until August 1956 did we reach our greatest strength, and that was only 400,000 men. The rest clearly would have to be provided by the population itself, but not before we could get the people to commit themselves on our side. This in turn required that we first give them security, which we could not provide because we were understrength. We were apparently caught in a vicious circle from which only strategy could free us.

The sudden increase in our forces in the spring of 1956 nevertheless enabled us to pass to the offensive. The FLN hopes for an early victory were thwarted. Both sides now had to prepare for the long pull. In our camp a phase of large-scale operations began.

The development of our military effort brought a reorganization of our command. Lieutenant-General Lorillot (replaced in late 1956 by General Salan) took the title of Commander-in-Chief of the French Forces in Algeria in addition to his functions as Chief of the 10th Military Region. Under him were three Army Corps commanders whose areas covered the old Algiers, Oran, and Constantine *départements*. Army Corps areas were divided into *zones* corresponding approximately to the new *départements*, each under a major- or brigadier-general. The next-lower level was the *secteur*, corresponding roughly to an *arrondissement*, with a colonel or lieutenant-colonel in charge. Then came the *quartier,* under a major, with a battalion or the equivalent in strength, and finally the *sous-quartier,* with a company under a captain or a lieutenant. For these last two levels, the civilian counterpart was usually at least one SAS officer, and sometimes several.

III. The Situation in Kabylia

The Kabylia I am referring to is the territory known as Greater Kabylia, as distinct from Lesser Kabylia to the east of it. Shaped roughly like a semicircle facing the sea, it extends for over 60 miles east-west and 40 north-south, with an area of about 2,500 square miles. Terrain, vegetation, and population make it strikingly different from the rest of Algeria and combine to create an ideal ground for guerrilla warfare. Kabylia has always been the particular headache of every conqueror of North Africa, from the Romans to the Vandals, the Turks, and the French. It was the last part of Algeria we penetrated during our conquest, and this as late as the 1860s. Ordinary banditry has always existed in more or less virulent form. Thus Krim Belkacem, wanted as a murderer, was already in a bandit maquis of his own before the insurgency started.

Kabylia is a chaotic, mountainous area culminating in the Djurdjura in the south, the highest range in Algeria with several peaks above 7,500 feet. It is not so much their height that creates difficulties but rather the deep ravines and the sudden, sharp differences of level. Any number of caves, some large enough to accommodate one hundred men in their long and twisted galleries, afford convenient hiding places. Large boulders provide ready-made firing and ambush positions as well as shelters against infantry and artillery fire and air-strafing. The following stories will give an idea of the terrain:

Bou Souar and Igonane Ameur, two villages in my *sous-quartier,* were about 1 km apart as the crow flies. Yet to go from one to the other took 45 minutes because of the ravine in between. My area, it must be noted, was far from being the most rugged in Kabylia.

In December 1957, our intelligence people in Tizi Ouzou identified the latest OPA boss of the town. We had his picture, moreover he was a hunchback, so we thought it would be simple to catch him. We knew he operated from Djebel Belloua, the peak dominating Tizi Ouzou. We spent weeks combing the Djebel, closely searching the villages, visiting every house, probing the walls, looking behind every bush and in every hollow tree. All in vain. Then one day we caught one of his assistants who led us to the man's hiding place: a small niche behind a little rock in a field terrace, in front of which soldiers and dogs had passed dozens of times.

Semi-flat ground is found only west of Tizi Ouzou, around Bordj Menaiel, where the Mitidja Plain around Algiers reaches the mountains of Kabylia.

Sharply contrasting with the Arab-populated areas of Algeria, Kabylia is heavily covered with vegetation. The Arab destroys trees, the Kabyle plants them. There are several natural corktree forests, the most notorious—for us—being the Mizrana (10 miles north of Tizi Ouzou) and the Yakouren (near Azazga, further east), both serving as traditional bandit refuges. Ravines are invariably thick with bushes the height of a man, often of the thorny type. The relatively denuded plateaux and summits are covered with briar bushes looking deceptively low; a man has only to lie down to be hidden. Kabylia being short of natural resources, the population's main income derives from arboriculture; olive trees, fig trees, and occasionally cherry trees grow by the thousands on every slope. Paths more fit for goats than for men are usually enclosed by six-foot-high prickly pear-cactus hedges screening the view and stopping men but not bullets.

One day a Kabyle arrested as a rebel messenger escaped in full daylight from my command post. He ran a few yards in front of the sentry, who fired and missed, and jumped into a small ravine. Within seconds a pack of soldiers—including fast-running natives—rushed after him. The man just disappeared in the "jungle." Another time three companies were combing a deep ravine in my *sous-quartier*. It was almost the end of the operation, and the combing party was no more than two hundred yards away from the static troops posted at the ravine's mouth. A *fellagha* was suddenly spotted between the two groups of soldiers. Rifles, submachine guns, and rifle grenades were fired at him. Then 150 soldiers went over the place, foot by foot. The man had vanished.

Kabylia's climate is temperate and thus favored the rebels, who necessarily live largely in the open and who did not enjoy the rich logistical facilities of the counterinsurgent forces. The annual rainfall is 45 inches, concentrated between October and February. Heat in summer is never oppressive for more than two or three days in a row.

The Kabyle population was estimated at 250,000 a hundred years ago. It is now more than one million. The Kabyles are aborigines belonging to the same Berber stock as the Schleuhs in Morocco. They have their own language, quite different from Arabic, but it is only a spoken one, for they never developed a writing system. In spite of some intermarriage with Arabs, they have generally retained their distinct physical and intellectual features. Blond, blue-eyed people are not uncommon among them. Of all the people of North Africa, they are the least influenced by Islam. They do observe the main religious rites such as the annual month-long fast, but not in a rigid way. The local Moslem priest has little moral or temporal authority. While the Arab society is monocratic, theirs is largely democratic. The political and social unit is the village, run by a *djemaa*, a local assembly in which each family is represented by its head. There have been cases of villages that federated into a higher unit, but never for long. Kabyles, however, have completely adopted the Moslem attitude toward women, who are kept in an extremely backward status.

Kabyles have a primitive yet definite talent for organizing, which puts them far above the Arabs in this respect. They have also an amazing sense of dialectic,[6] which often put to shame some of my young officers when they thought they could press a fuzzy propaganda line on the villagers.

The population density is almost as great as that of Belgium, about 260 per square mile. Clusters of villages and hamlets are perched on razor-sharp ridges, hidden on abrupt slopes in the most haphazard distribution. As security increased under French rule, Kabyles spread to the narrow valleys, and tens of thousands of individual houses were built outside villages and scattered throughout the area.

---

[6]   St. Augustin was a Kabyle. Kabylia was Christianized before the Arab invasion. In recent times a Catholic order, les Pères Blancs, has attempted to convert Kabyles. One day a chaplain told me proudly that the number of conversions had doubled in 1957, a unique case in all the Islam countries. "How many?" I asked. "Four!" Converts, he explained, had to leave their village because the community rejected them.

The scarcity of resources compared to the size of the population forces Kabyles to look abroad for a living. Usually, one-third of the males migrate to France for one or two years, another third take seasonal jobs in the Mitidja Plain or migrate to Algiers, and the rest stay in the village to take care of the families. They take turns doing this. The majority of the Moslem population in Algiers is made up of Kabyles, concentrated in the Kasbah. As a result of their constant migrations, they all speak French.

For years before the rebellion, the French Communist Party made a point of propagandizing and recruiting among Kabyles. Since Algerian Moslems could move back and forth to France without any control or visa, and, once there, could vote in the same capacity as French citizens, the Communist Party used to finance their trips just before election time so that they could register in constituencies where the contest was close. Pictures taken during communist riots in Paris in the early 1950s, notably during the anti-Ridgway campaign, show Kabyles in the front ranks of the demonstrators serving as shock troops for the Communist Party.

Few European farmers are found in Kabylia. Most of them are settled around Bordj Menaiel. In the largest centers live a few civil servants, shopkeepers, café and hotel owners, and small entrepreneurs.[7]

The French administration was more understaffed and more deficient in Kabylia than elsewhere, since there were so few European settlers. Kabylia as a whole was an *arrondissement* attached to the *département* of Algiers, with a *sous-préfet* and a staff of five or six assistants at Tizi Ouzou. While the European villages in and around Bordj Menaiel were self-administered *communes*, the rest of the territory was divided into *communes mixtes* (six, I believe) under a French *administrateur*.

---

[7] The above "facts on Kabylia" I had to discover and gather the hard way, by personal reading and observing. So amateurish was our Army Information Service that it never even issued a pamphlet on the basic, useful facts needed by officers in the field.

Tizi Ouzou was also a subdivision headquarters, and our regular peacetime garrison consisted essentially of one Senegalese and one Alpine battalion.

With its geographic and human assets, Kabylia was inevitably meant to become the main bastion of the rebellion. The administrative and military vacuum allowed Krim Belkacem and Amar Ouamrane, equipped with only 400 or 500 rifles (most of them shotguns), to acquire complete control of the population within a few months. By April 1955 our administration, the gendarmes, the police, and the Army had lost all contact with the Kabyles and were isolated. It was unsafe to leave Tizi Ouzou except in heavily protected convoys.

In addition to their success within their own region—*wilaya* III—the Kabyle rebels indirectly controlled the Kasbah in Algiers, and hence the capital of Algeria. Since the rebellion had not fared so well in other areas, Kabyle insurgents acquired a predominant position during 1956–57 in the movement inside Algeria, and they made efforts to capture its direction abroad, ultimately failing in this. Considerable rivalry existed—and still prevails to this day—between *wilaya* III and the other *wilayas* on the one hand, and between *wilaya* III and the External Organization of the FLN on the other hand. Kabyles complained bitterly that they were deliberately starved of weapons and equipment by the FLN Headquarters in Tunisia, that most of the arms convoys meant for them were stolen on the way by *wilaya* I (Aurès) or II (North Constantine). They could indeed have armed several thousand *fellaghas* had it not been for the lack of weapons.

In January 1956, when French reinforcements began to arrive in Kabylia, the area was reorganized administratively into a *département*, and militarily into a zone called, first, ZOK (Zone Opérationelle de Kabylie) and, later, ZEA (Zone Est Algérois). Major-General Olié was given civil and military powers. Incidentally, much has been made in the French press of the alleged Army complaints concerning the duality of civil and military powers in Algeria, presumed to have led to inefficiency in the fight against the rebels. It was often stated that the Army wanted full powers. From my experience, both in the field in Algeria and later at the Etat-Major Général de la Défense Nationale, where I saw affairs from a higher level, the accusation has not the slightest basis. Except in one or two instances where personality clashes occurred between a general commanding a zone and the local *préfet*, the dual system operated to the satisfaction of both sides. In some cases adjustments were required when a senior colonel commanding a sector found a junior *sous-préfet* as his civilian counterpart. But, as a general rule, civilian and military heads were solidly united by their common problems and difficulties. If there was indeed a conflict, it took place between the counterinsurgent leaders in Algeria, whether civilian or military, and the government in Paris. The best proof that duality of power was no problem is found in the fact that, when the Army was given full powers after May 13, 1958, this did not affect the administrative situation in the slightest degree.

The reinforcement in Kabylia consisted of the 27th D.I.A. (Division d' Infanterie Alpine) commanded by Brigadier-General Gouraud, to which were attached a dozen additional battalions bringing the total strength to about 30,000 men in June 1956. Some noteworthy facts about the 27th D.I.A:

Its staff had a 5ème Bureau, an innovation, theoretically in charge of psychological warfare and all problems pertaining to relations with the population. For many varied reasons, however—because the first immediate task of the Division was to crush the rebel bands, because General Gouraud was primarily concerned with military operations, because the 5ème Bureau had no means, because it was a sort of dump for annoying affairs—no eager candidate appeared to head it, and it was entrusted to a Major So-and-So, who found the whole business a terrible chore.

In addition to its organic platoon of L-19 liaison and observation planes, the Division had attached to it a unit of six or eight S-58 helicopters (SIKORSKY) and four BELLs or ALOUETTEs. The latter, lighter types were for the Division's own use. The former, heavier types, with a transport capacity of ten men at most, were merely stationed in the Division area and could be used by it, but the Army Corps at Algiers had first claim on them.[8]

---

[8] Still heavier helicopters ("Flying Bananas") were kept under direct Army Corps and Theater Command.

With the exception of the Division Headquarters Units, an artillery battalion, a cavalry company, and an engineer battalion, all units had been converted into plain infantry. When I arrived in Kabylia in August 1956, my neighbors to the north were a signal corps battalion, those in the northeast an antiaircraft battalion, those in the south an artillery battalion, and to the east a cavalry regiment, all organized and equipped like mine, which was a genuine infantry battalion. Their sophisticated equipment had been left behind in France at the time of their transfer.[9]

General Olié was transferred to another post in August 1956 and a *préfet*, M. Vignon, took over the civilian functions. The civilian-military liaison worked formally in the Etat-Major Mixte, a joint staff presided over by the *préfet* which met once a week. As the Préfecture was just across the street from the Division Headquarters, informal liaison between staff officers took place whenever the need arose.

The zone was divided initially into seven sectors (Bordj Menaiel, Draa-el-Mizan, Tizi Ouzou, Tigzirt, Fort National, Azazga, Bouira). The Tigzirt sector was suppressed in 1957 and its territory attached to the Tizi Ouzou sector (see Figure 1).

With troops at last available in substantial numbers in the spring of 1956, Kabylia was chosen as a test area where special efforts would be made to destroy the main rebel bastion so close to Algiers. The general idea was to break the rebels' armed forces and then to pacify the population. General Olié soon realized that, what with terrain conditions, the huge population, and the rebels' control over it, his 30,000 men were still below the requirements for the task.[10] Algiers could not send him a single additional company. He decided therefore to concen-

---

[9]   Even some Air Force personnel were fighting as infantry in Commandos de l'Air operating as part of the Theater General Reserves. The Navy had a Régiment de Fusiliers Marins busy in the Nemours Sector on Morocco's border. All gave a very good account of themselves. Many Air Force draftees were also assigned to Army units.

[10] No fewer than 70,000 French soldiers had been needed to quell a previous rebellion in Kabylia in 1872.

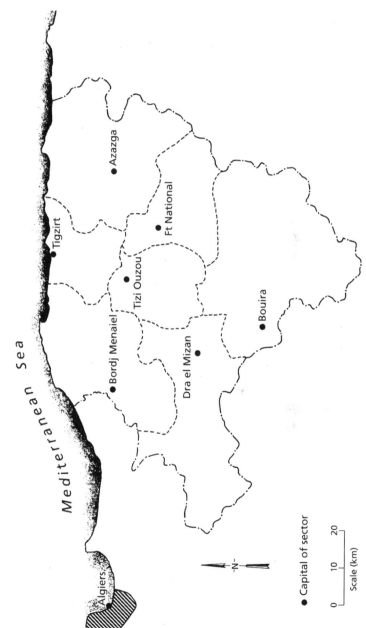

Figure 1
The French Sectors in Greater Kabylia (1956)

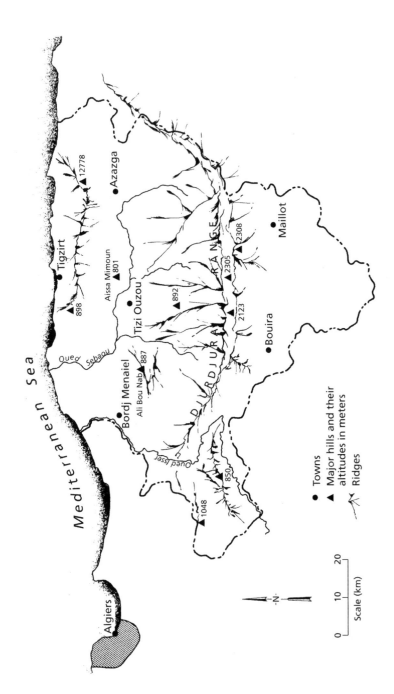

Figure 2
Terrain Features of Greater Kabylia

trate his efforts first in the "easy" part of the zone—the Bordj Menaiel, Tizi Ouzou, and Tigzirt sectors—and later to expand to the "difficult" one with the Djurdjura Range and the tough wooded area around Azazga.

The first step of the first stage in the process, i.e., destroying the main rebel forces, went quite easily. Rebel bands were roaming at will all over Kabylia. As both rebels and population were convinced that the former's victory was imminent, a huge number of last-minute volunteers had joined the insurgent groups, armed with all kinds of weapons including antique pistols, long knives, and axes. In May, June, and July 1956, large-scale operations struck hard at these irregular forces, with the result that thereafter only real *fellaghas* were left in the field, in groups no larger than a platoon. The eager volunteers disbanded and returned to their villages to serve as *mousseblines* (auxiliaries) or to reinforce the OPA, waiting to be called when the promised weapons arrived.

The insurgent remnants, chastened by these operations, lost a great deal of their aggressiveness. Survival became their main concern, not attack on French troops, except very occasionally when an ambush looked profitable. Fearing that the population would weaken under French pressure, they made a vigorous effort to maintain their grip over it. Consequently, terrorism started anew. Krim Belkacem devoted equal efforts to bringing some semblance of order into his military and political organization. *Wilaya* III was divided into four *mintakas*, and so on down the ladder. The small bands were made into platoons according to a primitive table of organization. Support services began to appear, and the emergence of political commissars, propaganda teams, and supply, medical, and intelligence units was evidence of a growing sophistication.

IV. The Sector of Tigzirt

The sector of Tigzirt extended over an area approximately 13 by 13 miles and corresponded roughly to the administrative limits of the *commune mixte* of Mizrana. It had no particular unity of its own geographically, demographically, economically, or otherwise. The sea (thank God) limited it on the north, or rather, I should say, sealed it; the eastern and western limits were somewhat artificially traced on the map; a highway from Tizi Ouzou to Tikobain served as its southern boundary.

From the sea southward the terrain rose to a long crest that crossed almost the entire sector, its highest point at 898 meters (about 2,700 feet); from there the land dropped to the valley of Oued Stita, beyond which stood Djebel Aissa Mimoun rather like an island. The northwest part of the sector was occupied by the Mizrana Forest, of which I will say more later. The forest naturally was the main troublespot.

Four good all-weather roads crossed the sector:

(1) a coastal highway from Algiers to Bougie, particularly dangerous to the troops in the section through the Mizrana Forest;

(2) a parallel highway along the main crest further south;

(3) a Tizi Ouzou-Tigzirt highway, dangerous in the Oued Sebaou gorges just north of Tizi Ouzou, which zigzagged from there around Makouda, and finally ran along the section bordering on the Mizrana Forest. Altogether a natural for cutthroats;

(4) the Tizi Ouzou-Tikobain highway joining the preceding one a few miles south of Tigzirt. This road was dangerous in its Aissa Mimoun parts.

Except for these highways and a few Army-built branch roads, there were only goat paths.

Tigzirt, a small town or large village, was the seat of the *commune mixte* and center of the command post of the sector. It was interesting for its Roman ruins.[11]

The civil administration consisted of the *administrateur*, two assistants, and a squad of gendarmes divided between Tigzirt and Makouda. I once asked some villagers in the Aissa Mimoun how often they had seen the *administrateur* before the rebellion. "Never." The invention of the automobile was the culprit. When the *administrateur* had a horse, he used to go everywhere. But in the last 40 years he had become roadbound and seldom bothered to climb the Djebels.[12]

The sector was commanded by Lieutenant-Colonel Lemoine,* Infantry, a man in his late forties. He had a small staff with a deputy, one intelligence officer, one operations officer, and two very junior officers doing odd jobs including (much later) psychological warfare tasks. Lt.-Col. Lemoine* was concurrently commander of the 93d R.I. (Infantry Regiment), but none of his battalions was under his direct command; they had been assigned to various other sectors.

The equivalent of six battalions was stationed in the sector when I arrived in August 1956: the 15th B.C.A. (Battalion de Chasseurs Alpins) in the north, whose area included part of the Mizrana Forest; one battalion of engineers in the northwest, including the rest of the forest; one signal corps battalion east of the 15th B.C.A.; the II/404 R.A.A. (Antiaircraft Artillery Regiment) occupying Makouda and the southwest part of the sector; my own battalion, the 45th B.I.C. in Djebel Aissa Mimoun; and the 11th Hussards Regiment (actually a battalion) at Boudjima-Tikobain in the southeast.

This represented the peak of our strength. When reservists were discharged in October–November 1956 after their six-month period of active duty was over, the sector strength fell to four battalions.

---

[11] Traces of Roman colonization were numerous in the area. Thus we still walked on a Roman road crossing the northern slope of Aissa Mimoun; I was told it was the remains of the Roman strategic highway crossing all North Africa. I saw many Latin-engraved stones at Bordj Menaiel.

[12] *Djebel* = mountain or hill.

Like the great majority of French officers, Lt.-Col. Lemoine* had fought in Indochina. He had no precise idea of what to do in our situation in Algeria except that *"il ne faut pas refaire la guerre d'Indochine."* He knew we had to win over the population, discouraged firmly any show of indiscriminate hostility toward Kabyles on the part of his units, always had his pockets full of candy for the kids, and a ready smile for the adults whom he treated with studied courtesy. "Look straight into the eyes of the people you greet," was his favorite formula, "their expression does not lie; this is how you can gauge their spirit and their inner thoughts." To me his greatest asset was his open mind and his willingness to accept suggestions, and we got along very well.

He learned a lot in his sector. He was so convinced he was right, and he had concrete proof to show it, that he pestered the zone staff a bit too much. Soon after his sector was merged with the Tizi Ouzou sector, he lost his command and was sent home, brokenhearted.

A sector in Algeria, as a rule, had no organic means. It was just a command organization, a kind of directing and co-ordinating brain with no logistical responsibility, entrusted with the noble task of fighting rebels and pacifying people. Command of a sector was therefore a very interesting assignment, and I do not know of any sector commander who was bored. They were all deeply absorbed in their job. So were the captains in their *sous-quartiers*, who did the actual work with their companies. The battalion commanders in between found little to do once their companies were statically established; they were too far from the population to have direct influence on it, too small a command to conduct interesting operations. Most of their time was taken up with administration and supply problems. They were bored and could find relief only when they could go into the field at the head of a battalion. It is not surprising that they thought only of military action and were reluctant to see their companies so encrusted in the *sous-quartiers* that they could not be gathered for operations. This fact, which had direct effects on the pacification effort, was to have curious results in the general attitude of the French Army in Algeria. Colonels and captains were the most adamant in their hostility and suspicions of French government policy; the majors remained spiritually uncommitted.

The picture on the rebel side was rather confused, as is inevitable in every insurgent movement. First, there was the rebel military and political organization. Our sector included two *mintakas* (zones) and three *nahias* (sectors). The permanent guerrillas within this framework numbered between 80 and 100 in the summer of 1956. Each small rebel band had a tendency to operate and remain in its own small area, except in an extreme emergency, because it found there its own operational and logistic facilities, and was very reluctant to accept poachers from the outside. This understandable attitude did not help larger-scale operations of the higher rebel command. Second, there were the occasional guerrilla visitors attracted by the relative safety of the Mizrana Forest, and their total sometimes exceeded two hundred.

Rebels rarely moved in broad daylight except in the forest. Even at night they never moved in large numbers, that is, in groups of more than fifty. Their moves were prepared by scouts, who contacted the local OPA and made *mousseblines* clear the way and ensure immediate security for the band. The OPA provided hiding places and food.

Aside from terrorism, their only regular military activity consisted in harassing our posts at night by firing a few shots from a safe distance, the obvious purpose being to make an impression on the civilian population.

V. The *Quartier* of Aissa Mimoun

From the time of my arrival until October 1957, my battalion's *quartier* covered most of Douar Djebel Aissa Mimoun (see Figure 3), an area 5 miles square northeast of Tizi Ouzou, limited on the north by Oued Stita (a dry river six months of the year, the embankments of which were covered with very thick bushes); to the west by Oued Sebaou (the largest river in Kabylia, passing through a deep gorge); to the south by the Tizi Ouzou-Tikobain highway; and to the east by an arbitrary line drawn so as to accommodate our neighbors of the 11th Hussards who occupied Tikobain and needed some maneuvering room (see Figure 4). The low alluvial land between the highway and Oued Sebaou further south was officially part of the *quartier* of our southern neighbor, the 1/93d R.A.M. (Mountain Artillery Regiment), but was in fact a no-man's-land, because the R.A.M. seldom crossed the river. Oued Sebaou was fordable during most of the year, except in some parts of the gorge.

The main physical feature of the *quartier* was the Djebel itself, a southwest-northeast ridge culminating in Hill 801 (2,400 feet). The southern slope fell more abruptly than the northern one and was carved by steep ravines. On it lived most of the population, about 15,000, settled in relatively large villages. Two unsurfaced roads (not shown on the map) gave access to the Djebel; one, recently built by the Army, led from a point north of the gorge to Akaoudj, the other from the Grand Remblai Farm midway up to Igonane Ameur to a point named Ighouna (not shown on the map).

The population could be divided into three groups:

(1) the poor, centered around Tahanouts on top of the ridge and spilling over onto the north slope;

(2) the less poor, on the central part of the south slope;

(3) the formerly rich—relatively so—around Akaoudj.

This economic division actually reflected a political division. Wealth was dependent on the amount of arable land, and since land

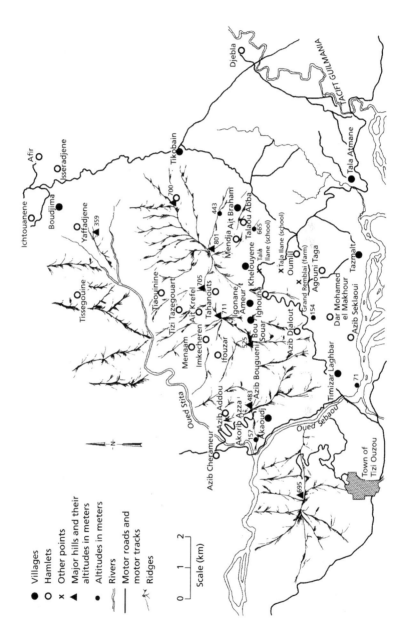

Figure 3
Aissa Mimoun

● Villages
○ Hamlets
× Other points
▲ Major hills and their altitudes in meters
• Altitudes in meters
〜 Rivers
— Motor roads and motor tracks
⋏ Ridges

Scale (km)
0   1   2

Figure 4
Deployment of the 45th B.I.C. (1 August 1956)

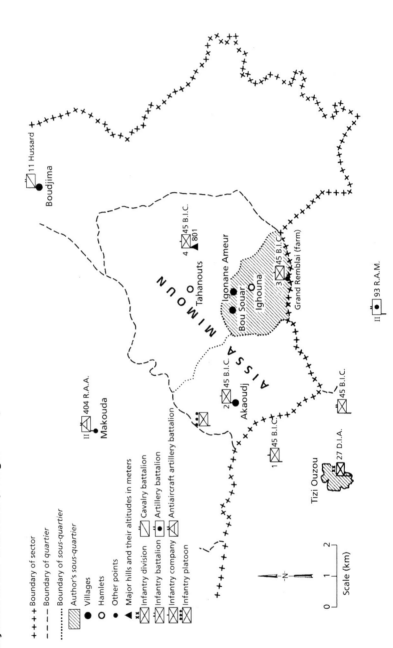

ownership had often changed in the past after tribal wars, the have-nots were obviously hostile to the haves, the more so as France had enforced peace throughout the area and thus had frozen the situation. I discovered, for instance, that the men from Akaoudj were markedly cold toward the other villagers; when I inquired into the reason, I was told that, when Kabylia had revolted against the French back in 1872, the males from Akaoudj joined the rebellion en masse—and were crushed. While they were away, the other villagers jumped on Akaoudj, looted the place, and raped the women. The French authorities, to punish Akaoudj, seized its rich land in the low area west of Oued Stita and distributed it as a reward to loyal Kabyles. Another somber history, which I never elucidated, concerned the enmity between the men from Bou Souar and those of Igonane Ameur, both of whom in turn did not look kindly on the villagers from Khelouyene.

The French power in Aissa Mimoun on the eve of the rebellion was embodied in a *garde-champêtre* (rural policeman), a native veteran of World War I who lived in a small hamlet near Tala Ou Abba. He was armed with a revolver, on the holster of which shone a brass plate engraved with the words: "République Française—La Loi." Against this opposition the rebels had a field day.

The insurgency in Aissa Mimoun started as a family affair. A 35-year-old man from Tahanouts named Oudiai recruited his first followers among his numerous relatives from Bou Souar and Igonane Ameur. He armed them with a collection of shotguns and old pistols and was thus set up in business. With a minimum of executions here and there, he established his power over the populace, which was in no position, even if it wanted to, to resist by force. The *garde-champêtre* was shot at and lightly wounded in the hand, very possibly in a fake assassination attempt. This gave him a reasonable excuse for shutting eyes, ears, and mouth for the duration of the war while still drawing his salary. His official ties with the administration made him indeed a likely intelligence agent for Oudiai.

Oudiai rapidly attracted to his group volunteers from the other villages and was soon officially recognized by the FLN as the boss of his *douar*. There being no opportunity to fight imperialists in Aissa Mimoun, Oudiai led his gang in several ambushes against civilian cars on the highways nearby. He expanded his territory southward as far as the foot of the mountain range on the other side of Oued Sebaou. He was thus in a position to harass traffic on every eastward exit from Tizi Ouzou, and he became a bad nuisance.

In between ambushes, he set himself to organizing the population according to instructions from above. He designated a boss for every village and hamlet, who in turn selected two assistants. These cell members' tasks were:

1. **To identify the enemies**, i.e., those villagers who opposed the movement, or who entertained publicly any doubt about its future victory, or who refused to pay their "voluntary" dues to the cause. (A sizable number of Kabyles fled at once to France despite the FLN veto. Three men from Khelouyene went into hiding. A wealthy oil-press owner from Igonane Ameur was murdered. A young World War II veteran from the same village was badly wounded.)

2. **To collect taxes.** The basic rate (500 francs, or $1, a month) was set deliberately low so that no adult could find an excuse for not paying; 1,000 francs a month were added for each family having a relative working in France; and special levies of up to 50,000 francs for the wealthy owners of oil press, bakery, and *café maure* (native pub). Fines were imposed for all sorts of reasons—for not paying taxes on time, for having failed in a logistic assignment, etc.

Taxes were collected in this way: each group of ten families paid to a representative, who turned the money over to one of the cell members. The latter would keep what was necessary for local expenses and pass the rest to the next-higher echelon. Very detailed accounts were kept. I often felt really touched to see such efforts to maintain honesty. This was, however, one of the few cases where honesty does *not* pay, for these accounts with the lists of donors, when we could seize them, were an intelligence bonanza for us. After several such accidents, the cell members got wise and camouflaged the names.

The money was used partly to buy supplies and equipment for the local guerrillas (food, canned goods, medicines, shoes, batteries), partly to pay a small salary to the fighters (2,000 francs a month), partly to pay *"allocations familiales"* (subsidies) to the families of guerrillas, patriots in jail, and "martyrs of the revolution." The total budget for Aissa Mimoun in early 1957 amounted to 900,000 francs a month. It was, of course, far less than we, the counterinsurgents, would spend in a day just to help the population, but the rebels' money was distributed in cash and without red tape, and that made a difference.

3. **To propagandize.** This was done generally during the daily meeting of the *djemaa* in each village. The village bosses received the propaganda line from one of Oudiai's deputies, who was the political commissar. Full meetings of the entire male population in the villages were called whenever the occasion warranted or when a guest speaker from higher up was available.

4. **To organize the population's support.** The support consisted in: (a) screening Oudiai's *fellaghas* from possible enemy incursion (whenever a group of *fellaghas* came to spend a night in the village, local *mousseblines* stood watch); (b) feeding the *fellaghas*, a burden that invariably fell on the wealthy families or on those whom the rebels were punishing for halfhearted loyalty; (c) procuring and delivering various supplies needed by the *fellaghas* (purchases were made at Tizi Ouzou, sometimes as far as Algiers); (d) hiding stocks of food for the *fellaghas*; (e) spying on the imperialists and their accomplices.

5. **To supplant the French administration.** Since no French administration existed at the *douar* level, no actual supplanting was possible, with the single exception of the judicial field. The rebels simply established an administration where there was none.

Justice was formerly dispensed by the *cadi* (native judge) at Tizi Ouzou. This was no minor function, for Arabs in general, and Kabyles in particular, are forever involved in complicated disputes. Therefore Oudiai's village bosses, in usurping this field, filled a real local need by arbitrating disputes on the spot.

When French reinforcements began to arrive in Kabylia in the fall of 1955, part of the population had second thoughts. Villagers from Khelouyene, who had been lukewarm from the beginning, worried Oudiai. He went to the village one day with his gang, assembled the males, and ordered them to destroy the school, a modern building erected in 1950 with two classrooms for sixty children and two apartments for the schoolteachers (who had left the area as trouble broke out). With Oudiai leading the way, the villagers carried jerrycans of gasoline and piles of wood, and they burned the school, the only one in Aissa Mimoun.

The following day a French cavalry platoon, sent up the hill to investigate, fell into an ambush at Ighouna. One soldier was killed and two were wounded. Both as a punishment and as a precautionary measure, the inhabitants at Ighouna were ordered to evacuate the place, and the Djebel population was warned that any man within two hundred yards on either side of the Grand Remblai–Ighouna road would be shot on sight. Ighouna, with several oil presses, two bakeries, and a *café maure*, had been the industrial center of the southern slope of the Djebel.

One of the most sinister spots in Aissa Mimoun was the highway through the gorge on the right bank of Oued Sebaou. It was a perfect ambush place, and Oudiai made the most of it. One day in February 1956, a convoy fell into a large ambush near Timizar Laghbar and we incurred some losses. The general then in command at Tizi Ouzou had had enough. He called Lieutenant Villon,* the SAS officer in charge of Aissa Mimoun.

"I will give you a company tomorrow. Go to Timizar Laghbar and tell the population to evacuate the village. At 9 a.m. our artillery will destroy it."

The next morning Lt. Villon* went to the village, announced what was in store, gave the people one hour to collect their belongings, and assembled them at some distance above the village to watch the show.

At 9 a.m. nothing happened.

At 9:30 still nothing.

At 9:45, feeling nervous, Villon* managed to contact the artillery by radio.

"For Heaven's sake, what's going on?"

"The general has cancelled the order. Timizar will not, repeat not, be destroyed."

"What a loss of face," confided Villon* when he told me the story months later. "Good luck in your pacification job. As for me, I have had enough and I have applied for a transfer to my old artillery battalion on the Tunisian border."

The 45th B.I.C., a new outfit with no tradition or history, was organized as an independent battalion in March 1956 near Algiers. Its table of organization (see Figure 5) followed the standard Type 107 especially devised for the particular demands of the war in Algeria. Its essential characteristics were:

(1) large combatant to support-service ratio;
(2) light armament (not a single machine gun except the 50-caliber ones mounted on halftracks and trucks);
(3) four combat companies instead of the usual three, hence greater tactical flexibility;
(4) extreme simplification of all logistic and administrative procedures for the combat companies. (Procurement and accounting of food, supply of ammunitions and equipment, payment of salaries, administration of personnel, all these routines were handled at battalion level.)

Total theoretical strength slightly exceeded 800 for the battalion and was set at 152 for combat companies. In fact, of course, the companies were always understrength. The C.C.A.S. (Command, Support, and Service Company) had been calculated too short for the tasks it was expected to fulfill, forcing the battalion commander to pick up men from the combat companies. Leaves, sickness, and temporary assignments to various special courses took away up to 15 per cent of the personnel. Owing to the shortage of draftees (we were then passing through the trough of the "classes creuses," with fewer men than usual coming of draft age), discharged servicemen were never replaced instantly man for man; for the same reason we also had an unusually large proportion of draftees unfit for marching or for sentry duty, or even for combat. I have seen infantry companies fall below

Figure 5
Infantry Batallion Type 107 (slightly over 800 men)

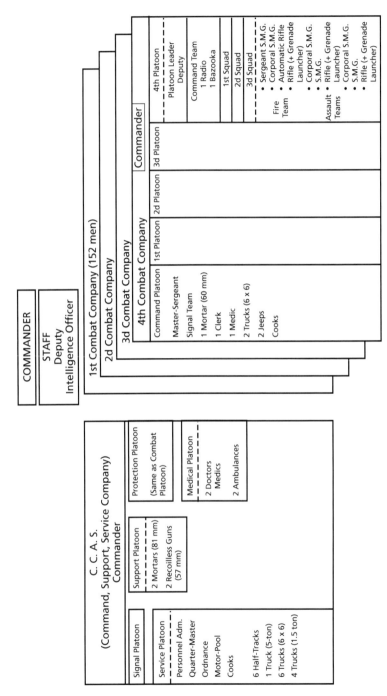

80 men, although this never happened in my battalion because we were Colonial Troops and as such came under a separate, independent branch in Paris, a fact that always helps.

Our men were French draftees, 60 per cent of them farmers. Thirty percent came from the southwest of France, the rest were a mixture from all the other parts of the country. We also had a sprinkling of soldiers from Black Africa, the Caribbean, and Pondichery.

Having been away from troop duty for so long and not knowing the true state of the Army, I expected to find reflected among the draftees the fact that 25 percent of the French people vote communist. I expected to have to deal with soldiers who loathed Army life, who would question the reason of this "colonial war." I was completely wrong. I never commanded soldiers of such quality, not even in 1944– 45 when we were fighting for the liberation of France. What struck me most was not so much their enthusiasm, which was high, but rather their reasonable, solid, businesslike attitude. My impressions were shared by everyone of my colleagues all over Algeria, and we could not help feeling elated to see such a generation coming up in France. For months and months my men lived in Kabyle shacks, in slums I might say, with no amusement, no girls, no French USO, nothing but work, sentry watch (four hours one day, two hours the next), ambush duty every three nights, patrols and operations in between. Yet never a complaint. Marvel of marvels, when we put a private in command of other privates, he did command with authority and initiative; one has to know the individualistic character of the Frenchman to appreciate our surprise.

As these men regularly wrote to their families, reporting what they saw and did in Algeria, we could slowly perceive a change in public opinion at home toward the Algerian War. By 1958 a great majority of the French people wanted to see the war ended, to be sure, but ended with the defeat of the FLN. "We have received too many kicks in the bottom," was the consensus.

We were also much luckier than the Metropolitan Army in regard to our NCOs. The Colonial Army, a prestige outfit offering assignments in exotic places from Timbuktu to Tahiti, attracts easily the best professional NCOs. Selection is stiff, and a sergeant has to be very good to be allowed to re-enlist. So rich were we in NCOs that the Colonial Army was forced to lend one-third of its low cadres to Metropolitan units. Three sergeants in my company had fought in Indochina, where two of them had been in command of one hundred natives in isolated posts with no other European around.

The battalion commander, Major Laval,* 42, his assistant, and four of the five company commanders were regulars with much combat experience in France, in Indochina, or in both. The intelligence officer, a schoolteacher in civilian life, and the last company commander, a colonial civil servant, were reservists who had volunteered for a two-year tour of active duty. In each combat company, there was a regular first or second lieutenant who could replace the company commander.

The battalion had first been engaged in operations around Rivet, a small European town 20 miles east of Algiers. This was the time when FLN victory seemed imminent and large rebel bands armed with anything from submachine guns to axes were roaming the countryside, destroying farms and crops, firing at civilian cars, and massacring French farmers and their families. One of my soldiers described to me once how a French family with whom his squad had been billeted was slaughtered:

"The grandmother and the 15-year-old daughter were tied naked to a chair in the kitchen. They had been raped and disemboweled. Their throats were slit from ear to ear. In another room was a two-year-old boy, his head bashed against the wall and his brains all over!"

Incensed by what they saw, our soldiers fell on the bands with everything they had, giving no quarter and no mercy. Since it was often difficult to tell a *fellagha* from a peaceful Arab, they fired on whoever ran. Very soon the rebels were routed and French farmers were breathing again. High-ranking military and civilian officers came from Algiers to congratulate the battalion. Newspapermen followed and took pictures. *Paris-Match*, the leading weekly magazine, printed on its cover a color picture of the battalion in operation. Then, in a pattern that was to be repeated so often, a segment of the press at home began to protest loudly against alleged repressive measures. Visitors from Algiers suddenly ceased coming, and in late May 1956 the battalion was transferred to Kabylia for "disciplinary reasons." It was there given a choice area, Djebel Aissa Mimoun, which had caused many headaches to the zone staff, what with the aggressiveness of the local rebels and its proximity to Tizi Ouzou.

In June and July the battalion took part in large-scale operations then going on all over Kabylia, and started settling in its own *quartier*.

I arrived when this phase was ending. Oudiai's band was estimated then at about 25 *fellaghas*, equivalent to a strong rebel platoon, who were divided into two squads, each under a sergeant. The battalion was deployed as follows:

(1) Command Post (C.P.) and Command, Support, and Service Company (C.C.A.S.): brick factory, 2 km east of Tizi Ouzou, at the fork made by National Road No. 12 and Communal Road No. 24;

(2) 1st Company: Djebel Beloua, 1.5 km north of Tizi Ouzou. The company was on loan to the Tizi Ouzou sector and did not come under the battalion operational command;

(3) 2d Company: Akaoudj;

(4) 3d Company: Grand Remblai Farm, 4 km east of the Oued Sebaou bridge on Road No. 24;

(5) 4th Company: Hill 801, with a small detachment at the burned-out school near Khelouyene;

(6) A school for corporals with 50 men detached from all the companies, under a lieutenant, was located for the duration of the course on the low land at Azib Cherameur, 1.5 km north of the junction of Oued Sebaou and Oued Stita.

Every company but the 4th could be supplied by truck; the 4th was supplied by mule convoy. Every other day, trucks from the battalion command post would bring their load to Ighouna; a squad of native muleteers from the Mule Transport Company of the 27th D.I.A. attached to the 3d Company would load the supplies and carry them up to Hill 801. Protection of trucks and mules was the responsibility of the 3d Company.

Each company in Aissa Mimoun had been given a *sous-quartier* (see Figure 4). The 3d Company had the smallest, because the company was the battalion's mobile reserve and was on immediate call for operations in the Tigzirt sector or in the zone.

● ➤ ● ➤ ●

I remained four or five days at the battalion command post. The second day I attended a meeting of all the sector's company commanders called by Lt.-Col. Lemoine* at Agouni Goughrane on the southern edge of the Mizrana Forest. I noticed on the way that we were taking no chances on this Tizi Ouzou–Tigzirt highway. My battalion's convoy of six jeeps was preceded by one halftrack, and followed by two 6x6 trucks loaded with a platoon and another halftrack.

The purpose of the meeting was to hear a lecture on pacification by a psychological warfare officer from Paris. The lecturer, a captain, had been captured by the Vietminh in Indochina and had spent a year in their prisoner camps. He described the Vietminh brainwashing technique. The key of the process, he said, was to start a dialogue with the prisoners, to break the psychological barrier between the prisoners and the political commissar.

"With us French officers, the Viets chose a subject to which they were sure we would be obliged to respond: cleanliness. They appealed to our pride, they told us how vital it was for us to keep clean so as to avoid diseases. They pointed out that their own soldiers managed to keep clean despite adverse conditions. It seemed so innocent that we swallowed the bait and we began co-operating with them on cleanliness. From then on, little by little, very subtly at first, bluntly later, they succeeded in forcing our co-operation on other matters and we could not avoid giving it, at least on the surface."

He explained how we could use the same approach to our profit here in Kabylia, by asking Kabyles to wash their hands and gradually leading them to give us their support. But there was a catch: the process worked only under mass-meeting conditions. It was very important to have the masses shout slogans; thus each participant would get a concrete feeling of the overall power of the masses and would lose his fear of the rebels.

When the lecture was over, Instruction No. 1 on Psychological Action was distributed to the company commanders. Other such instructions would reach us every two weeks, we were promised. The document explained how to organize the first mass meeting, with such details as where to locate the "claque" and how to give cues for applause and slogan-shouting.

(1) The meeting would start with a few minutes of slogan-shouting ("France means peace, FLN means misery!").
(2) Then the leader would tell an amusing story from the legend of Djoha, a picaresque figure in Arab folklore (the document contained a skeleton text of the story).
(3) This would be followed by a talk on cleanliness stressing the danger of dirt for oneself and for one's family (slogan: "Wash your hands!").
(4) A commentary on the Koran, the excerpt being appropriately chosen to show that violence without justice is wrong. [The Koran must contain everything.]
(5) A commentary on current events.
(6) Finally more slogan-shouting.
P.S.: collective singing if feasible.

Snickers and skepticism typified the reactions of the company commanders when the reunion came to an end. We did actually receive Instructions No. 2 and 3; the whole affair was dropped suddenly with no official explanation. I must say that Frenchmen are so distrustful of propaganda of any sort when it is directed at them that they can hardly imagine that it might work on others. After all, who can deny that propaganda can be a potent weapon? But this seemed really too ridiculous. Captain Orsini,* a colleague from another battalion, told me how he had actually tried to implement Instruction No. 1. He knew it would fail, but he just wanted to be sure so that he could give a piece of his mind to the psychological expert next time he appeared.

"When I asked the villagers to come to the meeting—males, females, and children, as the specialist told us—there was a great hullabaloo in the village. The men did not want their women to attend the meeting; it was unheard of, they would refuse to come. It would have been self-defeating to use force for this occasion, so I let the women skip the meeting. The men and the children came and sat sullenly. Now for the claque, all I could use were my own soldiers since not a single Kabyle has dared come out openly for us. The slogans were met with complete impassivity, no echo, just silence. The villagers heard the tale, the lecture on cleanliness, the Koran, the news, the final slogans. I might as well have talked to gorillas in the zoo. I lost face with them, that's all I got out of this meeting. I am glad, though, that I had warned my soldiers in advance not to take the show too seriously. I would have lost my prestige with them too."

For a long time "wash your hands" became a form of jovial greeting among the sector's officers.

The expert's logic was impeccable: the Viets had succeeded in a hostile milieu; for what if not hostile would be a group of enemy officers? The Kabyles under FLN control were a hostile milieu. Why shouldn't we succeed too? He must have forgotten that the French officers were prisoners, isolated from their normal environment, while Kabyle civilians were not prisoners and were living in their normal environment. I was to see other cases of such blind aping of the other side's methods, and always with the same result.

VI. The 3d Company and Its *Sous-Quartier*

I took command of the 3d Company on the 4th or 5th of August 1956, the day the company returned from a large operation in the area of Blida in the zone Nord Algérois. Its temporary commander, Lt. Perrier,* a reservist on active duty, remained with me two days and then went on leave.

The entire company was stationed in a dilapidated Kabyle farm, sharing the walled compound with the Aissa Mimoun SAS consisting of Lt. Villon,* a French sergeant, a French civilian radio operator, and two *mokhazenis* (native auxiliaries used as personal guards), one of whom was a Kabyle veteran from the nearby village of Djebla. Accommodations were miserable, to say the least, and rather depressing. Soldiers were piled in dark, dusty rooms; the open-air kitchen was dirty and located next to the mule shed; latrines had been dug haphazardly just outside the wall, were not kept up, and so attracted swarms of flies and wasps. Drinking and washing water had to be trucked in from the battalion command post because the local well was foul.

Defensive installations consisted of a string of barbed wire around the farm, shallow trenches outside the north wall facing the Djebel, and loopholes on the other walls. The company had never been attacked or harassed in that billet.

The platoons were armed with obsolete Springfield 1903 rifles, Thompson 45 submachine guns, Browning automatic rifles, and some MAS-40 French rifles used for grenade-launching. This armament was changed in early 1957, and we then received Garand M-1, MAT-48 French submachine guns much lighter than the Thompsons, and FM 24-28 automatic rifles as well as bazookas. The signal equipment consisted of one U.S. field telephone linked to the battalion switchboard, an S.C.R.-300 for battalion-company liaison, and five S.C.R.-536 for company-platoon liaison. These last sets were utterly useless in this hilly terrain and completely unreliable besides. When we went on to serious operations, we were provided with additional S.C.R.-300 for internal company liaisons. In the store of equipment I discovered a bugle. In

1947 in North China I had seen communist troops use a bugle with great effectiveness in combat. I found an amateur bugler among my men and copied unashamedly the Red Chinese. For simple orders such as Stop, Advance, Fire, Cease Fire, Attack, Operation Ended, etc., nothing can beat a bugle, and my fellow officers who smiled at first soon envied my one-man signal corps.

The soldiers' combat uniforms were in shreds after months of active operations. The men hardly differed from the *fellaghas*. They had been issued two types of shoes, one the regular leather and rubber-sole kind, the other canvas and rubber called "Pataugas" after the name of the manufacturer. Pataugas were preferred by the soldiers for their lightness; a pair lasted about two months (or sometimes one day, if we had climbed rocks). I found them still too heavy and unhealthy, and I tried canvas shoes with rope sole of the kind used in the Pyrenees; they were ideal while they lasted (about a month). This matter of shoes has some importance when one is running after Kabyles in their own terrain.

The lst Platoon was commanded by Lt. Berger,* a 26-year-old Cavalry reservist who had volunteered for active duty. His home was Algiers, where his family had been established for four generations. His views were that rebels were bastards, those who supported them—i.e., the entire population—even worse, and that force was the only way to treat the lot.

The 2d Platoon was under 2d Lt. Paoli,* a 22-year-old Corsican from Morocco doing his military service; calm, quiet, reserved, very mature for his age, and extremely reliable .

The 3d Platoon was commanded by a regular master sergeant, Vignaux,* 32, who had seen fighting in France and Indochina. Rather lazy but authoritarian, he cultivated a stupid, bovine look. He turned out to be a master at intelligence work and at gaining the confidence of the villagers.

The 4th Platoon was commanded by 2d Lt. Fontaine,* 21, a Parisian who had been with the company since the beginning and had

had some combat experience around Rivet. He had the temper and the brain of a young puppy, always ready to dash into blunders.

Soldiers were idle between operations. "They rested." Under the pretext that a war was going on, formal discipline had been greatly relaxed. Lieutenant Perrier* was a "just-follow-me" type of leader, high in spirit and aggressiveness but short on organization. A regular NCO, who was no longer with the company when I took over, had been so worried about the general idleness that he tried to keep the men busy building a vital "liaison-plane airstrip" outside the farm.

There was no contact at all with the population. Once in a while Perrier* took a patrol up the hill and toured the *sous-quartier*, not to visit the population but to hunt rebels. He never found any. At night two or three ambushes were set within a kilometer from the farm, on Hills 208, 237, and 190. Perrier* wanted to comb Acif Tiouririn, the ravine between Bou Souar and Igonane Ameur where, he was sure, guerrillas used to spend the day sleeping. Major Laval* would not let him do it. Just recently, the battalion had lost three men during an operation in a ravine on the north slope, all killed by shotgun blasts at point-blank by *fellaghas* who had been stumbled upon while hiding deep in the bushes. Laval* did not want a repeat performance.

Beneath the seemingly depressed look, however, the men were all high-spirited. Whatever apprehensions they felt when they first came to Algeria, they lost them chasing the rebels near Rivet. While they had no liking for discipline and army routine, operations excited them tremendously; platoon leaders always had a hard time assigning men to guard the billets when the company was about to go into operations; nobody wanted to stay behind.

However, as the rebels had been reduced in number and had found it best to avoid encounters with superior forces, it was more difficult to catch them. Operations in which my company had taken part recently had brought fewer and fewer results. Among cadres and men a feeling of futility was beginning to take hold. Thus they commented bitterly on the fact that in this Blida operation, in which 3,000 men had been involved during four days, the company had found no opportunity to fire a single shot.

As I took over my command, orders came relieving the company from mobile reserve duty.

PART TWO

The Struggle for Control
of the Population

I. The Strategic Problem

It was clear by July 1956 that a new phase had begun in the Algerian War. While the preceding period, from November 1954 on, had seen the rebellion expand and almost reach victory, the sheer size of the French forces at last available in Algeria frustrated the FLN's hope for an early decision. It made it impossible, moreover, for the rebels to hold safe territorial bases, a *sine qua non* for the development of a sizable regular army.

The rebels could, however, expand their guerrilla forces and fight a war of attrition, calculating that lassitude on the part of the French government and nation combined with outside pressure would force us eventually to give in. The success of the FLN strategy depended on the solution of three essential problems: (1) armament for the guerrillas, (2) the psychological effects of their operations, and (3) control of the Moslem population. For the French counterinsurgents, in turn, the strategy amounted to frustrating the rebels' efforts to solve these problems.

The rebels had no manpower difficulty in 1956. That was to come later, in 1957 and even more so in 1958, when they found it increasingly hard, and in the end almost impossible, to replenish their losses, owing to the waning enthusiasm of potential sympathizers, an unsolved armament crisis, and the logistic problem of feeding guerrillas that had become isolated from the population. But as of mid-1956, ten volunteers could easily have been recruited for every *fellagha* in the field, had it not been for the dire shortage of weapons. In fact, the guerrillas were forced to be choosy, and a patriot, if he wanted to be accepted into the maquis, had first to prove his worth by murdering a Frenchman or committing a terrorist action.

Armament for the rebels could only come from abroad, either delivered directly to the Algerian coast or smuggled across the borders. Local seizures yielded nothing, because the French fought too well, were too strong in the first place, and did not desert or surrender. Consequently, it was imperative for the French to seal off Algeria.

General Salan, succeeding General Lorillot as Commander-in-Chief, assigned first priority to this task. The Navy had no trouble taking care of the blockade. Algerian Moslems are not sailors (let us say, they had forgotten since their pirate days in the last century); and most of the fishing boats belonged to Europeans (the majority Spaniards) and could be easily controlled. In addition to coastal surveillance, the Navy watched, and occasionally—with no legal justification—boarded on the high seas, suspicious ships bound for Tunisia and Morocco. Thus, on October 17, 1956, a Greek ship under Egyptian charter, the 400-ton "ATHOS," was seized and brought to Oran with 70 tons of war material (12 mortars, 6 machine guns, 50 automatic rifles, 600 submachine guns, 2,000 rifles, 300,000 cartridges, and 6 radio sets).

On land, if the border with Libya presented no difficulty because of the Sahara Desert and the distance to the nearest rebel-infested area inside Algeria, the borders with Morocco and Tunisia would easily have required 100,000 men to control with reasonable effectiveness, given their length and the local terrain. To save personnel, it was decided to build an artificial electrified fence, a project which was completed along both borders by the spring of 1958. Until then, an estimated average of 1,000 weapons a month were being smuggled into Algeria.

Also, the rebels realized that they could achieve the greatest psychological effect on the French and on world opinion at the cheapest price by stepping up terrorism in the main cities, notably in Algiers, which served as headquarters to most French and foreign correspondents and thus acted as a natural amplifier. A grenade or a bomb in a café there would produce far more noise than an obscure ambush against French soldiers in the Ouarsenis Mountains. If European city dwellers could be provoked into blind reactions against the Moslems, so much the better. The No. 2 priority concern of General Salan, who saw eye to eye with M. Lacoste on these matters, was to deal with urban terrorism, especially in Algiers. Since Kabyles were dominant in the Moslem population of the capital city, special attention was paid to Kabylia, from where most of the terrorists came and were directed. Whenever a link was suspected between terrorist groups in Algiers and a rebel maquis in Kabylia, paratroopers, who all belonged to the theater reserves (they were highly in demand all over Algeria and hard to get), were sure to appear soon. Individual French settlers, with the exception of farmers, were not armed, for fear that they might act in blind anger. Those who were belonged to the carefully controlled Unités Territoriales, a part-time volunteer urban outfit supplementing the police and the Army in street patrols.

Finally, the rebels knew that their guerrilla forces would be lost if we ever succeeded in isolating them from the population. Therefore, even though they still enjoyed at the time a great deal of spontaneous support from the Moslem masses, they did not hesitate to terrorize the people at the slightest suspicion of wavering loyalty. Terrorism, a dangerous weapon because it often backfires, and one which the rebels had intended to use only for a short period in order to start the ball rolling, remained a constant form of their activity in rural areas, indeed the principal form in many places. I first knew that they were in trouble when I saw them going back to selective terrorism, and still later to blind terrorism—against Moslems—instead of expanding from guerrilla warfare to the higher stages of the insurgency process.

To defeat the rebels over the vast expanses of the Algerian territory was the task assigned to the bulk of the French forces, an important task in General Salan's eyes but one which nevertheless received only third priority. Once the grid of static troops had been established, with the emphasis on Kabylia, Salan considered his own task done; it was now up to the local area commander to deal with the situation in his Army corps or in his zone as best he could, with the occasional support of the theater reserves. Since the war in Algeria was tactically a multiplicity of small-scale affairs, no grandiose operation was conceivable, no large shifting of troops was warranted that would justify a more direct conduct of the operations by the Commander-in-Chief.

II. No Doctrine for the Counterinsurgent

As my activity fell within the framework of the static troops operating in rural areas, it is necessary to describe at this point how our task was conceived.

After the war in Indochina, after the nationalist uprisings in Tunisia and Morocco, after the limited experiment in the Aurès Mountains, the general consensus was that this war could only be won if we succeeded in divorcing the rebels from the population. Although the rebel forces were now broken into small, ineffective bands—this was already an achievement on our part—military operations could not by themselves bring a complete, definitive victory. On the one hand, guerrilla groups, precisely because of their small size and their small logistical needs, and also because of the terrain, were very elusive; on the other hand, their losses in personnel were instantly replaced and attrition would not produce effects for a long period. Weapons were what counted, but at the rate they were coming in, and considering how little armament guerrillas need to spread insecurity, attrition through capture of guerrilla weapons seemed just as slow.

The general directives from Robert Lacoste, the Minister-Resident in Algiers, which were widely distributed in the Army, insisted on the necessity to win over the population. In my zone, as everywhere in Algeria, the order was to "pacify." But exactly how? The sad truth was that, in spite of all our past experience, we had no single, official doctrine for counterinsurgency warfare. Instead, there were various schools of thought, all unofficial, some highly vociferous. While the majority of cadres lived in an intellectual vacuum, waiting for precise orders from above and meanwhile performing the routine combat tasks for which they had been trained all their lives, these different schools of thought were championed by minorities.

At one extreme stood the "warriors," officers who had learned nothing, who challenged the very idea that the population was the real objective, who maintained that military action pursued with sufficient means and vigor for a sufficiently long time would defeat the rebels.

They needed just one more regiment, or battalion, or company to do the trick. The 9th R.I.C. (Régiment d'Infanterie Coloniale) in the Bordj Menaiel sector was typical of this school. Its units did not deploy below company level until the spring of 1959. They were established in so-called "strategic positions" on top of the ridges, well apart from the population, where they controlled exactly nothing. They spent all their time in large operations. Precisely because of these tactics, the rebels grew in strength in that sector; as late as 1959, the area was considered the best hunting ground in all Kabylia, and any operation was sure to engage anywhere from 20 to 200 *fellaghas*.

I must say that the military system of awards and promotions was rigged in favor of the "warriors." Medals were given on the basis of valor in combat. If there was no combat because the local commander had succeeded in pacifying his area, too bad for him—no medal. It was no doubt much easier to assess the efficiency of an officer by glancing at the "score" (how many rebels killed or captured? how many weapons seized?) than by making an estimate of the support he received from the population; what criteria was one to use in this case?

At the other extreme were the "psychologists," most of them recruited among officers who had undergone the Vietminh brainwashing in prisoner camps. To them, psychological action was the answer to everything, not merely the simple propaganda and psychological warfare adjunct to other types of operations, conventional or otherwise. "You use force against the enemy," one of their leaders told me, "not so much to destroy him but in order to make him change his mind on the necessity of pursuing the fight. In other words, you do a psychological action." They were convinced that the population could be manipulated through certain techniques adapted from communist methods. Although the pure "psychologists" were few, they were very articulate. They managed to take hold of the professional French Army magazines in which, month after month, they published their thoughts and gave the impression that theirs was indeed the official doctrine. In fact, so ridiculous was their position when their theories were submitted to the test of reality in the field that the whole idea became the subject of standard jokes in the Army in Algeria. Psychological action was sunk with whatever valid points the theory might have had. Propaganda and psychological warfare never recovered from the disaster.

In January 1957 I had a long discussion with Colonel Goussault, chief of General Salan's 5ème Bureau in Algiers. Colonel Goussault is a brilliant officer who had served on General de Lattre de Tassigny's staff (a real distinction, for de Lattre had a genius for spotting fools and kicking them out), and who later headed our PsyWar section during the Suez expedition. In Algeria, he represented a variant of the "psychologist" school. He explained to me his plan:

"I have convinced Salan to select the Orleansville Zone as a test area. We will make a special military effort there. While this action goes on, a team of psychological action officers will comb the area looking for Moslems who have the leadership stuff—any Moslems, educated or not, pro-French or pro-rebel. We will secretly pick up these people from their towns and villages, we will bring them to a secret camp. There we will indoctrinate them in our own ideology. Of course, I expect some rejects. But those who pass the course will be infiltrated back into the area, still in complete secrecy. They will recruit followers and build up a pro-French movement rival to, but operating like, the FLN."

"I wonder what kind of ideology you think you can furnish them with. The rebels have an ideology, simple and effective because it appeals to passion: independence. What can you oppose to that?"

"Humanism, co-operation, social progress, economic development, etc."

"Precisely by what criteria are these potential leaders going to be selected?"

"Psychological action officers will simply investigate who is well regarded by villagers for any reason, not just because he is a notable."

"I can tell you from my experience in Kabylia that the only criterion that counts is the loyalty of the people, measured by concrete proof and not by words. I bet you that, barring a few happy exceptions; your potential leaders won't lift a finger for you once they are loose. Now a practical question: Do you really believe it possible to pick up men from a village without people's noticing it? Do you think they won't be investigated by the OPA and kept under watch when they come back?"

"It can be done, we can camouflage the whole thing, we can pretend they were arrested as FLN agents."

"From my experience in China, I can assure you there is not much room for rival movements in clandestine situations. Even professional bandits, and they were experienced, disappeared when the Chinese Communists came into an area; they were absorbed or eliminated. I don't deny the possibility of promoting rival movements on a small scale occasionally and for short periods, but this cannot represent our main form of counterinsurgency warfare; it will never bring decisive results. I will rather stick to my methods [see later]. Let's compare notes in six months. Meanwhile good luck."

I did not have to wait six months. Long before that Colonel Goussault had acknowledged fairly the failure of his plan.

In between the "warriors" and the "psychologists" stood the bulk of French officers left to their own devices with their practical problems. Colonel Blanc,* for instance, who commanded the Tizi Ouzou sector, ordered his men to "chat with the people at every opportunity" and thus earned the nickname "Li Fig Li Zolive" (i.e., "Les Figues Les Olives" pronounced in Kabyle fashion), because the usual chat between a soldier and a Kabyle farmer inevitably ended with a comment on the crop prospect. Or, there was Major Faivre* in another sector whose plan received wide distribution in the zone, with favorable comments from the zone command. His idea was to appoint by force in every village a chief, a political commissar, a team of propagandists, a man in charge of social affairs, a chief for the self-defense corps, etc. The proposal was duplicated at higher echelons, the document showing the elaborate and impressive organizational charts that we, in the Army, are so fond of. The designated men would presumably discover the joy of exercising power and end by co-operating willingly with us.

With all these fantasies, frustration was most intense at company level. The company commander in his *sous-quartier*, being directly in contact with the population, had the key job in the war. Echelons above him could always issue orders; he was the man who had to translate them into concrete action. And in the absence of sensible orders from above, he had to make his own if he wanted to achieve anything. He could not content himself with purely military tasks and let the local SAS officer carry the pacification job and work on the population. For the SAS officer was absolutely unable to operate as long as the area was not reasonably safe, and to make it safe required at least the control of the population, and preferably the co-operation of the population. In other words, the SAS officer was effective only when the basic problem was solved.

The army officer has learned in military academies that combat is divided into distinct phases: approach toward the enemy, contact with the enemy, test of the army's strength, attack, assault, exploitation of success, possibly retreat, defensive action, etc. For each phase, he has been taught, there is an appropriate standard deployment and maneuver for the platoon, the company, and the battalion, in accordance with the current doctrine. Therefore, the intellectual problem of the field officer in conventional combat consists in identifying the phase in which he finds himself. Then, all he has to do is to apply the standard answer to his particular situation. If he has a good memory, he can't go far wrong. Such a process unfortunately does not exist in counterinsurgency warfare. How much time and means to devote to tracking guerrillas or, instead, to working on the population, by what specific actions and in what order the population could be controlled and led to co-operate, these were questions that the *sous-quartier* commander had to answer by himself. One can imagine the variety of answers arrived at and the effects on the pacification effort as a whole.

III. My Own Theory

It is only fair to warn the reader that I too had an axe to grind. I had had broader experience in the business than most of my colleagues because I had been lucky enough to observe at first hand a revolutionary war conducted by the masters at the game, the Chinese Communists, in 1945–48. Immediately afterward, I was sent to Greece, where I expected to see another communist insurgency snowballing. I saw instead its defeat, a revealing experience. I had closely watched the events in Indochina and, thanks to my position in Hong Kong and to my relations with the British Army, I had studied the case of Malaya. Two trips to Manila and long talks with officials involved in the struggle against the communist Huks had acquainted me with the insurgency in the Philippines. I developed from my observations the embryo of a theory which I now intended to apply in the field.

There was no doubt in my mind that support from the population was the key to the whole problem for us as well as for the rebels. By "support" I mean not merely sympathy or idle approval but active participation in the struggle.

Such support is seldom spontaneous. Even when it is, it still must be directed and organized. Nor can it be imposed on the population entirely from without. It must come partly from the people, more precisely from the militant elements among the masses, from the "activists," to use the communist term. Support is thus acquired through an organization developed within the population.

In order to pacify, therefore, we had to identify those Moslems who were for us, to rely on them to rally the majority of the population, and together to eliminate the rebels and their militant supporters.

The question was, were there any potential supporters for our side in the population? I was sure of it. We had been in Algeria too long not to have influenced some people. In any case I had observed many times the validity of the axiom:

"In any circumstances, whatever the cause, the population is split among three groups: (1) an active minority for the cause, (2) a neutral majority, (3) an active minority against the cause."

True, the rebels had serious advantages over us:

(1) They had a dynamic cause appealing to the passions, while all we could offer was a line appealing to reason. Given time, however, reason would prevail. The best cause loses its power under war conditions, and peace then becomes the central issue.

(2) They had a headstart, having already set up their political organization among the population. This meant that we would have to destroy the OPA before we could establish our own.

(3) They were Moslems, and we were not. The rebel fish could swim better in Moslem water than the counterinsurgent land mammal. The more reason for us to rely on Moslem supporters.

On the other hand, we had in our favor our enormously superior material strength, our chief asset provided we used it fully and intelligently.

These were theoretical thoughts. They sounded good to me, but I realized nevertheless that they needed testing as much as I needed practical experience. Under what conditions would our potential supporters emerge from their present silence? How much risk were they prepared to take? Now that we were strongly implanted in the area and the rebels were on the run, would our supporters be convinced and come out easily? This is what I had to find out first.

IV. Indoctrination of My Company

My immediate task was to prepare my tool, the 3d Company, for the work ahead. After a few days spent touring the *sous-quartier*, checking the equipment inventory of the company, and listening to the cadres and the men, I called a meeting of all the personnel.

I explained the nature of this war. Our forces were vastly superior to the rebels. Then why couldn't we finish with them quickly? Because they managed to mobilize the population through terror and persuasion. And because of the support they got from the population, the rebel guerrillas were well informed on our moves, well screened, well hidden, well supplied, and consequently hard to catch. Moreover, those we caught would be replaced immediately and fighting would thus last a long time. It was therefore imperative that we isolate the rebels from the population and that we gain the support of the population. This implied that under no circumstances could we afford to antagonize the population even if we had to take risks for ourselves in sparing it. Operations of the type the company had participated in at Rivet, and more recently in Kabylia, were over. We no longer had to cope with large rebel bands. We would, of course, continue to hunt actively the remnants, but from now on we would devote our main effort to the population.

Perhaps influenced by Instruction No. 1 on Psychological Action, I told the men the wartime story of Hitler, Mussolini, and Churchill betting on who would catch a fish in a swimming pool. Hitler tried first using elaborate fishing equipment, but the fish would not bite. Mussolini dived into the pool, trying to catch the fish by hand; he was lifted from the water exhausted and half-drowned. Then Churchill sat quietly by the pool, lighted a cigar, and started emptying the pool with his teacup. "It will take time but I'll get the fish!"

"This is how we will proceed here," I concluded. The soldiers laughed, but it was obvious from the questions thrown at me that they were still skeptical. A private, a regular soldier who had risen to the rank of sergeant in the Foreign Legion, had fought in Indochina and

Korea, and had lost his rank after a brawl, summed up the general opinion:

"Sir, these Kabyle people, they are all bastards, they are all hypocrites, they all support the rebels."

"Our job is precisely to stop this support. If we lump together population and rebels—and this is what the FLN want us to do—we are sure to keep the population supporting them. If we distinguish between people and rebels, then we have a chance. One cannot catch a fly with vinegar. My rules are: outwardly you must treat every civilian as a friend; inwardly you must consider him as a rebel ally until you have positive proof to the contrary."

Through this lecture and a few others, and from the discussions among the men and the cadres, I managed to spot those who were in agreement with me. These were the men I intended to employ first in my operations. The rest, I thought, would be convinced by results—if I succeeded.

Near Hill 190, about 400 yards south of Grand Remblai, was a small hamlet, Agouni Taga. It was outside my territory, but since it was so close to my position, and since my southern neighbors from the I/93 R.A.M. seldom ventured north of Oued Sebaou, I decided to work on it. I also selected another hamlet, Oumlil, 1 km northeast of Grand Remblai.

I told 2d Lt. Paoli* and M/S Vignaux* to take their platoon to these hamlets, make a census, inform the population, and affix propaganda posters we had just received.

The census, a rather primitive affair (we just took the name and age of every inhabitant and painted a number on each house), was completed in two days. The population's attitude was outwardly cordial, either out of sincere feeling (because we were garrisoned so nearby that they had less fear of the rebels) or out of hypocrisy. We had no way of telling. Paoli* and Vignaux* commented on the news from Algiers' newspapers; the villagers listened attentively but silently. The posters were dutifully affixed on various walls. I asked if anyone could read. Nobody. So soldiers read the contents to the population.

Patrols discovered the following morning that all the posters had been destroyed. On my orders, Paoli* and Vignaux* returned to their respective hamlets, assembled the population, and said that from now on owners of the houses on which posters were affixed would be held responsible for their preservation. That very night I sent ambushes inside the hamlets. We had no more trouble there in regard to the posters. Vignaux* told me weeks later that one day, after a torrential rain, he saw at Oumlil a young boy leaning against a wall with his hand on a poster.

"What are you doing here?"

"The rain washed the poster away. My father tried to glue it back with cow dung but it did not work. So he told me to keep the poster on the wall."

"Fine, thank you, we will fix it now, you can go home."

It is impossible to assess the value of written propaganda. In my *sous-quartier*, and I suppose it was the same situation elsewhere, illiteracy was the rule. An educated Kabyle does not stay in his village where his education, a costly investment for his family, would be wasted. He usually put it to better use by settling in France or in a large Algerian town. In view of this fact I recommended that only posters with self-explanatory pictures be sent to me. The written ones I continued to receive I affixed outside the military posts in the villages; when a villager came to ask for a pass or for any other reason, the sentry read them to him.

The small incident I have related above, however, made me think that posters had a considerable, if unintended, value: they provoked the first battle of will between the rebels and myself over the population. Rebels tore them down or asked the population to do it. I asked the population to preserve them. This was a battle I could not lose because I was the stronger. Thus I won my first psychological victory.

V. An Operation at Sector Level

One day at the end of August 1956, Lt.-Col. Lemoine,* the sector commander, toured our *quartier*. He seemed surprised to hear Major Laval* tell him that Oudiai and his twenty-five rebels were still roaming the area. "What? Such a large band after so many operations? We must go after them. I'll see what reinforcement I can get from the zone."

The operation took place under Lt.-Col. Lemoine* a few days later. It was my first large operation. Since they all followed more or less the same pattern, I will describe it in detail.

The purpose was to catch Oudiai's band. We had no precise information on its whereabouts; we only suspected from various clues that the rebels were hiding in the valley of Oued Stita, the boundary between our *quartier* and our neighbor's to the north. It was therefore necessary that the operation cover the largest possible area, the entire Oued Stita valley (see Figure 6).

The participating units were divided into two groups:

(1) *"Le bouclage"* (the ring), with units remaining static on the periphery of the selected area throughout the operation. In other words, these units constituted a cylinder.

  Three battalions were assigned to the task:
  – the 45th B.I.C. on the Aissa Mimoun ridge, from Hill 493 near Akaoudj to Hill 700 at the extreme east;
  – the II/404 R.A.A. on the opposite ridge across the valley, from Ait Allahoun just south of Makouda to Tissegouine;
  – the 11th Hussards plugging the eastern end, from Yaffadjene to Hill 359 to a point 1 km northeast of Tikobain. Liaison with the 45th B.I.C. and the II/404 R.A.A. was its responsibility.

(2) *"Le ratissage"* (the rake), with units proceeding from the open end toward the closed one, combing the area and pushing the

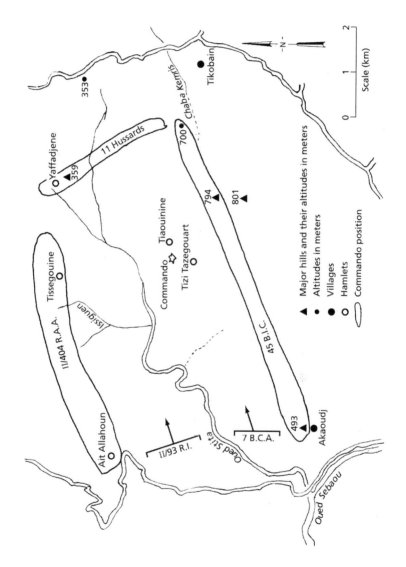

Figure 6
Operation Oued Stita

enemy toward the ring. In other words, these units acted as a piston.

Two battalions were assigned to the mission:

- the 7th B.C.A. (Battalion de Chasseurs Alpins) south of Oued Stita;
- the II/93 R.I. north of the Oued.

These two units were on loan for the duration of the operation. There were in addition:

(1) A 20-man commando drawn from the corporal school that was run by my battalion at Azib Cherameur. Its mission was to lay a strong ambush in the vicinity of Tizi Tazegouart and Tiaouinine (due north of Tahanouts) during the night preceding the operation.

(2) A 105mm battery from the I/93 R.A.M. At dawn on D-Day fire would be laid in the ravine from Hill 324 to Oued Stita (northwest of Ifouzar), in the deep ravine from Menaam down, and on the Issiguen ravine north of Oued Stita. The idea was to scare the rebels, if any, into running. The battery would, of course, provide fire support if needed.

(3) A platoon of light reconnaissance tanks from the 13th Dragoons, patrolling the highway between Tikobain and Boudjima to the rear of the 11th Hussards. Similarly, the six halftracks of the 45th B.I.C. would patrol the highway from Tizi Ouzou to Tigzirt north of the Oued Sebaou gorge behind the *ratissage* units.

(4) Air support was available on call from a flight of T-6s armed with rockets and 30-caliber machine guns stationed on a small airfield south of Tazmalt (outside the area shown on Figure 6) on the left bank of Oued Sebaou. An L-19 observation plane would be kept in the air over the operational area during daylight hours. Light helicopters for the evacuation of wounded and prisoners were also available on call; they were stationed near Tizi Ouzou.

A team of gendarmes was attached to each battalion. The "Gendarmerie" is a unique organization in France. It is a military unit administered and supported by the Minister of the Armed Forces; its men are recruited from among the best NCOs. But operationally it comes under the Minister of the Interior. Its mission is to serve as police in small towns that cannot afford a municipal police of their own, and in the rural areas (Gendarmerie Territoriale); it also provides company-size units for the maintenance of order in case of trouble and riots (Gendarmerie Mobile). Gendarmes are empowered with judicial functions; they work, in particular, as legal investigators for the judiciary system. Thus, in an operation like ours, the role of the gendarmes was to identify the dead and wounded on both sides and to make a manslaughter report. If the dead were rebels, the battalion commander would be charged with manslaughter, the case would go to a judge, and, of course, would be dismissed after a suitable number of months. If this seems ridiculous—and it was ridiculous—one must remember that there was officially no war in Algeria. When we met rebels, we had, in theory, to summon them three times in an unmistakable manner before opening fire. Legally, we could not enter a house without a warrant.

Only two platoons of my company were needed in the operation. I designated the 1st and 3d, and gave command of the whole to Lt. Berger.* But I went along to watch the show.

The company's mission was:

(1) to establish position between Hill 700 and a point halfway between this hill and Hill 794 to the west;
(2) to check on the population of the hamlet near Hill 700;
(3) to lay ambushes at night on D-Day at two intersections of paths about 1 km north of our position.

We left Grand Remblai at 4 a.m., arrived puffing at Hill 801, and reached the village near Hill 700 just before dawn. We waited in silence until there was enough light to see. Then Berger* ordered

Vignaux* to encircle the village, while he went in with his platoon to wake up and assemble the inhabitants. This took about twenty minutes. The houses were rapidly searched, and all villagers, including the children, were led to a small level area outside the village and there kept under guard by a small detachment furnished by Vignaux.* Berger* then did a quick reconnaissance of his position. His platoon settled on the right; Vignaux* took the left.

So far our radio (S.C.R. 300) had been silent. The sun rose, and we looked at the valley from our balcony. To our horror, Oued Stita was hidden under a layer of dense fog reaching the level of Tiaouinine. We heard a few brief submachine-gun bursts from that direction. Then silence again. On our radio channel, the 45th B.I.C. internal network, units now reported that they were in position and ready. At the scheduled time, the L-19 plane appeared overhead and the artillery began to fire in the ravines. Berger* passed the order to wear the red scarf around the neck. (The rebels had managed to copy and to steal French Army uniforms. There had been several instances when they passed as French soldiers, with unfortunate results for us. It was hard to tell, especially in large operations, whether a Moslem wearing our uniform was friend or foe, because we had many regular Algerian Moslem units, not counting Moslem auxiliaries in our ranks. To distinguish our men, therefore, we wore scarves in every operation. The color was different every day, and we changed the part of the body where we tied them—on the left shoulder, on the right, etc.)

At 8 a.m. everything was still quiet. The fog had lifted, and we could now see the thick vegetation on Oued Stita's embankments. With my binoculars I could see two of the 13th Dragoons' tanks on Hill 353; soldiers were visible also on Hill 359. Berger* suddenly thought about his neighbors to the right who had not yet made contact with us. He requested permission from the battalion command post to switch channels for a few minutes to get in touch with the 11th Hussards. Their main and subsidiary channels were both scrambled; Berger could not hear a thing. He ordered a sergeant to take half his squad on a patrol to a point 500 yards eastward and to return. No Hussards in the wood on our right. Just then, automatic weapons fired at us from below. I looked down and saw a group of soldiers with red scarves about 800 yards south of us. Some were standing up and pointing at us. No doubt the Hussards. Insults flew at them, with no effect because of the distance. A sergeant from our 1st platoon tied several scarves to a branch and agitated the flag over his head. The fire stopped. Berger* took some men and went down to see the Hussards and arrange liaison. The trip took him 45 minutes because of the difference in level. When he returned, I left the position and went to see the villagers.

Vignaux* was there, too, checking identity cards and comparing them with the names on a list of suspects the battalion intelligence officer had given us before the operation.

"I found these two," said Vignaux* pointing to two Kabyles sitting apart from the crowd.

"Who are they?"

"One is listed as a money collector, the other as a liaison man with the guerrillas. I have interrogated them already. They deny everything, of course."

The crowd was silent and was looking at me curiously. An old man got up and asked to speak to me.

"How long are we going to stay here?"

"As long as the operation lasts. We want to keep you out of the way so that there will be no confusion and no risk of your being shot by error."

"I understand, but we have not eaten and drunk since yesterday."

I authorized the women and children to go home, and told them to stay inside except for bringing food and water to the men.

At about 11 a.m., a patrol from the 4th Company brought us two auxiliaries. These men belonged to a group of six Kabyles from Tahanouts, Oudiai's own village. They had revolted against the rebels as soon as the 4th Company had occupied Hill 801 in June 1956. They had requested arms and had been incorporated into the company. I never found out why they opposed the rebels. They claimed they had acted out of loyalty to France. Possibly, but my guess was that it was just another instance of Kabyle rivalry. In any case, their defection could have meant a major breakthrough for us if properly exploited at the time, because they knew most of the active OPA members in Aissa Mimoun. The opportunity was missed, because we were not prepared for it and we lacked experience at the time. Our intelligence officer arrested several men here and there, and that was all. The defectors were used essentially in a military capacity, as auxiliaries, whereas they would have been invaluable in a political capacity.

They came now, at my request, to help identify FLN supporters among the villagers. They looked at the crowd and pointed at three men.

"This one made speeches against the French. That one often came to see Oudiai at Tahanouts. The third one denounced an anti-FLN farmer to the rebels."

I returned to Berger's* command post. The operation was proceeding uneventfully. In the afternoon, to relieve boredom, Berger* requested and received permission from Major Laval* to patrol the Chaba Kemris ravine in our rear, south of Hill 700. He left his three fire teams on position and took the rest of his platoon.

The ravine was steep, as usual, and densely covered with cork-trees and underbrush. Impossible to maneuver in this terrain if anything happened; soldiers twenty feet apart could not see each other. The progress was slow, with frequent stops to bring soldiers back in line. We combed the north slope going toward the mouth of the ravine until we were abreast of Hill 612; then we crossed to the other side and went up.

Suddenly shouts were heard. A soldier pointing his rifle at a bush said he saw something moving inside. Sergeant Boucher* told the soldier to cover him while he approached the bush, his submachine gun at the ready. Boucher* saw a leg. "Out now!" he shouted. And out came a young Kabyle, about twenty years old, shaking with fear. No weapon on him, no identity card. He denied that he was a *fellagha*. Then why was he hiding? He became afraid when he saw soldiers coming. Where was he from? From the hamlet near Hill 700. Where was he last night? He did not answer. We tied him and brought him to the place where the villagers were assembled. The auxiliaries from the 4th Company did not know him. Villagers confirmed that he was indeed from the hamlet, but they could not tell where he had been the night before.

Berger* reported the capture to the battalion command post and was told to keep the man with the other suspects.

The rest of the afternoon was spent reconnoitering the spots for the night ambushes and making sure the men from the 11th Hussards knew where they would be set up. The spots chosen were the crossroads 400 meters northwest and 1 km west-northwest of Hill 700. Each ambush consisted of a sergeant and six men. Just before night, Berger* redeployed his troops, drawing his men closer together around the platoon command posts.

The night was quiet except for a minor alert caused by a stray donkey.

The next morning went by with no event. At 1 p.m. we began to see the Chasseurs Alpins progressing slowly on the slope. At 3 p.m. they were abreast of us. At 4 p.m. the operation was over, we released the villagers, and left our position, taking with us the six suspects whom we handed over to the battalion intelligence officer at Hill 801.

Total score:

Rebel losses nil.

Our losses nil.

About 60 Kabyles detained for further investigation.

The submachine-gun bursts heard on the first morning had been fired by the commando. At dawn, one of the soldiers on the commando saw two armed *fellaghas* coming out of an isolated house outside the small hamlet 250 meters northeast of Tiaouinine. He fired at them; and suddenly a group of *fellaghas* ran out of the house, rushed toward Oued Stita, and disappeared in the fog.

In other words, Oudiai and his band had been within our net when the operation started. How did they manage to escape?

"That's easy," commented an officer, "in this sort of terrain an operation becomes worthless a minute after the first sunset. All the rebel has to do is to stay put during the first day, wait for the night, and then cross the *bouclage* as he pleases, unless he is really too unlucky. Our only chance is to meet rebels during the first few hours of the operation. Then we can hope to finish with them before night comes."

Going to the battalion command post the following week to settle routine problems, I talked to the intelligence officer about the suspects we had caught.

Three of the sixty had been good catches. The money collector from the hamlet near Hill 700 was indeed the local boss, and a brother-in-law of Oudiai besides. The young Kabyle hidden in the bush was probably a liaison man for the *fellaghas*, but he would not talk and so had been handed over to the police at Tizi Ouzou. The others were released after two or three days.

"What can I do? I have no certain information on them except what auxiliaries from the 4th Company tell me, and I can't entirely rely on that. These people do not talk, they know nothing, they have seen nothing, they are all very quiet citizens minding their family affairs and their fields. I am alone here for this job. If I were really to quiz sixty suspects, it would take me at least a month. And where would I put them all this time? *Ah, on n'est vraiment pas aidé!*"

VI. Occasional Contacts with the Population

We were living among ourselves at Grand Remblai, isolated from the population. Very few civilians came to the SAS office and, if so, generally to request approval for an application to go to France to work. Approval was granted automatically by Lt. Villon* after a rapid check of the list of suspects.

Second Lt. Paoli* and M/S Vignaux* repeatedly visited their respective hamlets nearby, continuing their propaganda work on the population and trying to make friends who would talk. So far they had met with no success. Villagers clammed up when asked if they knew anything about the *fellaghas*.

I devoted a great deal of time to improving the training of my soldiers. I had observed any number of mistakes during our military sorties. Two things had struck me in particular:

1. Soldiers in *bouclage* position showed themselves, made noise, and moved unnecessarily, thus inviting the rebels to try their luck elsewhere. I stressed that we were actually under ambush conditions, and that it was imperative to use camouflage and not to advertise our presence to the enemy. Moreover, as in an ambush, a clash with the rebels would be violent and brief. We had better be prepared for it behind organized firing positions.

2. In this sort of terrain, the first shots were bound to be fired by the rebels at a close distance. Our soldiers could not expect to see far ahead, particularly when moving. Nor could they expect much in the way of fire support from their comrades. Therefore, I paired off all my men; my orders were that they would always operate in pairs, with one man always supplying cover as his mate advanced. I insisted also that we fire our automatic weapons in bursts of four shots, so that we could nearly always tell whether the fire had originated with us or with the rebels. It was amazing to see how a little trick like that reduced confusion and improved our fighting confidence in the few cases when we did meet *fellaghas*.

I was shocked to discover that many of my men had not thrown a live grenade since their basic training days. I held firing-practice sessions with all weapons until the battalion ammunition officer objected. After this orgy, I had such sessions at least once a week during the entire time I commanded the company.

By order of the zone, the company operated a roadblock on the highway at Grand Remblai to check civilian traffic. Cars and buses were stopped and searched, identity cards were verified. I took advantage of this to insist that my men be courteous as well as firm when dealing with civilians. They were now to address Kabyles as "Mister" and to use the formal "*vous*" instead of the familiar "*tu*." It seemed ridiculous, even to me and probably just as much to the Kabyles at first, for Moslems themselves use "*tu*" with everyone. I stuck to my rule just the same, because it was an easy way to change the attitude of my soldiers and to place our relations with the Kabyles on a new footing.

Meanwhile we continued patrolling during the day and ambushing at night, with no result.

One afternoon, I took two platoons and climbed to Igonane Ameur, one of the two main villages in my *sous-quartier*. On reaching the village, I found a small group of Kabyles sitting idly in front of the small house which served both as mosque and as meeting place for the *djemaa* (local assembly). The spot, incidentally, enjoyed a magnificent view of the Sebaou valley and was a first-class lookout. They had seen us coming.

I told them please to call all the adult males for a meeting. They went from house to house. In an hour, thirty men had come nonchalantly, one by one. Second Lt. Fontaine* checked their identity cards and made a list of their names, while his soldiers glued posters on the walls.

"Is everybody here?" I asked a Kabyle.

"That's all we could find."

"The meeting will not start until you are all here. So go back and bring the other men."

To make sure, I sent soldiers behind them into the village. It took two hours to get the male population. I asked if they all understood French. No. Arabic? (I had the Algerian mule sergeant with me.) No. Would anyone volunteer to translate what I had to say? A young man of about twenty-five, with an intelligent face, very neatly dressed, offered his services.

"He must be the rebel boss to volunteer like that," whispered Sergeant Marceau.*

I asked who was the village chief. There was none; the president of the *djemaa* had gone to France and had not been replaced.

"You need a president so that we can deal with each other better. I ask you to elect one. I will come back in two days to meet him. But let's settle another problem now. Some of you waited two hours for this meeting to start because people were slow in coming. I don't mind waiting; I have all the time. But if you prefer meetings to go faster, I will bring my bugler next time, and I ask you to gather here as soon as you hear the bugle."

They agreed. I continued:

"I need volunteers to cut down cactus hedges between Ighouna and Igonane Ameur. Their work will be paid."

No volunteers. I pointed arbitrarily at ten men and ordered them to report to Grand Remblai the next morning at 8. Some of the men protested at once that they were too busy in their fields—sheer nonsense, because there is practically no farming activity in August.

"I am sorry. If you had a *djemaa* president, he could have designated you better than I did. So come tomorrow, no matter what your other occupations."

Sergeant Marceau* took their names. I ended the meeting with a propaganda speech:

(1) The case of Algeria was not to be confused with the cases of Indochina, Tunisia, and Morocco.
(2) We were here to stay, and those who did not believe it were in for a surprise.

(3) We had enough forces now to defeat the rebels. It was just a matter of time. Peace would return sooner if the villagers helped, but in any case ultimate victory was ours.

Just as we were about to leave, Fontaine* felt it necessary to comment on my speech to the audience:

"You have now heard the great chief speak. You better be prepared for trouble if you don't behave!"

I could not stop the fool in front of the public. On the way back to our quarters, I told him to leave speechmaking to me.

The next morning only three of the workers appeared. I sent a platoon to the village at once. Fontaine* found the seven other men sitting at their usual place in front of the *djemaa*. They would not come, they said, unless ordered to do so.

"You had your orders yesterday. This is a show of bad will. You will work today without pay."

A squad watched them while they cut down the hedges, just in case of rebel interference. When the day was over, I made a point of paying the three who had come by themselves, and dismissed the group.

I returned to Igonane Ameur the following day. Within 15 minutes after the bugle call, all the males were assembled, a visible progress. The posters, as I expected, had been torn to shreds.

"Who is your president now?"

No president.

"I need fifty men to finish cutting the hedges. Sergeant, take the identity cards of fifty men. They will report tomorrow morning at Grand Remblai. Now, who destroyed the posters? Nobody? Very well. We are going to affix new posters on several houses. The owners will be responsible for them."

In those days, a civilian who could not show his identity card was in trouble. There were identity controls during every operation in addition to the controls every day on practically every road and means of access to towns. A man without a card was sure to be arrested, investigated, and perhaps kept for several days. The rebels had once ordered the population to destroy identity cards, "an instrument of colonialist oppression," but they met with so much opposition that the order was never obeyed and was finally rescinded. Consequently, all fifty men from Igonane Ameur reported for work. They were paid 750 francs for the day (about $1.80), the standard wage fixed by the *préfet* of Kabylia. The SAS officer had a special fund for unemployment relief.

While the workers were busy clearing the path, a soldier discovered a small parcel behind a hedge; it contained a dozen shotgun cartridges and a primitive tool for filling them with powder. A villager had obviously found this way to get rid of the compromising ammunition.

The next time we patrolled Igonane Ameur we found one poster destroyed. The owner of the house swore he was innocent. How could he be responsible? Maybe it was done by people in the village just to bring trouble to him. He may have been right, but I could not back out. I called a meeting of the villagers. I had to decide what punishment I would inflict. This was a problem that kept plaguing every officer in the field during the war in Algeria. For, although many official or *de facto* regulations were decreed that we had to enforce on the population, never once did the authorities devise an efficient system of summary punishments for the violators. Inevitably, every officer made his own rules, with the result that punishments varied greatly from one *sous-quartier* to the next, to the confusion of the population.

I wanted to impose a fine high enough to serve as a deterrent, but not so high that the culprit could not pay it. One sheep, I decided. The man had no sheep. Eight thousand francs then (the current market price for a sheep). He had no money either. Fifteen days of work, in that case, would take the place of the fine. I told the villagers that the money from the fine would be spent on projects benefiting the village.

I now turned my attention to Bou Souar, the worst village in Aissa Mimoun according to my officers. Leaving two squads at Grand Remblai, I took the company up there before sunrise one day. Two platoons encircled the village and controlled the exits. The rest of my men entered the village as soon as the sun was up, searched the houses, and gathered the males.

The search produced nothing. A villager complained loudly in front of the assembly that a soldier had stolen an oil lamp from his house. Second Lt. Paoli* called the squad which had visited the house, interrogated the soldiers, had them searched by their sergeant. No lamp. The Kabyle still insisted. The sergeant swore he had personally led the search in the house. I asked the Kabyle when he had last used the lamp. "Last night, of course." I went to his house with him. "Show me your supply of oil." He could not produce any, nor could he show any container smelling of kerosene. He had been caught lying. I was to hear more complaints of this sort in future operations, as if the trick had been taught by the rebels in order to discredit French troops in the eyes of the population. I knew now how to handle the complaints, although I always checked carefully in case there might be a basis of truth. My soldiers were no saints, but I had warned them that anyone caught stealing from civilians would be court-martialed, and they knew I meant it.

We took the villagers to Ighouna, the empty hamlet south of Igonane Ameur. There I had them come one by one into a courtyard away from the group. A sentry stood outside to keep away intruders. Inside, Paoli* checked their identity cards against the list of suspects. Then a soldier entered the names in a book. Finally, they were brought to me in a separate room outside of which I had posted another sentry. I wanted to see if they were more inclined to talk when alone with me, safe from eavesdroppers. I started the conversation with innocuous questions, such as what was their job, had they served in the Army, had they lived in France, could they read. If they did not seem totally uncooperative, I would ask bluntly what they knew about the rebels, about the OPA members in the village. I put the question to a dozen men, who answered with the usual "I am very quiet, I mind my family," etc.

Then came an old man named Bekri.* I saw from his papers that he drew a pension from the French government. He had fought in the French Army in World War I, and had won the Médaille Militaire at Verdun.

"Have you seen any *fellaghas* at Bou Souar recently?"

He hesitated.

"Who is the FLN boss in your village?"

"Mon Capitaine, you must understand our situation. We are not afraid of you. The most you will do to us is put us in jail. The *fellaghas,* they cut our throats. Even if we want to help you, we cannot; too dangerous."

I pointed out that nobody could hear us now, nobody would know if he had talked. I would do my best not to compromise him in using the information he would give me. I was not going to be so foolish as to arrest the rebel supporters the minute he gave me their names.

"Who collects the money for the rebels?"

He fidgeted and finally blurted out, "Said Areski."* He told me where Said's* house was located and warned me that he had a pistol. I dismissed him for fear of keeping him long enough to arouse suspicions among the others. In fact, I threw him out of the room with a show of furor.

When the whole group had passed through, I had Paoli* designate twenty men, including Bekri,* to report for work at Grand Remblai the next morning. As arranged between Bekri* and me, he protested indignantly, saying flatly that he would not come. Just as loudly, I announced that he would come by force and work without pay as a punishment for his attitude. I don't know how well I played the part, but what a comedian Bekri* was!

I waited three days, during which I kept workers from Bou Souar busy fixing the truck road from Grand Remblai to Ighouna and continued my private interviews. Then Fontaine* and his platoon went one night to Bou Souar and brought back Said Areski.* They found no weapon in his house.

Said* denied everything. I handed him over to the intelligence officer. He still claimed to be innocent. He was sent to the police at Tizi Ouzou. He was released after four days. The police could not get a thing out of him, they said.

VII. Moving the Company Closer to the Population

We were now in September 1956. I had been at Grand Remblai long enough to realize that I would get nowhere if I stayed there. I was too far removed from my two main villages. Occasional contacts would never enable me really to control the population; I would have to move my company up the Djebel.

Ighouna seemed a good place. There was sufficient room for most of the company plus the mules; I could be supplied by truck; and the water problem was solved thanks to a small reservoir filled by a spring at Tala Ilane, also accessible by truck. I would be less than ten minutes' walk from Igonane Ameur and in a good position to place interesting ambushes at not too great a distance. The only drawback was the number of sentries (five) needed at night because of the irregular layout of the buildings. Major Laval* had no objection to the move, it being understood that Lt. Berger* and his 1st Platoon would remain at Grand Remblai to protect the SAS, ensure the safety of the convoys on the highway, and operate the roadblock.

I was glad to get away from the depressing atmosphere of Grand Remblai. The move, I was confident, would give my soldiers a clean start in the new field of activities I had in mind for them.

The first few days were spent cleaning the place, whitewashing the rooms, working on the defense installations, drilling the soldiers on the new defense plan. My telephone was hooked onto the existing line from Grand Remblai to Hill 801. I was soon ready to renew my work on Igonane Ameur, on which I decided to concentrate my efforts for the time being.

I went there almost every day with Paoli's* platoon, trying to talk with the villagers and to get information. We were beginning to know the inhabitants to the point where their faces were no longer strange, but I still could notice no change in their attitude; they remained as reserved as on the first day.

I was impatient to settle once and for all the question of a president for the village. I had spotted a man named Challal,* in his early fifties, dignified, calm, well-mannered; I had observed on several occasions that he seemed to be respected by the other villagers; he obviously was a notable, a natural leader. Moreover, he did not seem to be avoiding us deliberately. Our Kabyle auxiliaries from the 4th Company had nothing against him. When I asked him to become a candidate for the job, he refused adamantly. I could not persuade him. I looked around for other candidates; there were none.

One day I called a meeting of the populace.

"The time has come now for you to elect a good man as president of your *djemaa*. Since no candidate has come forward, I will designate one. If you want him, raise your hand."

Apprehension fell over the audience while I looked around for the man to designate. Heads were hunched in shoulders, eyes cast downward to avoid attracting my attention.

"I see M. Makour* over there. I am sure you all like him. Now raise your hand if you want him. No hand up? Well, sorry M. Makour* (who smiled with relief). Perhaps you would want M. Chabane,* the baker. He is a good man, too. Raise your hand if you vote for him. No vote for him? Sorry, M. Chabane.* Now I see a man with all the necessary qualifications, M. Challal.* If you do *not* want him, raise your hand. No hand up? Congratulations, M. Challal,* you have been elected unanimously!"

The villagers burst into laughter, appreciating the joke, while Challal* protested vehemently.

"You are now provisional president. Your mandate will expire when definitive elections have been held."

"*Non, mon Capitaine,* I will not carry out the responsibility you have thrust on me."

And he didn't. Hoping to work him around to it, I did not press the issue. I thus became known in the zone as the officer who had got a village chief unanimously elected by a show of no hands.

With the people of Igonane Ameur I used the process by which I had succeeded in getting information from Bekri* at Bou Souar. It worked, and an old man gave me the names of three villagers who were FLN agents. Challal* was one of them. Somehow I could not believe it and was reluctant to arrest him now that I had officially made him temporary chief of the village. Besides, how could I know that the informer was not deceiving me, denouncing men who might on the contrary be hostile to the rebels? Paoli* brought me for investigation the two other suspects, plus four villagers caught at random in order to camouflage the information and protect the source. I interrogated them separately, doing my best to intimidate them. Presumed innocents and alleged culprits, they all denied the charges. I kept them two days with no result. Then I sent the lot to the intelligence officer, telling him, of course, that I had nothing against the four decoys. He had no better results, and we released them.

During the month of August 1956, Lt.-Col. Lemoine,* worried about the lack of precise instructions on how to deal with the population, conceived with his small staff a 13-point program to be implemented in his sector. It was based on the idea that pacification would be achieved if we could gradually compromise the population in the eyes of the rebels. After all, weren't the rebels using the same trick? All the population needed to side with us—provided protection was assured by our forces—was a certain amount of mild pressure on our part so as to have an excuse vis-à-vis the rebels. The idea was expressed in the formula: "*Il faut mouiller la population*" (let's "wet" them).

Here is a translation of the document:

A SAMPLE PROCESS
designed to lead the population of a village closely protected by the Army to show its support for our policy

———

1. Hiring men for public works directly benefiting the villages (small-scale projects, cleaning wells, improving paths).
2. Hiring men for public works in the interest of the administration and the Army (building or improving automobile tracks).

3. Hiring men to work on strictly defensive installations (defense walls, watchtowers, pillboxes).
4. Paid requisitions of muleteers for a sortie meant to carry supplies (wood) to civilian and military authorities.
5. Regular use of Kabyle mule convoys (paid) to supply Army detachments and the population in the villages. Convoys will be protected at first, then left to themselves.
6. Requisition (unpaid) of muleteers for a small military sortie passing close to other villages. Mules will carry radio sets and batteries, etc.
7. Requisition of muleteers for a night exercise. Stop and have them remain on alert status.
8. Kabyles will keep watch with soldiers in the post protecting the village.
9. Kabyle guides for night patrols.
10. Night patrols with fire.
11. Arming Kabyles. Weapons withdrawn after each sortie.
12. Weapons left at night in Kabyles' houses kept under our sentries' watch.
13. Official distribution of weapons to the population. (Simultaneously officers will challenge veterans in shooting contests; pictures will be taken of Kabyles mixing with soldiers, etc.)

I applied the program to the Igonane Ameur villagers up to point 11 while my company was stationed at Ighouna. The last three points were implemented after I had established a platoon in the village itself. The only significant opposition was met on point 8. Two of the eight Kabyles selected to stand watch at night in my camp protested energetically; one of them left the village the next day and joined the *fellaghas* (he was caught eighteen months later).

The program did not accomplish what it was meant to do. It was not sufficient to implicate the population to make it switch sides, for there was still too much of either genuine support of the rebellion or fear of the *fellaghas* and the political cells.

One Sunday in September 1956, when the program had generally been completed in the sector, Lt.-Col. Lemoine* organized a large
meeting of the population for the official distribution of arms (shotguns). The meeting took place at Agouni Goughrane on the edge of the
Mizrana Forest in the presence of *Préfet* Vignon and General Gouraud.
Five thousand Kabyles were brought by trucks, carrying banners with
the name of their village. The place was decorated with flags, the division band was playing martial airs, whole sheep were roasting over an
open pit for the classic *mechoui* (the Arab barbecue). Lt.-Col. Lemoine*
and the *préfet* made speeches; then the distribution of shotguns began.
A delegation from each village marched to a large table, and the *préfet*
congratulated the men on their loyalty and handed them the arms.
When Igonane Ameur's turn arrived, two of the ten men I had selected
balked.

"Go ahead, don't be afraid," said the young Kabyle who had
offered me his services as interpreter the first time I went to Igonane
Ameur, "it's only a show, they won't let you keep the guns."

And this is precisely what happened. As soon as we were back at
Ighouna, I retrieved the weapons, as I had been ordered to do. Neither
the French authorities nor the population had been fooled by the
show.

The program nevertheless had plenty of merit. I found it invaluable, if for reasons quite different from its official goal. It served me as
an excellent way to establish contact with the population, to force the
villagers to respond to my will, to make them realize that *fellaghas* could
not prevent me from getting a measure of forced, but still useful, co-
operation from the population. The money earned by the hired workers
was badly needed, and, even though they made a show of being forced
to work, I knew that genuine volunteers would have flocked to us had
it not been for the rebel-imposed terror. The program was equally good
for the morale of my cadres who had been given concrete things to
do and were kept busy doing them and imagining ways and means
to circumvent opposition. During all the time we were implementing
the program, my soldiers worked in close contact with the population.
When we completed this mechanical process, the atmosphere had per-
ceptively changed at Igonane Ameur.

At the end of this period, I received the visit of a "Loudspeaker and Pamphlet Company." Three such units had been hastily formed in Algeria according to the U.S. Army table of organization; they were each operating in one of Algeria's three Army Corps areas. For equipment they had a public address system, tape recorders, a movie projector, mimeograph machines, still cameras, and a photographic lab. Among the specialists were interpreters and artists or cartoonists.

A lieutenant arrived the day before to prepare the operation, which consisted, he explained, in:

(1) an exhibit of propaganda pictures on plywood panels;
(2) native music on tape recorders;
(3) a general propaganda talk (the loudspeakers would carry the words to the villages up on the crest, a mile away);
(4) a propaganda talk geared to the local situation (I would have to provide the topic and the necessary information);
(5) a movie show in the open at night.

The lieutenant wanted immediately to visit the villages to take pictures of the inhabitants for the panels. He also offered to print whatever pamphlets I needed here. I ordered a thousand small stickers with the words "The Army Watches," which I planned to have posted by my soldiers on houses and other conspicuous spots during their night sorties. I sent patrols at once to notify the villagers in my *sous-quartier* to come and see the show the next day. They replied they could not stay for the movies for fear of a *fellagha* ambush at night. I promised them military escort.

The show took place as scheduled. The villagers' pictures made a great hit, and they clamored for copies when they recognized themselves or their friends. The movie part was a complete flop. The first movie was a cartoon, the second one a short on the economy of olive trees in rural villages of Kabylia, the third an old war picture of the First French Army fighting in the Vosges Mountains in 1944/45. They excited no interest.

"Can't you get better pictures than that?" I asked Captain Chauvin,* the Loudspeaker and Pamphlet Company commander.

"*Mon pauvre ami*, it was difficult enough to get these in Algiers from the Government Cinematographic Service. Their catalogue contains very little of interest."

"Can't you use commercial movies? My wife wrote me the other day that she saw in Paris newsreels of the Suez expedition. This is what I want the villagers to see, the Egyptians on the run, not culture of olives in Kabylia."

"I have no money to rent commercial movies."

As usual, propaganda was fine as long as it cost nothing. Several months later, if I may anticipate somewhat in my account of events, I attended a joint staff meeting at the Préfecture in Tizi Ouzou. The *préfet* announced that he had received a 5-million-francs appropriation for propaganda in Kabylia in 1957.

"Sir," I exclaimed, "that makes only 5 francs per Kabyle."

"I know but that's all we have."

Using 500 artillery shells and 10,000 gallons of gasoline for an operation was quite all right, for these were expenditures long accepted by government routine. But expenditures for a new field of activity such as propaganda—or let's just call it "information"—was sure to raise a row among finance comptrollers.

In view of the success of pictures with local people, I asked Captain Chauvin* why he was not provided with Polaroid cameras. He had never heard of them; he would try to get some. (He never did.)

Returning to our camp that night, after we had safely escorted the villagers to their home, I overheard Sergeant Marceau* discussing the show with a colleague:

"What do these fools think? That Kabyles here have never seen a movie in their life? That they can be impressed with magic lanterns like tribesmen in the Congo? Why, all the villagers here have lived in Paris, Marseille, or Lyon!"

It was also at this time, in October 1956 if my memory is correct, that Force "Z" deserted to the rebels. The idea of this force had been conceived by secret service people, who sold it to the government in Algiers. Working outside regular channels, they recruited "secretly" a group of 200 Kabyles, who were supposed to establish an anti-rebel maquis of their own. As anybody who knew the situation could have told the organizers of this scheme, the 200 Kabyles passed *en bloc* to the other side soon after they were armed, taking with them all their weapons and ammunition. The zone had to launch at once a large operation near Port-Gueydon with the help of paratroopers. A hundred deserters were killed or captured and the same number of weapons recovered.

To sum up the situation at this stage, the big question was how to assess the loyalty of the Kabyles. The theory that the population would join our side once it felt protected from the threat of rebel bands had proved wrong. The idea that we could forcibly implicate the population on our side had not worked.

It was clear to me that the major stumbling block was the OPA. We would make no progress as long as we had not purged the villages of the insurgent political cells. But how to identify the rebel agents? This was the problem I had to solve.

VIII. A Platoon Detached to Igonane Ameur

In mid-September 1956, Major Laval* authorized me to establish a platoon at Igonane Ameur. I hoped in this way to tighten control over the population and to get the information needed to purge the village. I selected for this task my 2d Platoon, the main criterion being the personality of its leader, 2d Lt. Paoli,* in whom I had entire confidence. I made a few changes in personnel, replacing "warriors" with "pacifiers."

After months of continuous operations my men's fatigues were in tatters. I wanted at least the 2d Platoon to arrive in the village with better-looking outfits. My request was turned down, the zone quartermaster preferring to hoard his stores.

We had made several discreet reconnaissance efforts and had found two relatively large houses opposite each other in a narrow lane in the center of the village, not far from the fountain which was the focus of village life. The owners were in France, and only their wives and children lived there. I told "provisional mayor" Challal* that I was requisitioning the houses, for which rent would be paid, and asked him to relocate the families.

The houses were impossible to defend against a resolute attack. They could easily be approached at night; they were dominated by terraces and other houses directly to the north; and defenders had no extended field of fire. We improved the situation slightly by building a watchtower protected with sandbags, opening loopholes in the walls, surrounding the two houses with barbed wire, and at night closing the lane. I arranged with the 4th Company on Hill 801 that, if the post was attacked, I would block the attackers' retreat toward the foot of the Djebel while the 4th Company would move down toward the village. Paoli* was linked to my command post by telephone (the line was never sabotaged) and given an S.C.R. 300 radio.

The day the platoon settled in, I called a meeting of the villagers. I told them my soldiers were there better to protect them from rebel pressure. I asked them to come directly to me if they had any complaint about the behavior of my soldiers, in whom I had complete confidence. I explained how easy it would be for rebels to infiltrate and attack or harass the detachment; but in that case, of course, my soldiers would fire back with every available weapon and I could not guarantee that civilians would not be hit. The villagers' interest, therefore, was to see that no such rebel action took place. My warning was well understood, for only two light harassments occurred in the eighteen months I stayed in the *sous-quartier.*

Once settled in the village, my soldiers did not need to be told any more that they had to be on good terms with the population. They realized very well that their safety depended upon it, and never did I receive a complaint from the villagers.

The platoon was supplied daily from Ighouna by two young civilian muleteers who came and went without escort. Nothing ever disappeared. At first, food was sent to the platoon ready-cooked, but it arrived cold and soup was spilled, so that thereafter we only sent raw food to be cooked on the spot.

A thorough census was the first step toward controlling the population. We had learned from our first experiment at Oumlil and Agouni Taga, the two hamlets near Grand Remblai, that we needed more information than we had previously asked. We registered every inhabitant regardless of age and sex. We noted the name of those who were said to be away, and tried to get their present address in France or elsewhere in Algeria. We noted every case in which we could not be shown a recent letter or a postal money order, for the absent person could then be presumed to be with the guerrillas. We found five such cases at Igonane Ameur. We unraveled the family ties among the villagers. We checked their sources of income. All these data were recorded in a central book; for every male above fifteen we made a card on which we would note any further information.

Each household was provided with a family census booklet in which we noted the name, age, and sex of every member; the family head was made responsible for reporting any change. This was designed to help house-to-house investigations in case we ever needed to conduct such searches. Every house in the village was numbered, and on the outside wall we painted a summary of the census in this way:

No. 54 (house number)

Abboud* (family name)

8/7 (total no. of persons in family/no. actually in house)

Control also meant that my soldiers had to know every villager by sight. To hasten the process of acquaintance, the village was divided into sections, to each of which the same team was always assigned. It did not take more than a week for my soldiers to be able to spot immediately any new face in the village.

Control, finally, implied that people's movements were subject to certain regulations. Drawing on my experience in China, I decided on two simple rules:

(1) Nobody could leave the village for more than twenty-four hours without a pass.

(2) Nobody could receive a stranger to the village without permission.

The rules were announced to the population at a meeting, together with the fine in case of violation (a sheep). Passes and permissions were not refused unless we had some definite reason; I simply wanted to know who was moving, and we kept a record of passes granted. I am convinced that the system inhibited the FLN agents in the village and gave the inhabitants a valid alibi for refusing to work as messengers or suppliers to the guerrillas.

Every day, I sent Paoli* the newspapers from Algiers (received a day late), in which I underlined the news I wanted him to communicate to the villagers. Occasionally, I would send him a note telling him to emphasize a point of local interest. Every evening, Paoli* went to the *djemaa* and talked with the villagers who had spontaneously assembled there, as was their custom. Once in a while he would call a general meeting.

I had the feeling that collective propaganda could not be as effective as propaganda conducted on a person-to-person basis, because the villagers were reluctant to express their thoughts publicly. For this reason, and also because I noticed that all the work load fell on Paoli* while his men's potential was not fully used, I devised the following system: Paoli* would brief his men every morning on a single propaganda point and send his teams to their sections; on meeting a villager, the soldiers would develop the point (for instance, "every sick person should come to our dispensary for treatment" [see below]); and the soldiers would note the man's reaction to the talk. I did not expect great results; I wanted primarily to give my soldiers a feeling that they were actively participating in the pacification work. When after two weeks I checked on the notes made every day, I saw to my surprise that I could form an opinion about the villagers' feelings: I could see that some had responded to our propaganda, that others had obviously been hostile, that still others had remained noncommittal. Months later, when the village had been purged and pacification was well advanced, the picture I had received by this mechanical process corresponded almost exactly to the genuine attitude of the villagers.

Whenever a villager came to the post to ask for a pass or for other reasons, Paoli* used the opportunity to interrogate him. The results were extremely meager. People who talked blamed everything on the young Kabyle who had fled to the maquis after his night of sentry duty at Ighouna; he had been the chief rebel agent in the village, he had collected the money for the rebels, etc., but now that he was gone nobody was co-operating with the rebels any more. We did not buy the explanation. Once or twice we were given names of FLN supporters. I interrogated them at Ighouna, but failed to get anything worthwhile.

A villager came to see me one day requesting permission to open a *café maure* at Igonane Ameur. My first impulse was to agree; after all, if the man could make a living that way, why not? But I remembered on second thought that *cafés maures* were the ideal place for the rebels to disseminate propaganda, rumors, and *mots d'ordre*, or to contact agents.

"How can I be sure that you won't work for the rebels?"

"Sir, I swear on the Koran and on my family that I am wholeheartedly for the French, I hate rebels."

"This is what everybody tells me. Can you prove what you say?"

"How? If I could, I would do it at once."

"You pay taxes to the rebels. Don't deny it; I know everybody does it. I don't blame you, I understand your position. But you can at least tell me to whom you give the money."

He hesitated, denied he ever gave money, and left. This gave me an idea. Why shouldn't we use bureaucratic pressure to get information? I arranged immediately with the SAS officer that every Kabyle from my *sous-quartier* who requested something from the administration be first sent to me. Many were the villagers who applied for a visa to France. Invariably I would tell them:

"I cannot grant you a visa unless I am certain you are not a rebel supporter. As you well know, the FLN organization exists in France too, and they assassinate and sabotage just as much as here. You cannot at the same time refuse to co-operate with us and ask a favor of us. So, who collects the money in your village?"

Invariably they refused to talk. But I was confident that my approach would pay off sooner or later, for I had in my hand the ultimate weapon—bureaucratic inertia.

I was naturally furious when I discovered that a man to whom I had refused a visa had gone to France anyway. I investigated and found that our tight control over movement to France was actually a sieve; a visa could be had easily in Algiers for a price. There was nothing else for me to do but to complain about this state of affairs through official channels and to impose the usual fine on the man's family.

I was really stretching my imagination at that time to find a way to break through the wall of silence that met my every effort to obtain intelligence. A recent instruction from the zone staff on counterguerrilla warfare stated pompously that intelligence was the key to success, as if we did not know. But how to get it? I wished they would tell me. The eighteen-year-old son of the man who had been murdered by the FLN before our arrival, a likely prospect, would say nothing because he was too terrorized. Serrad,* the World War II veteran who had been seriously wounded by FLN terrorists, returned to Igonane Ameur from the hospital. He requested to serve as an auxiliary with Paoli's* platoon. When I asked him who had tried to kill him, he replied that he did not know; it had been too dark when he was shot at. He was still visibly afraid. He always moved from his house to the post looking sharply around, his right hand holding a pistol ready in his pocket. He talked to nobody in the village, and nobody talked to him. I stationed three soldiers every night in his house to protect his family; he still did not feel safe enough to talk.

One day the master sergeant who commanded the 4th Company detachment at Tala Ilane brought me the local barber from Tala Ou Abba, a village about 2 miles east of Ighouna. The barber, an elusive character, had been caught carrying a list of names on which small sums of money had been inscribed; he had on him the total of that money, about 45,000 francs. Undoubtedly a money collector for the rebels. I interrogated him in vain. He lied or refused to talk when confronted with the evidence. After two hours of effort, I ordered him to be tied and kept under watch by the sentry. Some minutes later, I heard shouts in the courtyard and a burst of submachine-gun fire. The prisoner had requested permission to go to the latrine; once untied, he had tried to escape, but not fast enough. He died on the way to the hospital. Gendarmes came to Ighouna, interrogated the sentry and me, made the usual manslaughter report, and the case, of course, was dismissed months later.

One thing I was determined to avoid: that we rule by day while the rebels ruled by night. I consequently increased the number of our ambushes. Patrolling at night seemed to me a stupidity, for the man who moves is necessarily at a disadvantage against the one who waits for him motionless. From Ighouna I sent out four two-hour ambushes every night, each by a four-man team. Lt. Berger* at Grand Remblai and Paoli* at Igonane Ameur each had out two three-man ambushes a night. In order to discourage villagers from receiving rebel visits at night, we often set ambushes inside houses. We also used to throw small stones at doors and roofs and to whistle softly—the usual signal of the rebels. When a villager inside carefully opened his door, as happened two or three times, he was in for a surprise. Reports of this ruse of ours spread so fast that villagers no longer dared to respond to the signal. They were reluctant to open their doors at night even to us.

Paoli* noticed after a while that whistling was heard whenever his men left the post for an ambush. He could not locate the origin of the whistling. I found the recipe to stop it. Several nights in a row, Paoli's* men made numerous false sorties; when whistling was heard, a nearby house, chosen at random, was thoroughly searched, the search lasting a good two or three hours. The nuisance, I suppose, made the villagers stop the whistlers. Also, Paoli's* sentries whistled themselves and probably provoked false alarms.

I opened a dispensary at Igonane Ameur the very day I established a post in the village. The job was given to a soldier who had received first-aid training in his boy-scout days and had worked for a while in a French hospital. It was obvious from even a superficial look at the village that sanitary conditions were terrible. In spite of all their contacts with Western civilization, the villagers were still clinging to their fatalistic philosophy and deliberately ignoring the simplest hygiene principles. They seldom washed—although water was not lacking, since a modern reservoir had been built in the village in 1947; they defecated in the streets; they lived in windowless houses with just a narrow hole in the ceiling to let the smoke escape; they shared accommodations with donkeys, sheep, and chickens.[1] T.B., sores, ringworm, and eye diseases were prevalent.

I therefore expected hordes of customers. None came. Paoli's* patrols grabbed children in the streets who had sores, and we took care of them. In most cases, with simple medicines, improvements were spectacular. Today an ignoramus armed with antibiotics and sulfa powder is more efficient than a good doctor of thirty years ago. I warned the parents that they would be held responsible for not bringing sick children to the dispensary. We took advantage of the house-to-house census to spot sick women, and had the family head bring

---

[1] Reading at the time "Count Belisarius" by Robert Graves, a story of the sixth-century Byzantine general who expelled the Vandals from North Africa, I found a description of Berber life which could have applied to the twentieth century. The book, incidentally, relates the eternal story of the overseas theater commander and his troubles with his home government. *Plus ça change....*

them in for treatment. The battalion's doctor came twice a week to treat villagers. As I had often noticed before, once a measure had been ordered the people complied with it. Soon the dispensary had visitors from morning till night, and we had a problem because we were rapidly exhausting our army allotment of medical supplies. Besides, we could not get special drugs for children and women from army sources. At first, my soldiers bought them with their own money from Tizi Ouzou drugstores. When I found out about it, I talked the SAS officer into supplying us.

I also opened a school in the *djemaa* building. Parents raised much opposition, saying they needed the young boys for herding the animals and for helping in the fields. I went over the family census list; when a family had only one boy I left him out of school, but I ordered that all the other boys come. We had about sixty boys aged between eight and fourteen. We organized two classes. The schoolteachers were draftees, one a plumber and the other a farmer. The results amazed me. The competence and devotion of the improvised teachers were matched by the eagerness and intelligence of the boys. The alphabet was mastered in a week, and within a month the youngsters were reading stories from their primer. Walking through the village, I could hear boys singing French children's songs.

Reflecting on who might be our potential allies in the population, I thought that Kabyle women, given their subjugated condition, would naturally be on our side if we emancipated them. The rebels had done nothing for them. I had, of course, to proceed very carefully so as not to antagonize the males too much. I decided to start with the young girls. Once my boys' school was running smoothly, I called a meeting of the population and ordered that girls from eight to thirteen (the marriage age) be sent to school in the afternoon. (The boys had their course in the morning.) I ignored the protests, and soon I had two more classes.

Adult Kabyle women were generally kept indoors. Going to the fountain was their only opportunity to go out, and they made the most of it, meeting, chatting, and laughing together. I noticed that there was always an old man sitting nearby. A sergeant told me the man was certainly in charge of keeping an eye on the virtue of the females, for the males had found that women at the fountain were glancing and smiling too much at my soldiers. If I had the fair set with me, I thought, I was on the right track.

I was struck by the fact that Kabyle children, on the whole, were apolitical; the rebels had not mobilized them as the Chinese and Vietnamese Communists had always done. Veterans from Indochina in my company had made the same observation. It was tempting to take advantage of the rebels' oversight. I could not, however, bring myself to do it. This war was already bad enough for children to be involved in. I took care that they were kept busy in school and in organized outdoor games. Of course, when a child inadvertently gave us some information, we opened our ears. One day, for instance, Private Boyer,* one of the teachers, jovially asked young Mourad,* 12, if everything was all right.

"Yes," replied the boy, "but if we had guns and ammunition, you soon would be out."

As the boy was by nature friendly to us, this was obviously something he had heard from his father. So an entry was made on Mourad* Senior's card in our files. Nevertheless, I discouraged any attempt by my cadres to use children as informers.

One day in October 1956, the government tax collector came to my *sous-quartier* to collect the annual tax from the inhabitants. The process had been irregular since the beginning of the rebellion owing to the deterioration of the situation. I was ordered to give the collector official protection and assistance. So I sent patrols to the villages and hamlets and notified the inhabitants. They came to Ighouna the next day, village by village. The tax collector, a Moslem civil servant, checked each name on the list and took the money against a receipt.

The amount varied from about one to twelve dollars. I was watching the operation and noticed to my surprise that not a single villager had forfeited. When a man was absent ("He is in France," or "He is away"), a member of his family paid for him. Even men known to be in the maquis, even Oudiai himself, paid his taxes by proxy.

"Isn't that amazing?" I asked Lt. Bauer,* the new SAS officer. "What does it mean?"

"It simply means that the tax collector is all that these people have known of the French bureaucracy for years and years. He personifies to them the French government, administration, and power. They all know from experience that they could get away with murder but not with tax evasion. Besides, taxes are low. So, in order to have peace, and perhaps out of an old reflex, here they are."

Lt. Bauer* had recently replaced Lt. Villon* in the Aissa Mimoun. A Foreign Legion cavalry officer, he had specialized in native affairs in Morocco. He applied for a transfer to a Legion unit in Algeria after Morocco became independent, but was instead assigned to an SAS job. He was very bitter about it. He had lost any illusion about the Moslems in Morocco, where he had seen them turning suddenly from genuine friendliness to murderous savagery on the eve of independence. He was even more bitter at the French government. One day in his area in the Morocco Atlas, he told me, the local Moslem chief had said to him:

"When I was your age, Lieutenant, I staked all my future on the word of a young French lieutenant like you. Today I don't even believe in the solemn word of honor of your President."

Whereupon the *caid* took out of his pocket the latest issue of *Le Monde* and pointed at the huge headline: "Sultan of Morocco Back From Exile." The French government had sworn that the deposed Sultan would never again rule in Morocco.

Notwithstanding his feelings, Lt. Bauer* was a disciplined, conscientious, and able officer. We worked together very well after he realized that I had other goals in mind than distributing candies to local children. The fact that his colleague from Tikobain, Lt. des Loges,* had recently been assassinated just outside his office did not deter him from taking risks. (SAS officers were a choice target for FLN terrorists.)

In order to show that the overall situation was improving, Algiers decided during that period to renew the draft of young Moslems for the Army. The majority of Moslem Algerians in the French Army were professional soldiers. For the sake of applying the law equally to all citizens, however, every Moslem was subjected to conscription like the French at home. Most of them were discharged after medical examination, but they still had to come before the draft board. I received a list of eight names for my *sous-quartier*. Six were located, two were missing ("in France"). The six reported to Ighouna as told, and we sent them to Tizi Ouzou. Only one was drafted.

By October 1956, a slight thaw was noticeable at Igonane Ameur. All was quiet on the surface. On the basis of "you order, we obey," the villagers were doing what I wanted. Thus, every night four villagers reported to the post for sentry duty; the night rebels harassed the post, and the villager on duty even fired back at them with his shotgun.

I had reached the main line of resistance.

IX. Company Routine

While working on the population, I naturally kept the company busy tracking the *fellaghas* in my *sous-quartier*. We also took part frequently in operations in the *quartier* or outside. In the latter case, the battalion had to provide one or two companies formed for the occasion by drawing platoons out of each company; command of these temporary companies was given, by turns, to every company commander.

In the absence of intelligence on the whereabouts of the rebels, operations in my *sous-quartier* were simply a small-scale model of those I have already described for the sector. Thus I decided one day to search the ravine between Bou Souar and Igonane Ameur. We had often seen lights flashing at night, and we thought that *fellaghas* might be hiding there. I checked with Major Laval* in case he had other projects in mind for this large ravine, but he authorized me to go ahead.

The 1st Platoon from Grand Remblai made a *bouclage* at the mouth of the ravine on the highway. The 2d and 3d Platoons established fixed posts with automatic rifles on both sides of the ravine; the 60mm mortar took up position with one of these posts; and the rest of the two platoons advanced with the 4th Platoon to cover it while it searched the ravine.

We were all in place a half-hour before dawn and started when it was clear enough. We discovered several small caves with traces of burned candles, ashes, and empty cans. The river bed was a chaos of boulders, cascades, and thick bush, and it took us five hours to reach the highway below.

It was the rule that every isolated unit, no matter what its size, always kept a group of soldiers on the alert, ready to intervene if anything happened. I had a squad for this task in my camp at Ighouna; the platoons detached at Grand Remblai and Igonane Ameur maintained a team of four soldiers. An officer or NCO was also constantly on watch in every post.

The prevention of loss or theft of weapons was an important affair. Each man had a chain by which to attach his weapon to his wrist. At night, weapons were collected and padlocked on racks. Frequent drills were necessary to make sure that no time would be lost in distributing the weapons in case of emergency. Particular care was taken in regard to ammunition. Cartridges and grenades were counted, and every man was responsible for his allotment. After firing exercises or operations where mortars or rifle grenades had been used, we made sure that no unexploded shell was left lying around.

In case of emergency, an isolated unit anywhere in Algeria, provided it was equipped with an S.C.R. 300, could always ask for help on Channel 12, which was monitored twenty-four hours a day at *quartier*, sector, and zone level. It was also possible to request help on Channel 16, which was reserved for permanent air-ground liaison. Every military plane flying over Algeria kept a receiver open on this channel. This system worked so well that help in the form of tactical support planes would appear within half an hour of an S.O.S.

Twice a day at various hours patrols were sent along highways and motor tracks to prevent possible ambush against convoys. The roads in Algeria were classified into three categories:

(1) those on which no escort was necessary, such as the Tizi Ouzou–Algiers highway;
(2) those on which an escort of one armed vehicle was necessary, such as the Tizi Ouzou–Tikobain highway;
(3) those on which armed convoys were necessary, such as the Tizi Ouzou–Fort National highway. (In some cases L-19 planes provided air observation during the move.)

These regulations were in force from dawn to dusk. At night no traffic was authorized, at least in Kabylia, except for operational purposes or in an emergency.

No road ambush took place in my *quartier* while I was there. However, one of my successors, a captain, was killed in 1959 by a rebel commando 200 yards from Ighouna, together with his jeep driver and a sergeant.

Jeep and truck drivers were provided with bulletproof vests. Steel helmets were compulsory for personnel in Army vehicles.[2]

From Agouni Taga, the small hamlet south of Grand Remblai, one had a magnificent view over the entire south slope of Djebel Aissa Mimoun. On Major Laval's* orders, I installed an observatory there, linked by telephone to Grand Remblai. This kind of direct observation, however, never gave us any worthwhile information.

I will now describe briefly our daily routine at this period.

The NCO of the day woke up the company at 6:30 a.m. The company assembled at 7:00 a.m. after dressing and breakfast (black coffee and bread). The 1st Sergeant read the list of men due for sentry duty for the next 24 hours, assigned soldiers to the various chores, and organized the daily convoy of two trucks to the battalion command post. By that time the sick and the men on leave from Igonane Ameur, if any, would have reported to Ighouna and boarded the trucks. The 1st Sergeant personally inspected the escort, checked their arms and ammunition, and then announced the departure of the convoy by telephone to Grand Remblai and the battalion. I went along with my jeep when I had business to conduct at the battalion command post.

We had been warned by Zone Headquarters that schedules and itinerary of convoys must be varied in order to avoid ambush. This was a fine idea, but in practice we had only one possible itinerary, and the distribution of food and supplies at the battalion command post took place in the morning at an hour that could not be changed because of various logistical imperatives at zone level.

The trucks stopped at Grand Remblai, picked up the mail and any sick men, hooked a water tank to a truck, and continued to the battalion command post. Then one of the trucks went to Tizi Ouzou to deliver the outgoing mail and pick up the incoming. This was the most popular assignment in the company, for small as Tizi Ouzou was, it was still a town with shops and cafés and a few European girls in the

---

[2] My zone issued regular monthly reports, which were read to the soldiers, showing the traffic accident statistics. Losses from this cause equalled our combat losses.

streets. At the main café my men were usually greeted with derision by the "warriors" of the 9th R.I.C. "Pacifiers," they were called. They resented it bitterly at first, but they had the last laugh when they compared results with the other fellows during 1957. The convoy finally returned to Ighouna shortly before noon.

On the day set for supplying the 4th Company on Hill 801, a squad from Igonane Ameur stood waiting for the mule convoy at the village *djemaa* and escorted it to Tahanouts. The muleteers were not armed except for their chief, a Moslem sergeant. He was a draftee from Laghouat in the North Sahara, and a member of a sect, the Mozabite, hostile to the FLN. The situation was very embarrassing, but by tacit agreement nobody on either side made any remark about it. Through this muleteer sergeant I managed to obtain first one and then a second saddle horse from his company. From then on I seldom moved in my *sous-quartier* except on horseback, and I even used my horse on operations in the *quartier*.

Once in a while I organized an exercise in the morning for the entire company: an attack on a *mechta* (house)—there was an isolated ruin of a *mechta* not far from Bou Souar—or a *ratissage*. In this case we always notified our neighbors lest they mistake the noise for the real thing.

One of my constant minor troubles came from the abundance of game, particularly partridges, in the area. Soldiers and officers moving on jeeps or trucks along the highway below me seldom resisted the temptation to fire a few shots. This naturally provoked an alert. In a way it was good exercise for my soldiers, but I was worried about the "cry wolf" effect.

Lunch was around 12:30. Then the men rested until 2 p.m., most of them sleeping in anticipation of night watch and ambush. In summer the noon hours saw a torpor settling over all of Kabylia. Once in a while I sent patrols out or went on operations during these hours just to show the rebels that we were not completely asleep.

Our activity in the afternoon followed the same pattern as in the morning. Dinner was at about 6 p.m. During the night, ambushes went out. Sometimes I sent them simultaneously to different places, sometimes I spaced them at different hours. Occasionally I staged an alert.

Often in the night native dogs barked in the villages. I thought at first that it was an indication of people moving, and who other than *fellaghas*? The dogs, as I later found out, merely barked at jackals. I had flare mines with trip wires disposed around Ighouna. They lasted no more than a week, activated by jackals.

When a sentry reported seeing persistent lights in the Bou Souar ravine, we fired two or three mortar shells in the general direction.

Every summer for more than two months, fifteen to twenty of my men were incapacitated by virus hepatitis.

As can be seen from this description, the activity of the bulk of my company at Ighouna was devoted principally to routine military operations. I was practically the only one constantly engaged in pacification work. At Igonane Ameur, on the other hand, Paoli* and his men were busy with their particular tasks, such as propaganda, schooling, medical treatment for the population, controls, etc. I was impatient to station my entire company in the villages.

Second Lts. Paoli* and Fontaine* were suddenly transferred to the Bordj Menaiel Sector at the end of October 1956. They were replaced by Warrant Officer Pierre,* a regular NCO from Martinique who commanded a platoon in the 4th Company, and by 2d Lt. Dubois,* a young schoolteacher draftee fresh out of the reserve officers school.

I was furious at losing Paoli* just when he had become well acquainted with his village and with the special tasks I demanded. I pleaded to keep him, offering a more senior officer instead (Lt. Perrier,* who returned to my company as my assistant). But the transfer order had come from Paris, and there was nothing to be done about it. This movement of personnel was a constant plague in this sort of war where stability is so necessary.

Lt. Berger,* whose contract had expired, did not renew it. He was not interested, he told me frankly, in the kind of work we were doing. He had joined the Army to fight rebels, not to be "nice to the population."

●　●　●

November 1, 1956, was the second anniversary of the rebellion. A general strike by all Moslems in Algeria had been announced in rebel broadcasts from abroad. The zone command had warned us of a step-up in guerrilla and terrorist activity, and ordered us to increase patrols and controls.

On the morning of November 1, W/O Pierre* telephoned me from Igonane Ameur. No children had come to school, the streets were empty, all the villagers were staying home, and even at the fountain no women had appeared. I went to Bou Souar and found the same situation. I assembled all the adult males there and took them to Ighouna, where I put them to work clearing a helicopter landing strip.

I climbed next to Igonane Ameur, where Pierre* had already gathered the males at the *djemaa*. I asked them why they were not working. No answer. I interrogated several of them singly in Pierre's* office. Who had passed them the order to strike? They did not know, they just heard that a strike was on. Heard from whom? They could not tell, they did not remember. I returned to the *djemaa* and told the villagers that, since they were all so patriotic, a mere 24-hour strike did not seem enough. Consequently they would have to stay at home until further notice, more precisely until they told me who had given the order to strike and organized the movement. Every day they would be brought, one by one, to W/O Pierre* for interrogation. The women would be escorted to the fountain every morning between 8 and 9; children would come to school as usual.

The 24-hour curfew lasted five days. My soldiers made sure by visiting the houses that the children were fed; in case of doubt the children were brought to the dispensary and given milk and food provided by the SAS. School boys and girls were fed after school. On the fifth day two villagers gave the name of the culprit, a man named Oudiai from Bou Souar, a cousin of the local rebel chief.

I was not surprised. I had already arrested him (see the next section).

X. Accidental Purge of Bou Souar

Looking at the events retrospectively, I think I merited a break for all my efforts. I was at the end of my wits when the break came on November 2, 1956. I was eating lunch with 2d Lt. Dubois* at Ighouna when the orderly reported a Kabyle outside wanting to see me. I was in a bellicose mood, what with my Igonane Ameur curfew. If the man had come to ask a favor, he had chosen the wrong day. I went out and saw a frail old man sitting astride an ass. He gestured to be helped down. We sat him on a chair in my office and I waited a long time while he was puffing and recovering his breath. Then he spoke slowly, with great difficulty but clearly.

"*Mon Capitaine,* they are all bastards, s.o.b.'s. I will tell you the names of all the gang working for the *fellaghas* at Bou Souar. The chief is Amrane.* You will recognize him because he lost his left hand in an accident. Be careful, he has a pistol."

"How do you know all this?"

"Amrane* is my nephew, he lives in my own house, and that is where they have all their meetings. He thinks I am too old and too sick to understand what they say, but I have listened, and this is how I know."

"Why are you giving me this information?" He looked surprised at my question.

"Aren't you against the *fellaghas*? Me, I am for France, I hate them, that's why I came to see you."

He gave me a list of fifteen names, the cell boss Amrane,* his two assistants (one of them cousin Oudiai, the only literate Kabyle in the *sous-quartier* and consequently the chief propagandist), Said Areski* (marked as the liaison man with the *fellaghas*), the *mousseblines* (auxiliaries), and the chief supporters of the movement, including among them a woman, a young widow. He disclosed their activity in great detail, what actions they had participated in, when they had stood watch for the *fellaghas*, how much money they collected.

"Is there anybody like you whom I could trust in Bou Souar?"

"No, the people there are all bad."

Then he told me he had T.B. His nephew was trying to starve him to death. That morning, when he knew his nephew had gone, he managed to escape the house unnoticed and come to see me. I gave him 5,000 francs, and called the SAS officer to arrange that the man be given a bed and protection at the Tizi Ouzou hospital. I telephoned Major Laval,* told him the news (we used English for confidential information), and requested two platoons to reinforce my company for the operation I was planning.

Bou Souar was tightly encircled the next morning at 4. At 5 a.m., while it was still dark, teams designated in advance entered the village and went to the various houses to catch the men on the list. They walked in their socks to avoid noise. Dogs barked, but no villager woke up, thanks to the jackals. At H-Hour, set at 5:30, the men penetrated into the houses. I was standing near a house next to Amrane's,* a place owned by a certain Gabsi,* who was listed as a *moussebline.* Just as the team was about to go into the house, Gabsi* emerged and was instantly seized. He started to scream at the top of his lungs, as if he were being slaughtered, yet my soldiers were not rough with him at all.

"Shut him up," I barked at Sergeant Marceau,* "he's giving the alert."

Marceau* was already strangling Gabsi.* From Amrane's* house came noise of a scuffle, and out came Amrane,* kicking and screaming. I was seeing him for the first time. He had been caught just as he had half disappeared into a hole behind a pile of wood in the courtyard. The hole went several yards underground to a thick bush in the ravine. This is how he had always managed to escape when we searched the village. His name did not even figure on our preliminary census list.

One by one, suspects were brought to the gathering place, properly tied, and laid on their stomach. From the looks on their faces when they saw each other, I was certain I had made a good catch; they knew that I knew. When they were all there except for Said,* who had been missing from the village that night, I gave the encircling cordon the order to search the village thoroughly. Meanwhile a squad searched Amrane's* house for his pistol, although he denied ever having possessed a weapon. We emptied the house and granary, displaced the pile of wood, probed the walls, lifted every tile on the roof, searched the ravine near the escape hole, and found nothing.

I returned in triumph to Ighouna, leading the group of captives, separated from one another by ranks of soldiers to prevent their exchanging talk. In the largest courtyard behind my office my soldiers dug holes long enough to allow a man to lie in them and covered with barbed wire. The prisoners were led to their tombs and watched by two sentries.

I was determined this time to handle the case myself. I no longer had confidence in the police at Tizi Ouzou; nor could I rely on the battalion intelligence officer, who always had too much paperwork to concentrate on interrogating prisoners. I asked Lt. Lefevre,* who commanded the 4th Company, to lend me one of his auxiliaries as interpreter for a few days. When he arrived, I had the prisoners brought to me, one by one. I did not interrogate them at this stage, but gave them instead a short speech:

"As you can guess, I have much information on your activity with the *fellaghas*. You can be sure that I will get from you, one way or the other, what I don't know. Now my policy is to release you if you repent, no matter what you did. If you do not repent, you will be punished severely. I will know you repent sincerely when you give me a full confession of your past activity. The choice is yours. Think it over, I will interrogate you tomorrow." Then, without waiting for their comments and affirmations of innocence, I dismissed them.

The first day I fed them exactly as I did my soldiers, and I even allowed them to purchase soft drinks from our small canteen. The second day they appeared again before me and denied everything. They were innocent, it was all a tragic error, they hated the rebels, they did not understand why they had been arrested.

The third day I cut out food, and had only water given to them. The battalion doctor was visiting my company.

"Doc, I have a bunch of tough customers here. How about using truth serum?"

No, he could not help me, for it would violate his pledge. Besides, truth serum effects were not what they were supposed to be.

I started interrogating the woman, who was marked on my list as "the hostess with the mostes'." She screamed hysterically, scratching her face with her nails. I could not get in a word, so I sent her back to her tomb. The next candidate was probably the richest man in the village; he had the largest house, the best field. He did not look like the revolutionary type. He was indicated on the list as a regular host for the *fellaghas*, a food supplier and occasional watchman. Obviously a minor offender. I tried persuasion:

"Look, Amar,* I know what you have done. I am convinced you were forced to do it. Tell the truth and you will be released."

He denied everything.

"If you fear that rebels will know you have talked, let me assure you that they will have no way of knowing because I will keep the fact to myself. In any case everybody in the group will eventually talk, if only by force, so the rebels will never be able to blame a single suspect. When did you last receive *fellaghas* in your house?"

I repeated the question, but Amar* persisted in his denial. I told Bakouch,* the auxiliary, to take him away and bring another prisoner. Bakouch* was rather long in returning. The new prisoner was again a minor offender. I was interrogating him in the same fashion, with the same result, when Sergeant Marceau* reported with a broad smile that Amar* begged to see me urgently.

"All right, take this man away and bring Amar* in." I did not recognize Amar.* He was black from head to foot, all covered with soot. I took Marceau* aside.

"What happened?"

"Sir, Bakouch* locked Amar* in one of the ovens in the bakery and told him that if he did not talk, he would light a fire under the oven. Within ten minutes Amar* was screaming to be let out, and he says he's ready to talk now."

And thus I got my first confession. When Amar* finished, I let him have a shower, and he cleaned his clothes; he was given a substantial meal and led back to his tomb. Bakouch* and the sentry who escorted him made a great show of pushing and kicking him so that the others would not suspect anything. I inspected the miraculous oven. I changed into an old coverall and had myself locked in. It was of course dark and silent as a grave inside, psychologically very impressive, but otherwise quite harmless. I called all my cadres:

"This oven system works well, and I am going to use it. But I warn you that I will not accept initiatives of this sort in the future. If you have an idea, tell it to me first."

I wish to make myself clear to the reader on this score. Insurgency and counterinsurgency are the most vicious kind of warfare because they personally involve every man, military or civilian, on both sides, who happens to be in the theater. No one is allowed to remain neutral and watch the events in a detached way. While the insurgent does not hesitate to use terror, the counterinsurgent has to engage in police work. In order to achieve any result, he has to overcome the prisoners' fears, not their fears of the counterinsurgent but their fears of what the insurgents will do to them if they give out information. If anyone seriously believes that mere talk will do it, all I can say is he will learn better when confronted with the problem. This police work was not to my liking, but it was vital and therefore I accepted it. My only concerns were: (1) that it be kept within decent limits, and (2) that it not produce irreparable damage to my more constructive pacification work.

This is why, being an amateur in the field, I wanted to stay in complete control of the action and not be led by eager and still more amateurish subordinates. As for moral twinges, I confess I felt no more guilty than the pilot who bombs a town knowing of the existence of, but not seeing, the women and children below.

Pretty soon I received complete confessions from all the minor offenders, including the woman. I knew in detail most of the activity of the three bosses.

Of these, one made a full confession and even offered to serve me as undercover agent. Cousin Oudiai resisted the oven treatment and still proclaimed his innocence. I did not care; I knew enough about him. Amrane* needed a lot more pressure before he would talk, but talk he did except for these vital pieces of information: who was his boss, and when, how, and where he made contact with Oudiai and the *fellaghas*. He claimed he did not know his boss; he had only met him twice at the Saturday market at Tizi Ouzou; he did not know his name; he could only give a vague description of him. As for contacting *fellaghas*, he maintained that it was the other way around: they contacted *him* through Said,* and he never knew in advance when they would come. (This was a patent lie, because the others told me they had been warned sometimes two days in advance to prepare food and accommodations for Oudiai's band.)

Amrane* also told me this, which I consider his most significant statement:

"Sir, the inhabitants of my village, and those of other villages as well, they know everything. If a man tells you he has never given money for the *fellaghas*, that he has never stood watch for them when they stayed in the village, that he has never seen *fellaghas*, you can be sure he is a liar. He who tells you he does not know the OPA boss in his village is a liar." Here was the key to the systematic, easy approach I was looking for. Now I would be in command of the events instead of waiting for a break. All I had to do in order to purge a village was to proceed in two stages:

1. I would arrest simultaneously four or five villagers on whom I had a shadow of information, or who had simply committed some minor offense. The key was to arrest them at the same time, for it was hopeless to expect that a single suspect would ever talk; he would be too afraid that the rebels would trace the disclosure to him. Arrested in a group, on the other hand, suspects would be more inclined to talk, for they would find safety in numbers.

2. This first group—provided a cell leader had not accidentally been included in it—was almost certain to lead me to the bosses, whom I would then arrest.

Three of the prisoners mentioned another Oudiai as an important man in the rebel organization, not merely in Bou Souar but for the whole of Aissa Mimoun. They did not know exactly what was his role; they thought he might be a liaison man between his cousin Oudiai, the rebel chief, and other higher rebels in Tizi Ouzou. The man lived in an isolated house in the ravine about 1 km south of Bou Souar. One of the informers offered to serve as guide.

Lt. Perrier* was sent one night to arrest him. The house was encircled, a soldier beat on the door. No answer. Perrier* and another soldier climbed the wall and saw a man inside the courtyard climbing the opposite wall to get out. They alerted the rest of the party. Oudiai* jumped outside and was shot dead.

The interrogation took me a week, with the help of 2d Lt. Dubois.* When it was all over, I proposed to Major Laval* that I establish a platoon at Bou Souar; otherwise there would be no way to prevent *fellaghas* from exerting pressure on the villagers and thus rebuilding their OPA. To make the move I would have to bring to Ighouna the 1st Platoon still stationed at Grand Remblai; I would leave behind there just one squad for the protection of the SAS. Major Laval* agreed. We consulted Lt. Bauer* from the SAS, who had no objections. We had already investigated the billeting possibilities at Bou Souar. The most convenient house, because of its size, belonged to Amar;* it was 100 yards away from the western limit of the village and located in a hollow, but we had no choice.

On November 10, 1956, Dubois* took command of the 1st Platoon and settled in Bou Souar. That same day, I assembled all the prisoners with the exception of the three cell members. I read each confession to the whole group, and they put their fingerprints on the documents as signatures.

"You have all talked, you have not hidden the truth. Only I know that you have talked. As I promised you, you are free now. You can go home."

The three cell members were sent to the battalion intelligence officer with a full report. Amrane* and cousin Oudiai were interned by decision of the *préfet*. When I left Kabylia in July 1958, Oudiai had been paroled and was back in Bou Souar. I never heard of Amrane* again. I requested that the third man, who had offered his service as an agent, be kept in prison for a month, so as not to expose him in the eyes of the rebels. However, he disappeared as soon as he was released.

When I went to Bou Souar that afternoon to inspect Dubois'* instal-
lation, I was mobbed by a crowd of women as soon as I reached the
first house in the village. They hugged me, tried to kiss my hands, and
recited all the Koran's blessing on my head. They were thanking me for
the return of the prisoners. They apparently had thought they would
never see them again.

I spent the first few days at Bou Souar following the move of the 1st
Platoon. I expected a reaction from Oudiai's guerrillas, and we sent
out three ambushes every night for a week. Nothing happened. In fact,
Bou Souar was never harassed.

Dubois* repeated there all that we had done already at Igonane
Ameur in the way of a census, informing the population, educating
the children, rendering medical assistance, and having villagers share
sentry duty with our soldiers. We had some experience this time, and
there were fewer trial-and-error moves. A delegation of villagers from
Igonane Ameur complained to me soon after the opening of the school
at Bou Souar. They were griping "because we are the only village in all
Kabylia where girls go to school; we want the girls back home." I told
them I had been only experimenting and, now that I had found the
experiment worthwhile, I was planning to extend it to other villages.
Then I directed Dubois* to open classes for Bou Souar's girls.

The change in the attitude of the population at Bou Souar after
the purge was amazing, a real honeymoon. No longer did the villagers avoid talking to my soldiers. I didn't have to force the sick to visit
the dispensary. Even the women came, and often unaccompanied. The
villagers visited the Army post in such numbers to buy beer and soft
drinks from the local canteen that I had to warn Dubois* against possible treachery; I lectured his men on the need to be ever vigilant and
on guard—although in a most discreet way. As the surest sign that I
had hit straight at the OPA, the villagers were smoking again quite
openly.

Time had come now to approach the next step in my program, i.e., to find local leaders and enable them to function. I had this goal in mind when I asked the prisoners who, in their opinion or to their knowledge, had been hostile to the rebellion. Their answer was disappointing. Nobody had been hostile; perhaps the least sympathetic men were Bekri,* the old veteran (see page 88) because he was drawing a pension from the French government, and Cheurfa,* the local Moslem priest.[3] Bekri* was on the verge of senility, and I did not like to rely on Cheurfa* and become associated with the priest in the eyes of the population. Islam is not exactly a progressive religion, and the first thing we would have to do if we wanted to lift Algeria out of its morass was to shatter the backward Islamic way of life.

In the absence of any clearly reliable men, the only thing I could do was to call the villagers to elect their leaders themselves, and then to test those leaders, support those among them who had leadership ability, and hope that our policy would slowly convince them that ours was the better cause.

If the method worked, it meant that I had found a tested, systematic approach to the pacification of Algeria. But even if it worked, might not people object that it was a mere fluke? The answer to this argument was within my reach, for I would soon apply the process to every one of my villages. Again, people could object that success was due chiefly to my personal ability and wide experience, and that it could not be repeated by just any officer. Hence I could prove the validity of my method only if I contented myself with a directing role, letting my subordinates execute broadly-sketched but precise tasks. Dubois* would serve as my guinea pig in this case.

"Get the population in Bou Souar to elect a provisional mayor and six councilmen. Do not influence them in their choice, otherwise the elected people will appear as our stooges and we won't be able to fire them if they prove to be no good. They can elect anybody they

---

[3] I found later that all the priests in Aissa Mimoun had been less than enthusiastic about the rebellion, which, in spite of the religious trappings adopted for tactical reasons, seemed to them a dangerous lay revolution.

please, including those who have previously worked for the OPA. If you have any problem you can't solve, call me."

The elections took about a week. I attended the first meeting of the population, in which Dubois* explained why it was necessary to elect a provisional government for the village. French authorities, he said, were prepared now to make a considerable effort to raise the standard of living of the people, to modernize their way of life, to invest substantial sums in the improvement of their community. These things could not be done without the co-operation of the villagers, we could not and would not decide arbitrarily what was to be done. Dubois* added that the local government would not be merely a useful tool for us, but that it would serve just as much as the population's lawyer and representative vis-à-vis the French authorities.

From Dubois's* reports I learned that the elections did not occasion much enthusiasm. No candidates appeared until the very last day. The villagers finally elected Bekri* as mayor; among the councilmen was Gabsi,* the man who had tried to give the alert when we raided Bou Souar.

Challal,* the man I had in mind for the job of mayor at Igonane Ameur, disappeared from his village the very day I lifted the curfew, immediately after the arrests were made at Bou Souar. His family told me he had gone to France. They later produced letters he sent from Saint-Etienne, a town in Central France where many local villagers used to go. Thus, the information I had received on him was true. I had not believed it because I had been unable to corroborate it.

XI. Expansion of My *Sous-Quartier*; Purge of the Other Villages

At the end of November 1956, my company was distributed as follows:

Command Post, Command Platoon, 3d and 4th Platoons (less one squad) at Ighouna
1st Platoon at Bou Souar
2d Platoon at Igonane Ameur
One squad at Grand Remblai

Having occupied the two most important villages in my *sous-quartier*, I still had two combat platoons with me at Ighouna, where they could not be used as they should in pacification work. I did not like to see them wasted in futile military operations. I sought naturally to aggrandize my *sous-quartier*. I offered to take over the entire area within the jurisdiction of the 4th Company on the south slope of Aissa Mimoun, a piece of real estate which included the villages of Khelouyene Mendja, Ait Braham, Iril Ou Abba, and Tala Ou Abba. The 4th Company could thus devote its activity to the north slope.

Major Renard,* a classmate of mine at Saint-Cyr, who had just replaced Major Laval* as the battalion commander, accepted the proposal. The small detachment of the 4th Company, which ruled over this area from his post at the burned-out school at Tala Ilane, moved to Hill 801. I replaced it with my 3d Platoon (see Figure 7) under 2d Lt. Bringuier,* a recent arrival in my company.

I had still another suggestion in line with this reshuffle. Now that my company was so dispersed and that three of my platoons were engaged essentially in working on the population, I saw my immediate military task as that of affording a reasonable degree of safety to my detachments and to the population they controlled. This would not preclude, of course, the continuation of small offensive operations against the guerrillas whenever the opportunity presented itself, but it would rule out *a priori* operations to the detriment of the pacification

Figure 7
The Enlarged 3d Company *Sous-Quartier* (December 1956)

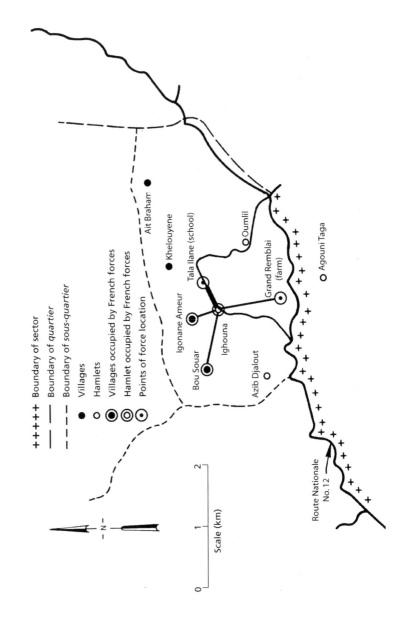

+ + + +   Boundary of sector

———   Boundary of *quartier*

– – –   Boundary of *sous-quartier*

●   Villages

○   Hamlets

◉   Villages occupied by French forces

◉   Hamlet occupied by French forces

◉   Points of force location

Ait Braham

Khelouyene

Tala Ilane (school)

Oumlil

Grand Remblai (farm)

Agouni Taga

Igonane Ameur

Bou Souar

Ighouna

Azib Djalout

Route Nationale No. 12

N

Scale (km)
0   1   2

work. Since what I was doing in my *sous-quartier* (dispersing my company in order to occupy the villages) would eventually become the general practice in the battalion—and Major Renard* concurred—there was a definite need for a small commando operating in the *quartier* to go on tracking the *fellaghas*. The time to organize it was now. Short as I was of personnel, I offered one sergeant and four men as my company's contribution to the commando. The idea was approved, and the 20-man commando was organized immediately. Lt. Perrier* became its leader, and it was based at Ighouna. The commando operated most of the time on the north slope of Aissa Mimoun.

I took my first leave around the New Year of 1957. The day after I returned from Paris, a party of soldiers from the I/93 R.A.M., our southern neighbors, stumbled by accident upon a group of rebels near Azib Seklaoui in the low land between my *sous-quartier* and Oued Sebaou. They killed thirteen and captured one wounded *fellagha*. I immediately sent Lt. Perrier* with his commando. The battle was well over by the time they arrived, but they were able to collect several weapons that were lying around, including a Colt .45 pistol in a white holster. This, we knew from our Bou Souar informants, was Oudiai's own pistol. I notified the battalion intelligence officer, gendarmes were dispatched to the spot, and Oudiai's body was formally identified. An interesting piece of news for us, and we wasted no time in spreading it among the Aissa Mimoun inhabitants. To make sure that no doubt was raised by the rebels concerning the death of our local public enemy no. 1, I suggested to Major Renard* that a delegation from each village look at the dead *fellaghas* on the pretense of identifying them. This turned out to be an excellent idea, for rumors were already spreading that Oudiai had managed to escape.

It was ironical that Oudiai, the man who had eluded us for so long, should have met his end in an accidental encounter with our neighbors who were not specially interested in him. Of his original band, seven *fellaghas* were now left.

Another event that took place in January 1957 was the arrival in my company of eighteen Moslem draftees. One was a Kabyle, the others were Arabs. They had just finished a period of two months of basic training at the battalion command post under 2d Lt. Bringuier.* With them came also a Moslem master sergeant, a regular NCO, who had fought in Indochina. I assigned them to my detached platoons, not wanting to keep them at Ighouna where I detained and interrogated prisoners, and where no direct pacification task was undertaken.

We treated them exactly as we did the French soldiers, except for food (they did not eat pork). They behaved in a normal way, mixed easily with their French comrades, and took part in every operation, firing at *fellaghas* with just as much gusto when the occasion arose. They never discussed the war or political events, differing in this respect from the French soldiers. We saw to it that sentry duty was never given simultaneously to two Moslem draftees. When M/S Ben Ali,* at Tala Ilane, was the NCO of the day, 2d Lt. Bringuier* and M/S Vignaux,* who was now his assistant, split the night between them to check on Ben Ali* discreetly. We never had any trouble with them, however. Most of these Moslem draftees being illiterate, I had them attend classes in schools with the local children whenever their duties allowed it.

Their story has an unfortunate ending. In the summer of 1957, when they were well accustomed to us and were participating eagerly in our various activities in the villages, they were suddenly transferred to various Metropolitan (as opposed to Colonial) Army units in the zone. We were sorry to see them go. I hated particularly to lose Kacem,* my bodyguard, a man endowed with Herculean strength and the happiest temper. The men themselves felt very bitter about the transfer. Their mail was checked occasionally by the intelligence officer, and I remember seeing a letter in which one of them wrote how much he hated the idea of being assigned to a Battalion of Chasseurs Alpins because "in the Colonial Troops [where he was] there is no racism." (Not that there was racism in other French troops.)

Several of the Moslems deserted right after their transfer and joined a band of *fellaghas*. They made a successful ambush against a convoy near Fort National and were killed in the pursuit.

The history of the purge in my newly-occupied territory may be divided into three periods: (1) preliminary work and intelligence-gathering; (2) arresting the OPA members; and (3) occupying the villages.

At Tala Ilane I gave Bringuier* responsibility for the whole territory, telling him to concentrate on Khelouyene and Ait Braham, the two main villages.

A rough census was gradually made. In order to facilitate the work, I had aerial pictures of the entire Aissa Mimoun taken at low altitude, which enabled us to spot every isolated house and to make certain that none escaped our attention. We immediately opened at Tala Ilane a dispensary and a school for the Khelouyene children. The battalion doctor agreed to give a two-week medic course to two of my soldiers. Lt. Bauer* gave me SAS money to provide a meal a day to the Khelouyene children at the school. We hired a local cook and asked the villagers to pay his salary, which they did willingly.

The people in this area east of Igonane Ameur seemed from the beginning more open than those we had met so far. Although they did not show any sign of overt friendliness, although nobody dared smoke in public, we had the definite impression that they were glad to see us. Bringuier* had spotted a dozen veterans and retired professional soldiers as a likely source of intelligence. His first invitation to them to come to lunch met with a minimum show of reluctance. It was followed by many others, and with the help of generous libations of Algerian wine, tongues loosened up. Thanks to this pleasant technique ("simple, but it works," said Vignaux,* the initiator), I was soon in possession of enough information to arrest a first batch of suspects who, according to my theory, would lead me to the real bosses. They were sixteen in all, at least two from each village and hamlet.

Unwilling to get myself tied up in the time-consuming work of interrogating the prisoners, I gave the job to a Sergeant Levy* from the commando, a *pied-noir* from Algiers, lawyer in civilian life, who had volunteered as a reservist for the duration of the war. He had enough brains and good sense, I felt, to handle the job properly. As a matter of fact, we were greatly helped by the example of the purge at Bou Souar.

When the prisoners were told that they would be free, no matter what their past activity, provided they told the whole truth, they knew we meant it. As a result the "oven treatment" was needed only for two difficult cases, of men who were cell members.

It took about a week to get the picture of the FLN political organization in the area concerned. Just as I was about to throw out the net a second time for the big fish, I received a visit from a man named Ahmed Asli from Khelouyene. A World War, I veteran, he had opted for full French citizenship status after that war. "I always voted the French ballot," he told me proudly. When the rebellion broke out in Aissa Mimoun, he tried to organize opposition to the rebels, and he narrowly escaped several assassination attempts by Oudiai. Finding no support from the French authorities, he was driven into hiding in the Djebel, then at Tizi Ouzou, and finally in Algiers, where he felt relatively safe. He had heard there of our efforts to clean up the Djebel and had returned to help us. He gave me the names of the most active FLN supporters he knew. His information jibed with what I already knew from the prisoners.

In the next two or three days, another veteran from Khelouyene, named Boukrou, and two villagers from Ait Braham came to denounce the rebel political leaders. This was highly interesting to me, not so much for the information (I had that already), but because these men had taken a considerable risk in offering it, and their loyalty to us was beyond doubt. In these men I had at least a core of politically reliable people on which to build my own political machine.

It remained only for me to finish the purge. But a major complication set in. Major Renard* told me I could not establish a detachment at Ait Braham after the purge, as I had intended. The veto came from General Gouraud himself, the zone commander, who thought that my company was already too dispersed to have any military value. I protested indignantly, arguing as follows:

1. So far in the history of the war in all Algeria, not a single isolated post, not even when the garrison consisted only of four or five French civilian farmers, had been lost as a result of a determined attack by the rebels. Why, then, would it be unsafe for me to disperse my company still further?

2. Had I not contributed my full share of men for operations outside my *sous-quartier?* I would continue to do so, even with a detachment at Ait Braham.

3. Wasn't the risk in not controlling and protecting the population much greater than the risk of dispersion?

Renard* and Lt.-Col. Lemoine* sympathized with me but said they could not budge General Gouraud. I was surprised that moving a platoon within a *sous-quartier* was a decision to be passed upon by a zone commander. This was no way to win a war, it seemed to me. (I kept this last thought to myself, of course.)

I was stuck now with my sixteen prisoners. I could not release them until I had arrested the bosses. I could not tell them why, though they had all confessed, they were not being released. I kept them at Ighouna under a relaxed regime.

I met General Gouraud a month later when he accompanied to Bou Souar a high-ranking official from Algiers (see below). I explained to him the situation, expecting a rigid "no." To my surprise, he agreed instantly. To this day I don't know whether he had changed his mind or whether he had been misinformed by his staff.

This incident is as good an opportunity as any to broach the subject of one of my strongest complaints during my tour in Algiers, namely, the lack of appreciation by higher levels of the situation and problems at the grassroots. Different perspectives give different views; this is normal, and it is not what I am speaking about. My complaint revolves around the fact that the critical tactical work in this insurgency was carried out, naturally, by the junior officers directly in contact with the population. The real problems developed at their level. Some of them were pretty obvious and were perceived also by the top echelons. Others, which were not so apparent even when they were important, completely escaped attention at higher levels. One example I have already mentioned was the problem of a well-established, uniform system of punishments against people who violated one of the many regulations imposed by the circumstances. Another was the ease with which Moslems circumvented our control of movement between Algeria and France. When I said to a Kabyle "You won't go to France unless...," it was important for me that he didn't. When I affirmed that no Kabyle could really be trusted until he had given positive proof of his loyalty, I had dozens of cases to support my assertion.

Important strategic decisions were made in ignorance of these real problems. Theories were elaborated on the basis of intuition. The gap started between the *sous-quartier* and the *quartier* levels and was, of course, amplified at every echelon above. What made it worse was the illusion of the higher echelons that reports from below and inspections from above were giving them the complete picture of the situation. There were two solutions in my view: One, and by far the best, would have been for the civilian and military officials from higher echelons to spend days, perhaps a week, with the officers at the grassroots, instead of just passing through or inspecting. The other was for the same commanders to set up a team of observers to do that job for them.

In spite of my pleading and numerous invitations, no one ever came to my *sous-quartier* for more than a short day, except the *U.S. News and World Report* correspondent, who certainly got a better picture during his four-day stay than he could have received by any other means.

So conscious was I of this information gap between the different levels that I used myself to spend several days with my various detachments. I always learned something.

The day after General Gouraud's decision, I arrested all the OPA bosses and moved to Ait Braham a detachment made up of soldiers from the 3d and 4th Platoons. Once more I saw the atmosphere changing radically overnight: villagers smoked, mixed freely with the soldiers, came often to the post to buy drinks and talk with us, and co-operated in every way. Kabyles even volunteered to join our forces.

Two cell members from Mendja had fled just before their arrest. Three months later I received a phone call from the 4th Company announcing the surrender of two *fellaghas* at Tahanouts. They were the same two men. This is the story they told me.

After I had arrested the first group of sixteen suspects, all the OPA members guessed that they would be denounced. They therefore contacted the *fellaghas* and asked to join the maquis. They were turned down. The local guerrilla leader told them he had no weapons to give them, and the food situation had become increasingly difficult in the maquis because of our movement regulations and our control. Moreover, the guerrilla leader usually would accept only men who had shown their mettle by committing a terrorist act: "Go and kill a French officer and we'll take you." (This was, of course, a very elastic rule, applied only where large numbers of volunteers were eager to join the bands. The rebels became far less choosy when they had suffered losses and had to replenish their manpower.)

The OPA bosses were bitterly disappointed and resigned themselves to their fate, except for the two men from Mendja who fled to the north slope of Aissa Mimoun, wandering by themselves for several days. The guerrilla leader finally relented and took them into his band made up of the remnants of Oudiai's gang. They stayed in the area for two months, at first without weapons, later with a shotgun each.

The main concern of the guerrillas was to escape our search. They slept or remained hidden during the day, not daring to move. Their moves took place only at night. As the cells were being progressively destroyed, they were now cut off from the population. They still attempted to collect money and food, but they had to do it themselves, going cautiously into the small unoccupied hamlets and isolated farms. Whenever they asked people in these hamlets to collect money for them, they were refused; the villagers complained it was too dangerous.

After two months of this life, five of the nine guerrillas in the band suggested leaving the area and joining a larger maquis in the Mizrana Forest. The leader, "Sergeant" Smail,* refused but was unable to impose his decision, and the group split. The two men from Mendja went to the Mizrana Forest, stayed there a month, and deserted one night when their band made a sortie toward Makouda. I learned from them that my Djebel was considered a lost area by the rebel chiefs in the Mizrana. *Fellaghas* were forbidden to cross it without express orders.

The two men were processed by the police at Tizi Ouzou. As they had committed no major crime—to the knowledge of the police—they were released rapidly and returned to my area. I offered them a choice between going back to their village and joining the *harka* (a unit of full-time local auxiliaries called *harkis*) which I had just formed (see below). But they requested a visa for France, not daring to expose themselves to the reaction of their fellow villagers.

With the purge completed in my *sous-quartier*, I reorganized now my company's deployment. Since I had four occupied villages and only four platoons, I could not assign an entire platoon to each village and still keep a reserve with me. I consequently ignored the table of organization and reduced the strength of the platoons to between twenty and twenty-five men according to the size and situation of the village. In order to save more personnel, I moved my command post and all that went with it to Tala Ilane.

The dispersal of my company over the area between Bou Souar and Ait Braham—a distance of 4 km as the crow flies but actually much more because of the terrain—forced me to pay more attention to the possibility of an ambush against my numerous patrols moving back and forth between their posts and my command post. I elaborated a new plan for defense against ambushes, based on the principle that units stationed below the point of ambush would quickly establish a defense line, while units stationed above would rush to the spot. We had frequent drills at all hours of the day, and I had these drills made as public as possible so that the population could see that we were ready to cope with rebel incursions. It took from five to ten minutes between notice of the event and reaction. The system was adopted for the other companies and co-ordinated for the *quartier* by Major Renard.*

A few days after we had evacuated Ighouna, I received a delegation of villagers from Igonane Ameur. The olive crop had just been harvested, and they now needed to use the oil presses at Ighouna. Could they reoccupy the empty hamlet?

"You know why the population was evacuated from Ighouna? Because of frequent rebel ambushes there. I am using the road every day for my trucks. If I let you settle there again, how can I be certain that you won't co-operate with the *fellaghas?*"

"Sir, we all are hostile to the rebels."

"Why don't you show it more? For instance, I asked your village several months ago to elect a mayor and a council. Where are they?"

W/O Pierre* reported the next morning that the villagers had assembled at the *djemaa*. In the afternoon Igonane Ameur had its first municipal government. The mayor was a man named Abboud,* the wealthiest man in the village (rich by any standard), who owned the largest oil mill at Ighouna. He resigned two months later for business reasons (he was running a small truck transport company) and was replaced by a man named Haddad,* a metal worker just back from Saint-Etienne in France; The name means "smith" in Arabic, and the smith in Moslem villages is next to the bottom in social standing, just a notch above the butcher. Abboud* and the villagers had evidently pulled a joke on me, or so I thought. But if they really did, they made a serious mistake, for Haddad* turned out to be the second most efficient mayor in the area.

Once I had let Ighouna be reoccupied by the villagers, all those who had been displaced long before my arrival because their isolated houses were close to the road from Grand Remblai to Ighouna requested permission to return. I had no objection provided they accepted one condition: if an ambush took place on the road, and they had given no warning while they could, they would be held responsible. They accepted, and from then on I had a large string of civilian watchers along the road. I checked their vigilance one day by sending five *harkis* disguised as *fellaghas*, and, sure enough, a young boy came running to my command post to warn us. He had been sent by his father.[4]

In February 1957 (I am not sure of the date), the FLN ordered another general strike all over Algeria. I think it was to coincide with the U.N. debates on the Algerian question. I made a tour of my *sous-quartier*

---

[4] No system is foolproof. The special rebel commando sent to kill Captain Hermanna,* my successor, infiltrated at night, entered the two houses nearest the spot selected for the ambush, tied and gagged men, women, and children, and remained hidden there until they spotted the jeep on the road.

that day. Everything was normal, farmers were out in their fields, children had all gone to school, women chatted as usual at the fountains. Except at Igonane Ameur. There the new mayor Haddad* and the villagers had gone overboard to show that they were not taking part in the strike. The entire male population equipped with picks and shovels were working on improving the motor road from Grand Remblai and the paths. They were organized in large gangs, each under a councilman. That evening I received a phone call from Colonel Boissot,* the Zone Chief of Staff:

"Congratulations, Galula."

"Thank you, Sir, but what for?" Maybe I was being promoted.

"We had a plane flying all over Kabylia today to check on the strike. The only place where the pilot reported any civilian activity was your *sous-quartier.*"

Paradoxically, the first village I had occupied, Igonane Ameur, was now the only one I had not purged systematically. I was reluctant to do it because, at least on the surface, the population was co-operating with us ostentatiously since the hasty departure of Challal,* the OPA boss. I had to find out whether he had been replaced, as I strongly suspected.

On the first Saturday of March 1957, I established a roadblock in front of the battalion command post on the highway from Aissa Mimoun to Tizi Ouzou. M/S Vignaux,* assisted by two soldiers from each of my posts, stopped every villager from the *sous-quartier* on his way to the large weekly market at Tizi Ouzou, and noted down the amount of money he was carrying. On the way back in the afternoon, he checked every man for the money he had left and his purchases. A man from Igonane Ameur could not explain what he had done with 32,000 francs he was carrying on the way out. He was arrested and confessed to being the FLN tax collector in his village. He refused to tell who was helping him and to whom he had handed over the money. He was sent to the police and later to a prison camp.

Even though the people at Igonane Ameur, too, were smoking publicly and chatting openly with the soldiers, I was not sure that a rebel cell did not still exist—even though it might be dormant. I let it go at that and decided I would apply my purging system only if I noticed a change for the worse in the population's attitude.

PART THREE

The Struggle for the Support of the Population

I. The Situation in Algeria in the Winter of 1957

A wit in my battalion used to say:

"We will win this war all right, not because we are so clever but because the FLN are more stupid than we are."

Events were bearing him out, for, in spite of all our minor and major blunders, the general situation had taken a turn for the better by the early months of 1957. We were muddling through in strength, the rebels in weakness, and this made a difference.

There had been the Suez campaign and the stunning defeat of the Egyptians by the small Israeli Army. True, the affair ended in a smashing political victory for Nasser, and the FLN leaders realized more clearly than ever that perhaps their main front was not in Algeria but abroad. Nevertheless, to the masses of Algerian Moslems, who had access to enough objective information not to believe the Egyptians' claims of a brilliant military victory, it seemed that the French were not so degenerate after all. They had reacted with the full support of the French population at home.

Then, five top leaders of the rebellion, including Ben Bella, had been neatly caught during a flight from Rabat to Tunis. Their capture, I admit, had little effect on the direction of the rebellion, because the movement was too loosely organized to crumble under such a blow. Also, the rivalry among Arabs being what it is, their elimination gave impetus to the other leaders' scramble for the top. On the other hand, the event confirmed the masses in Algeria in their suspicion that the French had perhaps been written off too soon.

A third important event abroad was the slaughter of French civilians by a mob at Meknes in Morocco following the capture of Ben Bella. It was one more proof that European minorities could not be entrusted to a militant nationalist Arab government born in terror. An agreement with the FLN being impossible, it remained to settle the issue by force, and French strength was tangible while the rebels' was not.

Inside Algeria, the *quadrillage* of static troops covered the entire territory. Its density was not always in keeping with the demands of the situation, but nowhere could the rebels claim a hold on safe bases. They were on the run everywhere, ineffective even as a guerrilla force, incapable of co-ordinating an operation by two *katibas*, able only to terrorize the population. They had not succeeded in sabotaging the economy, which, on the contrary, was booming (as reflected in the number of Algerian Moslem settlers in Morocco who were returning to Algeria, and were easily finding employment there, because conditions had deteriorated so much since Moroccan independence). Everywhere the French forces were opening roads and building permanent SAS *bordjs*, camps, airfields. Low-rent apartment houses for the Moslems were replacing slums at an amazing rate in every town. Millions were being invested in the Sahara. These were not signs that the French were preparing to leave.

Last but not least, the French won the battle of Algiers. In the latter part of 1956, the rebels staged an orgy of blind terrorism in the Algerian capital. A large bomb killed or wounded seventy civilians, mostly Europeans, in a dance hall; another bomb hidden in a lamp post at the busiest bus stop killed or maimed eighty people. These are cases I remember, but there were many others. The responsible authorities felt control slipping from their hands; if the drift was not halted soon, there would be no way to prevent a reaction of blind anger by Europeans against Moslems and to stop God knows what other foolish moves against the French government.

Under the Special Powers Act, the 10th Paratroop Division of General Massu, just back from Suez, was given authority to assume police functions and to clean Algiers. General Massu proceeded from the fact that the terrorists were operating from within the Kasbah, the old native town, and he controlled all its exits and the streets leading to it. So effective was our control that several terrorists who succeeded one day in leaving the Kasbah found themselves unable to dispose of their time bombs and blew up with them. Massu's second assumption was that, willingly or not, the population of the Kasbah had fallen completely under the control of the terrorists, and therefore any Moslem suspect knew his immediate FLN boss and could lead to him. Time was short since bombs were exploding at an alarming rate, and consequently there was no time for the niceties of regular procedures. The police, either because of FLN infiltration or because it had never been designed to cope with such a situation, was totally inefficient, and the paratroopers had to handle the job themselves.

In ten days the terrorist organization was dismantled so completely that Algiers became free of terrorism for at least two years. Only one terrorist leader escaped, M. Ben Kheda, who subsequently became President of the Algerian Republic Provisional Government (later to be eliminated by Ben Bella). The most impressive lesson of the battle was expressed half-jokingly by a paratrooper colonel: "Give me one hundred resolute men and I will terrorize a city like Paris." For the total rebel terrorist organization, we found, amounted to no more than five hundred people, including the minor supporters. They had been able to terrorize and almost to paralyze a city of 700,000 inhabitants.

It was a major victory, the concrete proof that we could really break the back of the rebellion. The FLN and their supporters in France and abroad naturally did their best to spoil it, and a virulent campaign against "tortures" followed immediately upon our success. If there was a field in which we were definitely and infinitely more stupid than our opponents, it was propaganda.

The threat from the rebel forces having been lifted in the preceding months, our operations had generally dwindled to small, though numerous, affairs. The main concern now was to win over the population. The need for a valid political platform to support our action became increasingly urgent, and both the French government and the Parliament endeavored to devise a program. Independence was ruled out, at least for the time being and as long as it entailed handing over Algeria to the FLN, a group considered far from representative of the majority of Moslems. The choice thus narrowed down to two possibilities:

1. Complete integration of Algeria into the French system. It meant, not that Algerian Moslems would be transformed overnight into Frenchmen, but simply that they would be given exactly the same

rights (though not yet the same duties) that French citizens enjoyed, with the same opportunities for betterment in terms of education, social security, jobs, and salary. While in an Algerian framework the Europeans would always remain a minority, eternally exposed to the risk of being swept away, in a Franco-Algerian combination the Moslems would be the minority, yet they would have nothing to fear considering the humanistic, liberal traditions of France. Integration had long been the goal of a large number of Moslems in Algeria. It was until recently the very platform of Ferhat Abbas, and it still had considerable appeal. The European settlers who had been opposed to it were slowly rallying to the idea under the pressure of events.

2. A federation or confederation of France and Algeria. Algeria would receive some sort of internal autonomy and thus preserve its personality, but essential links with France would be maintained. The idea had few supporters in Algeria. To the Moslems it seemed to offer all the disadvantages of the past system and no benefit; the Europeans saw it as a dangerous step toward full independence without guaranty.

While integrationists and federalists quarreled inconclusively in the Parliament, the French government came out with a practical interim three-step program designed to take the wind out of the rebels' sails without prejudicing the future. The formula was (1) ceasefire, (2) elections, (3) building of a new Algeria. Feelers were put out to the FLN leaders in Rome, who rejected the proposal. Incidentally, the mere fact that the French government had contacted the rebels, albeit unofficially, when it became known, increased the toughness of the FLN cadres in Algeria, reinforced the Moslem population's reluctance to commit itself prematurely on our side, and infuriated those in the administration and in the armed forces who were exerting themselves to obtain this commitment.

It was also decided that it would be useful in any case to start the democratic education of the Moslem masses. This was the essential purpose of the municipal reform conceived in Algiers at that time. The old *communes mixtes* under a French *administrateur* would be dissolved and replaced by smaller, self-governing *communes*.

II. The Municipal Reform

I do not know exactly who was responsible for the carving of the new *communes* in Kabylia. I was told it was the work of a young French anthropologist well acquainted with the area and the Kabyles. All I know definitely, however, is that neither the SAS officer nor I was consulted insofar as the Djebel Aissa Mimoun was concerned. We both learned officially one day that four *communes* had been created in my *sous-quartier*, namely Bou Souar, Igonane Ameur, Khelouyene, and Ait Braham, and we were shown their boundaries on a map.

As it happened, large tracts of farm land owned by the people of one *commune* were included in another, and hamlets traditionally related to a village in *commune* A were now part of *commune* B. We also seriously doubted the possibility that four such small communes, each poor in economic and human resources, could operate efficiently. Only one adult Kabyle, cousin Oudiai,* was literate in my entire *sous-quartier*, and he was now in jail. Where would we find the men competent enough to administer four *communes*? But these were relatively minor problems. The timing of the reform was the major one.

The municipal reform was to be implemented all over Kabylia as soon as possible; February 1, then March 1, were given as the imperative target dates. Considerable pressure was exerted from Algiers on both the *préfet* and the zone commander, who in turn put the heat on the lower echelons, down to the SAS officers and the *sous-quartier* commanders. The reform presented no great difficulty for me; I was almost ready for it. Only I did not want to implement it until the purge was completed—which would not take too long in any case—because I knew too well what would happen if I did: assuming that I could force the villagers to elect anybody, only FLN stooges would have emerged from such elections.

Considering that my *sous-quartier* was the most advanced in Kabylia in regard to pacification (I had talked to enough colleagues from other areas to realize it), I was certain that a reform conducted under such conditions, with no regard to the reality, would be a fiasco, and indeed this is what happened elsewhere. Wherever "elections" were held, the new mayors happily collected their salary from the Préfecture and took their orders from the FLN, to whom they gave a slice of their income. When villages in Kabylia were finally purged, mayors and councilmen were found to be the rebel cell bosses or their puppets. But since they now had official positions, it was not so easy to dislodge them, for the *préfet* had to publicize any change in the form of an administrative decree published in the official Algerian Gazette, and this was likely to provoke annoying inquiries from Algiers.

M. Vignon, the *préfet*, came to my *sous-quartier* at the end of February 1957 to inaugurate the new municipal council of Igonane Ameur. The mayor, Haddad,* with his tricolor sash, the councilmen, the children, and the population were assembled in the village square near the *djemaa*. When the *préfet* appeared, the school children sang songs, the population applauded, Haddad* made a short speech, and the *préfet* made another. After the ceremony the *préfet*, the council, Lt. Bauer* from the SAS, and I met in the *djemaa* to discuss village affairs. The *préfet* was obviously struck by the sincerity and even the heat of the discussion. In other municipalities he had visited, mayors and councilmen had been sullen or just yes-men. Here were villagers who openly complained about my refusal to grant visas for France or about the idea of sending girls to school, who turned down a proposal made by a councilman to begin by building a city hall and insisted that a real school was needed more. He noticed the easy relations between my soldiers and the villagers, the friendly curiosity of the women, the unobtrusiveness of our military apparatus. Here was a place where pacification really worked. (I learned all this from Lt. Bauer,* who got it from the Secretary General of the Préfecture.)

"When will you be ready for the inauguration of Bou Souar's municipality?" he asked Lt. Bauer.*

"Any time you would like, Sir, we are ready for it now."

"I will tell you when."

When the Secretary General returned to his office, he invited M. Robert Lacoste, the Minister-Resident, to attend the ceremony at Bou

Souar and see for himself. My *sous-quartier* was begininng to be a show place.

M. Lacoste accepted, but at the last moment he had to fly to Paris for a cabinet meeting. In his stead came the Director of Political Affairs in Algeria, M. Lucien Paye (who became Minister of National Education under M. Debre in 1960), accompanied by a host of various civil servants from Algiers. The party arrived at Bou Souar by helicopter with M. Vignon and General Gouraud.

It was a repetition of what had occurred at Igonane Ameur. On his way back to Algiers, M. Paye commented to his staff that he had not been fooled. What he had just seen at Bou Souar, he said, was just a show, cleverly staged, to be sure, but faked just the same. "These people want independence, they care for nothing else. So don't tell me they were sincere!"

While we were meeting with the mayor, Bekri,* and his councilmen in the small house serving as a temporary *mairie*, one of M. Paye's assistants stayed outside to look at things and chatted with Sergeant Royer,* the head schoolteacher in the village. Royer* told him his problems, how eager the children were to learn, how much he needed books and equipment. The assistant promised to help him.

"Here's my address in Algiers. If you need anything, just write me."

Some weeks later Royer* wrote him a letter. Thereupon the assistant burst into M. Paye's office and said:

"Sir, read this letter. When a sergeant, and not a regular but a draftee, describes the situation in his village in such terms, when he shows so much enthusiasm in his work, I just can't believe it is faked."

I was told M. Paye was shaken in his convictions. I must confess I was equally shaken to find that the Director of Political Affairs, the number 1 adviser of M. Lacoste in Algeria, did not believe in any outcome of the war but independence.

I will come back to my work with the newly-elected local leaders. Meanwhile I must describe an operation in which I was closely involved.

III. Cleaning Tizi Ouzou

Tizi Ouzou ("The Pass of Genista" in Kabyle, genista being a spiny shrub) is the capital of Greater Kabylia, located about seventy miles east of Algiers, to which it is linked by a railroad and a good highway. The town lies at the foot of Djebel Beloua, a 2,000-foot mountain covered with trees and shrubs and strewn with small villages.

The city actually comprises two towns: the old one (or Kasbah) in the north, touching the slope of Djebel Beloua, a maze of narrow twisted lanes with inward-built houses; and the new one (or European town) spread south of the Kasbah, with relatively broad, straight streets intersecting at right angles. Slightly detached from the town on a hill is the Bordj, an old Turkish fortress serving now as the command post of the Tizi Ouzou sector.

The total population was about 20,000. Of these, 3,000 were Europeans; mostly small businessmen and shopkeepers, lawyers, bank clerks, and civil servants, whose number was increasing rapidly as Tizi Ouzou was now the seat of a Préfecture. The Kasbah was exclusively populated with Kabyles, while a mixture of Europeans and Moslems shared the new town.

Being the seat of the zone headquarters with its attached units (Military Police, Signal Company, Ordnance Repair Company, Quartermaster Company, Medical Company, etc.), Tizi Ouzou had a large garrison, but none of these units had any direct responsibility in policing the town; they were responsible only for their own immediate safety, although the MPs, when patrolling the town looking for delinquent soldiers, were naturally on the alert for terrorists.

Every Saturday a large native market attracted from 10,000 to 15,000 Kabyles from the surrounding areas; they came on foot, by donkey, or by bus, and met in the large open market place just outside the town on the road to Algiers. The market was, of course, the ideal spot for the rebels to collect the money from the rural agents, to pass orders, and to spread rumors and propaganda.

Tizi Ouzou had been from the first a hotbed of terrorism. Several times a week the siren on the city hall's roof would scream lugubriously: a terrorist attempt had just been committed. At once the Kabyles fled from the streets, the European shopkeepers popped out of their stores pistol in hand, the various units in town established cordons in front of their billets and at assigned spots, and the police rushed in, most of the time too late. When a terrorist (real or presumed) had been spotted, a wild chase took place, and sometimes innocent Kabyles running in the streets received bullets meant for the right target. The terrorists used the Kasbah as their normal refuge. Most of the Kasbah exits had long been obstructed with barbed-wire fences, a simple measure which reduced somewhat the frequency of terrorist attempts on the other side of town, but not in the sections nearest to the Kasbah.

In February 1957 the situation became so bad that the zone decided to move a company into the Kasbah itself. The 1st Company of my battalion was chosen for the mission and transferred from its position on top of Djebel Beloua. Major Renard* was on leave at the time; therefore, as the senior officer in the battalion, I drafted the orders for the 1st Company and went to the zone to have them approved.

My plan was to follow in the Kasbah what I had done in my *sous-quartier*, that is, to contact the population (hiring workers for local projects, information meetings, person-to-person propaganda), to control it (census, check on movements), to enforce school attendance by the children (the existing schools were boycotted), to eliminate the OPA, to stage elections for local representatives. These aims were accomplished. I wanted the company to be spread by platoons within the Kasbah, but the Chief of Staff of the zone rejected this last point. Within a month after the 1st Company had moved in, the situation had improved magically in the Kasbah, but terrorism still persisted in Tizi Ouzou.

The terrorists now came from the rural areas, most of them young villagers who had been given a pistol or a grenade and asked to prove their ruthlessness before being accepted by the maquis. The rebels concentrated their terrorism on Tizi Ouzou because they knew it would get much publicity. The rate of attrition of the terrorists was greater than before, since they could no longer escape and hide so easily in the Kasbah, but ignorant volunteers were not lacking. One day the police caught a 12-year-old shoeshine boy who had thrown a grenade in the railway station. A man had given him 500 francs for throwing the object.

One day in early April 1957 I was ordered to report at once to Brigadier General Lacomme, the zone deputy commander.

"We are going to clean Tizi Ouzou and I have a special task for you. You will be in charge of the psychological action during the operation, which starts tomorrow."

I was to learn much later from General Lacomme that the *préfet* had wanted me to direct the entire operation, appointing me mayor of Tizi Ouzou and delegating to me his special powers for maintaining order in the town. General Lacomme had strongly objected for two reasons. I was merely a captain, and as such, even armed with the *préfet's* delegation of power, I could not get the same degree of support from the Army units and from the various civil services as could General Lacomme if he were so delegated. He wanted also to protect me, for, in his eyes, the operation consisted principally of unpleasant police work; it would be better for me if I was not singled out as a target by pro-FLN papers in France.[1]

General Lacomme took me at once to the briefing for the operation. Major Lebel,* the zone's G-2, explained the operation:

Step 1: Under the command of the colonel commanding the Tizi Ouzou sector. Force "A" encircles the European town before dawn. Force "B" enters the town at dawn, each platoon going to its assigned section with a team of gendarmes and municipal policemen. The inhabitants are ordered to stay home. Gendarmes and police enter every house, check the identity of the residents, and eventually arrest people on a list (about 80 names).

---

[1]   An early report of mine on conditions in Kabylia had been expurgated and printed in a restricted Army bulletin in Algeria. *Le Monde* got hold of it and devoted two pages of its valuable space for three days showing how "fascism was guiding the French Army in Algeria." *L'Humanité*, the communist daily, published twisted excerpts from *Le Monde* and promised to disclose the name of this "Captain from Kabylia." I was prouder than if I had been awarded the Legion of Honor.

Step 2: Under Major Lebel.* The prisoners are assigned to four temporary interrogation camps staffed and supported by various field units stationed around Tizi Ouzou (one of them my battalion). Their intelligence officers conduct the interrogations and meet every day with Major Lebel* at the Tizi Ouzou sector command post to bring him the information collected.

Step 3: Under Major Lebel.* The leads are followed and the FLN leaders arrested.

I had taken no part in the planning and was now abruptly confronted with this plan. When it was my turn to speak, I inquired if any public address truck was available. No. How could we ask the population to stay home during the check, or pass any official notice? Apparently public relations problems had not been considered at all. A hurried phone call was made to Tigzirt requesting that a sound truck be sent at once; it arrived at night just in time for the operation. I also objected that it was wasteful not to take advantage of such a thorough house-to-house check to make a complete census, which would facilitate control later. After some discussion, I was finally supported by General Lacomme, but it was too late to organize the census properly and to print census sheets with all the useful entries. I asked, finally, what provisions had been made for ensuring that the rebels would not rebuild their OPA. None, but if they did, we would repeat the process. It was too late to discuss the problem, for the unit commanders had to leave and get ready for the next day. The meeting was adjourned.

The operation took place as planned. The municipal police (about thirty men, including ten Moslems under a *commissaire*) were given no task except to enter the house and make the primitive census on the first day; they did not take part in the intelligence work. The chief of the Sûreté and his four French assistants participated in the intelligence meetings but did not interrogate the prisoners until they had first been processed by the field units' intelligence officers; the Sûreté people concentrated of course on the big fish.

The interrogation camps had been hastily improvised. In one, the prisoners were kept in tents and had every opportunity to communicate with each other; in another, they were housed in an empty wine-storage tank, with their feet tied, watched by a sentry; in still another camp, each prisoner was kept in a large wine drum open at both ends and laid horizontally on the ground. The pressure techniques—and the results—varied greatly from camp to camp; they had been left to the initiative of the intelligence officers, with strict orders not to exceed decent limits, i.e., to avoid injury of any sort to the prisoners, who might be released at any moment without notice. The pressure consisted generally in forcing the prisoners to stand in uncomfortable positions.

Confessions came in day after day, and Major Lebel* was able to identify and reconstruct the chain of command of the OPA, whose leaders were promptly arrested. The real boss, however, was a rebel sector chief who manipulated the OPA from the outside through liaison agents; he escaped capture. Among the subordinate OPA members in Tizi Ouzou was a Kabyle working at the Préfecture. The chief interpreter for the *préfet* was also found to have given money, and occasionally information, to the rebels. The *préfet* was shown the evidence, but he refused to have the man arrested or dismissed; he argued that FLN terrorist pressure was such that we had to expect and close our eyes to incidents of this sort. This was the beginning of a feud between the *préfet* and the Sûreté chief, who was transferred to another post some months later.

I was in a difficult position. I had a task but little authority and still less the means to accomplish it. Thinking of the necessary post-purge work, I insisted from the beginning with Major Lebel* that the prisoners be asked who, in their opinion, had been hostile to the FLN in Tizi Ouzou. But he was too concerned with his immediate intelligence work to press the matter with the intelligence officers. I also argued with General Lacomme on the necessity of making the population itself participate in the control, by creating a "Dispositif de Protection Urbaine" (city protection system) along the lines of what had been done with success in Algiers. Under such a system, the population is organized on a voluntary basis—with block, street, and if necessary building leaders, who are armed and take part in the defense against terrorists, one of their tasks being to check on and report any strangers in their areas of jurisdiction. The *préfet* opposed the idea, because he feared that only the European civilians would join the organization. It was a risk, I argued, but there was no harm in testing the idea, and since the Europeans, legally or illegally armed, were always in the streets after a terrorist action, we might as well channel their energy in a preventive enterprise. No. All I managed to accomplish was to issue an order to the population in the name of General Lacomme, making it an offense for a house owner not to report within twenty-four hours any visitor from out of town. The order had no effect, because the municipal police had neither the time nor the personnel to enforce it.

In the field of information and propaganda, there was not much I could do, since I was given no means, no personnel, no money, and no equipment except one sound truck. The Psychological Action officer for the zone, a major, had nothing to offer except a stack of old pamphlets.

"Can't you get me a tape recorder?"

"I have pestered Algiers for two months to get one for myself!"

I phoned Colonel Goussault, the chief of our Psy branch in Algiers, and promised him a sensational tape in exchange for a tape recorder. I got it the next day and went to the hospital. There I recorded an interview with a young *fellagha* who had just been wounded in a small operation. The result was found so interesting that it was broadcast by Radio Algiers for several, consecutive days. The *fellagha*'s statement— true or false but in any case genuine—was that rebels who wanted to surrender, and they were many, could not do so because they were constantly watched by their leaders. In his case, he had had to kill his sergeant in order to surrender.

We did not have a single newspaper in French or in Arabic for the Kabyles. True, the great majority of the Kabyles in the Djebels were illiterate, but those in the towns were not. Besides, they were all curious, and I am sure that a newspaper written for them—one that was sold, not distributed free—would have been read and discussed all over Kabylia. I once sent my henchman Sergeant Levy* to visit the local bookstores in Tizi Ouzou and to see how many copies of *Le Monde* were sold and to whom. The statistics: fourteen in an hour, twelve of them to Kabyles.[2] (Levy* took advantage of his visit to a bookstore to chat with the Kabyle owner and to ask if he had by any chance a 1952 nationalist book on the black list. The owner, persuaded that he was dealing with a sympathizer, cautiously produced one from the back of his store and offered Levy* more literature of this kind. I put Levy* in touch with the Sûreté, and the game was played until the Sûreté arrested a group of important FLN bosses at Tizi Ouzou and Algiers.)

I attempted to supply the population with news. I organized two propaganda teams with men borrowed from the Military Police and from the 1st Company in the Kasbah. They circulated in the sound truck and attracted fairly large crowds. With the help of a police interpreter, I composed propaganda talks recorded on tape and related to the purge in Tizi Ouzou. The gist was that we were only after the FLN leaders, and that the people who had only been forced to support them had nothing to fear from us if they told the truth.

Thinking that live propaganda was the best, I particularly wanted to show freshly captured *fellaghas* and have them describe in their own words how life was in the maquis and how they had been treated by us after their capture. Unfortunately, the phenomenon was a rare one owing to the nature of combat in Kabylia. I had great hopes one day when I heard that a group of rebels had been cornered in a cave. When the dust settled, most of them were dead, and the rest wounded and bound for the hospital. Using all the resources of all the French forces in Kabylia for a period of two weeks, I only managed to get hold of three prisoners who were in good condition. They addressed the population in the Saturday market. I learned later from various officers in the field that their talk had undoubtedly made an impression on the villagers, for they spontaneously reported it when they returned home. I had General Lacomme sign a note urging all units in the zone to

---

2   I attended once at Grand Remblai a meeting of the sector SAS officers presided over by M. Vignon. The officers complained bitterly about the bad influence of *Le Monde* on the population. "Very bad in my area," said one, "four copies are bought every day." "Worse in mine, six copies," said another. "It's fine in mine, only one copy. "The circulation of this newspaper was literally an accurate barometer of the success of pacification. Not one copy was read in Aissa Mimoun, fortunately.

capture more prisoners even if it entailed greater risks for ourselves. Henceforth, when awards were given out, the emphasis would be on the number of *fellaghas* captured rather than killed.

When Major Lebel* finally announced to me that he was ready to release a large number of suspects, I had them brought to me one by one. These men had all confessed their activity, they had all given some sort of support to the rebels, and consequently they all shared some guilt. I decided to bluff. Quoting the terms of the law concerning those who participated in a plot against the security of the state, I told them they could easily get a stiff prison sentence, from two to five years. (They squirmed.) We knew, however, that they might have been forced ("indeed, this is the truth"). We were therefore prepared to be generous ("Allah bless you"). But there was a condition (?). They must not do it again ("never, I swear"). Promises were not enough, they had to show they meant it ("certainly"). All they had to do was to say publicly to the people in Tizi Ouzou that they had given aid to the rebels but that they had now seen the light. Some of them blanched when they heard the condition, but they all accepted. So for a week the sound truck was busy broadcasting live confessions. Of course, the men would certainly deny in private what they had said publicly, but while their public speeches were heard by thousands of people, how many would hear the denial? My fellow officers from the 1st Company reported to me that the population's reaction in the Kasbah had been surprisingly good. What particularly impressed the audience was the fact that the prisoners had been released in spite of their guilt, which could not be doubted, not only because the population by and large knew very well the OPA practices, but also because the speakers had quoted precise facts and figures. The popular conclusion was that it was cheaper to tell the truth than to resist. Of the fifty or so prisoners who were thus released, about fifteen became active supporters of the 1st Company, either because they had been won over or because they were afraid of the rebels. They volunteered for various civic jobs, and some even passed information.

I was really sorry that what the 1st Company was doing in the Kasbah could not be extended to the rest of Tizi Ouzou. While the Kasbah ceased to give us trouble, terrorism persisted in the European town, although to a lesser degree. The OPA was rebuilt shortly after, less efficiently but still.

I returned to my company after four weeks in Tizi Ouzou, glad to be again first in my village rather than second in Rome.

IV. Testing the New Leaders

To pick up once more the thread of events in my Aissa Mimoun *sous-quartier*, the situation there, in March 1957, was as follows: I was well in control of the entire population. The census was completed and kept up to date, my soldiers knew every individual in their *communes*, and my two rules concerning movements and visits were obeyed with very few violations. My authority was unchallenged. Any suggestion I made was promptly taken as an order and executed. Boys and girls regularly went to school, moving without protection in spite of the FLN threats and terrorist actions against Moslem children going to French schools; some of the children had to walk a long distance from hamlets and isolated houses. Every field was cultivated.

Village by village, I had eliminated the OPA, systematically everywhere, except at Igonane Ameur where I had used more haphazard methods since the population was already co-operating with us, at least outwardly. A municipal council had been elected in each *commune*. While I had experienced some difficulties in trying to find mayors for Bou Souar and Igonane Ameur, candidates had not been lacking elsewhere, particularly when it was found that the job carried with it a salary of 1,500 francs a day, quite a sum in rural Kabylia. In fact, several villagers from Bou Souar began complaining to me that their mayor, Bekri,* was no good—too old and inefficient—and hinted that they would do the job much better. Without any prodding on our part, the villagers from Khelouyene elected Asli, the very man I had had in mind. I did not know well Derradji, the new mayor of Ait Braham, but I had good information on him.

The remnants from the original guerrilla band raised in Aissa Mimoun were no longer a problem. Guerrillas from other areas, to my knowledge, did not venture onto the southern slope of Aissa Mimoun. I nevertheless maintained the same precautions against ambush or treachery, lectured my soldiers against overconfidence, and punished severely as an example the few cases of laxity I discovered. Thus a newly arrived NCO was reduced to private and fired from the battalion for having behaved as on a picnic while he was supposed to protect a group of civilians operating a bulldozer near Oumlil. We had our usual four or five ambushes out every night; patrolling was constant during the day, if only because of the liaison and supply moves between my posts and my command post at Tala Ilane. Despite the present dispersal of my company, I was able to provide one platoon for operations outside the *quartier* and up to two inside.

My goal now was to win the support of the population through the newly elected leaders. The immediate problem was to find out how good they were. There could be only two valid criteria—loyalty and efficiency. As to loyalty, I had full confidence only in Asli and the four men from Khelouyene and Ait Braham who had spontaneously offered me good information when it was still dangerous for them to do so. As for efficiency, they all needed testing except perhaps Haddad,* the mayor of Igonane Ameur. The tasks ahead would provide ample opportunities for it.

The first task was to run the municipal council that managed village affairs. Asli and Derradji regularly gathered the councils on their own initiative; Haddad* did it less frequently; Bekri* never. Asli, Derradji, and Haddad* directed the meeting with authority and common sense; Bekri* was really too senile; and the only man who seemed active in his council was a farmer living (unfortunately for me) in Azib Djalout, a hamlet 2 km south of Bou Souar. Asli was bossy and bellicose, Derradji imaginative and friendly with his associates, Haddad* very businesslike. Thus, by just watching the meetings I could form an opinion on the character and qualities of the participants, and I soon was able to make up my mind as to whom I could count upon.

The council meetings were always attended by the chief of my detachment in each *commune*. I had to fight against my subordinates' tendency to take charge of the meetings. A certain amount of paternalism was unavoidable owing to the ignorance of the councilmen, but I did not want to take responsibility from them. True, we could run things better than they did, but it would have been self-defeating both for my immediate testing purpose and in the long run. A corporal or a soldier served as secretary, for no councilman could read and write. The secretarial problem was solved in an unorthodox fashion in 1958 for Khelouyene and Igonane Ameur, when the two brightest boys in school were hired for the job. One was 14, the other 13, they had then been in school two years, and they did extremely well.

The day the *communes* were established, a flood of official notes and literature was forwarded to them from the Préfecture and the Sous-Préfecture, as if the *communes* had had the same experience, traditions, and facilities as those of Metropolitan France. The new mayors received the *Journal Officiel d'Algerie* containing the texts of new laws and decrees, circulars asking the local statistical results of the last agricultural season and the forecast for the coming one, etc. I arranged with the SAS to filter the flow and pass along only what was immediately relevant. Together with Lt. Bauer* I visited the *préfet* and we suggested:

(1) that mayors and some councilmen be given a short course on administrative matters;
(2) that the official procedures be simplified and adapted to the situation;
(3) that a simple booklet with the essential administrative rules be compiled for the immediate benefit of my subordinates and for the long-range benefit of the mayors.

M. Vignon promised to look into the matter, but I was so much in advance in comparison with the other areas of Kabylia, where they were still struggling against guerrillas and exerting themselves to control the population, that the locally elected leaders had to wait until late 1958 to receive some sort of training. Meantime we helped ours as best we could.

As soon as the purge was over and the council elected, I planned to enter with fanfare the new constructive era and to substantiate the "New Algeria" slogan. This was the time to replace the stick with the carrot as an instrument of policy, to find out what the population wanted, and if possible to give it. If the new council could not begin its career by bringing marked improvements in the life of the villagers, it would be sunk and we with it.

The Préfecture had received emergency appropriations for just this purpose. Thus 1,500,000 francs had been earmarked as an inauguration gift for the *communes* of Bou Souar and Igonane Ameur, 500,000 francs for Khelouyene and Ait Braham. Why the difference? Nobody could tell me except that a bureaucrat in the Préfecture had allotted the sums without consulting Lt. Bauer* or me. It was annoying because Asli and Derradji knew about it and could see no reason for the discrimination; on the contrary, weren't their *communes* the most eager to participate actively in the building of "New Algeria"? Since the appropriations were now officially entered into the Préfecture's books, no change was possible; we would have to wait for the coming regular budget.

Since the *préfet* had kindly asked me to visit him any time I had a problem he could solve, I took him at his word and told him how important it was for us to use the appropriations as a political weapon in a time of insurgency. If we did not make any difference between a *commune* where the population co-operated and one where it did not, what incentive would the villagers have to go along with us? Nobody, after all, ever accused the United States of not being a democratic country. And how does the administration in power there build up and consolidate its political machine if not by patronage? I therefore insisted, in a meeting attended by SAS officers and *sous-quartier* commanders, that appropriations for the next budget be made on this basis. The *préfet* agreed entirely, except that in actual practice he avoided the kind of meeting I had suggested and consulted only the SAS officers. The result for my *sous-quartier* exceeded my expectations: when the normal budget was finally made, my *communes*, which were the most successfully pacified, had more money than we could reasonably use. As a taxpayer I felt it necessary to apply the brake and to veto needless expenses.

The first council meetings were devoted to studying what projects could be done. At Bou Souar the council wanted to build a new mosque. I flatly refused. I was highly suspicious of this sudden religious fervor in a Kabyle village. Besides, while church and state were separated in

France, the French government had continued subsidizing the Islamic Church in Algeria, and, although this was still official policy, there was a growing feeling both among the educated Moslems and among us that Islam was the real obstacle that had prevented the Algerian masses from moving into the 20th century. When the French arrived in Algeria in 1830, they found a local Jewish minority in the same state of underdevelopment as the large Moslem majority. Both groups were given the same opportunities, yet only the Jews took advantage of it, and to such an extent that in two generations they became completely assimilated in terms of education and consequently in terms of social and economic advancement. Why should we continue to promote Islam? If the villagers wanted to repair the shabby existing mosque, they would have to do it at their own expense.

The council suggested next building a motor road from the highway below to Bou Souar via Azib Djalout. We turned it down because it was not needed yet, it would cost far more money than we had, and a motor road linking Bou Souar to Akaoudj and hence to a good highway was planned and would be built with special SAS funds. What about the water problem? we suggested. Bou Souar got its water from two small springs below the village. The flow was abundant in winter but down to a trickle for the rest of the year. With a reservoir, the village would have enough water the year round. The idea was adopted. Then Bekri* wanted to build a real *mairie*. No hurry, we said, but a schoolhouse was urgent, for the house we were using was not conveniently located and was in bad condition. The project was also approved, and we kept the mayor and the council busy finding the best location for the school and negotiating the purchase of the land.

I went along with 2d Lt. Dubois,* Bekri,* and a councilman to have a look at the springs. There they were all right, but what to do? None among us had any competence in hydraulic engineering. Lt. Bauer* tried to get us some help from the civil works engineer at the Préfecture, but he was rebuked. "For years," he was told, "we had to do with miserly appropriations; and now suddenly we are drowning in money, but we have no more personnel than before." We tried civilian contractors, but they too were swamped with work offers all over Algeria, and they naturally accepted only the largest, fattest, easiest contracts. So I turned to Army engineers. General Guerin, the new zone commander who replaced General Gouraud in April 1957, ordered the 72d Engineer Battalion to help me, and a young officer came, made the plan, and directed the work on the reservoir.

The school at Bou Souar was built by the villagers under the guidance of a soldier from my company who was a mason in civilian life.

The single biggest headache in connection with these projects was to get the actual money, for we ran into a tremendous barrage of red tape. The French administrative system for financial matters is built on the assumption that everybody is a potential thief; treasurers are apparently recruited on the strength of their innate suspicion, and trained to multiply obstacles and safeguards. So, although we had money appropriated, we could not get it because we had first to furnish a precise plan on how it was going to be used, or because we had to produce receipts signed in triplicate by the village workers, or even because the *commune* of Bou Souar had been misspelled "Bou Couar" in the *Journal Officiel*. We were in danger of paralysis. At that point I exploded and went to pester the *préfet*. Couldn't he fire the treasurer and get a more co-operative man? Impossible, a civil servant cannot be fired except for serious cause clearly specified by law. Could he have him transferred? Impossible, the treasurer came directly under the Ministry of Finance and was independent of the *préfet* (another of these famous safeguards). M. Vignon knew all about the man, but we had to put up with him.

I was to encounter many other cases of red tape of this sort. Thus we received a note from the Préfecture's Education Department requesting that school children be insured according to regulations against accidents occurring in school or on the way to school. The premium was very reasonable, 100 francs a year. The parents promptly complied. Some time later we were informed that the children could not be insured because our school buildings did not conform to the official standards; they had no lavatories, no running water, no enclosed courtyard, no electricity. Indeed not—the school at Ait Braham, for instance, was just a group of Army tents; there was no flat area at all to serve as a courtyard, and we had to level off the razor-sharp ridge in order to set up the tents. It is significant to note that no regular Ministry of Education official ever attended the annual distribution of prizes in our school, although the *préfet* himself made a point of doing so.

At Igonane Ameur the money was spent building a school and a motor road up from Ighouna. This road was useful to transport olives and to bring construction material into the village; it was also useful because of the large number of villagers employed in the project. At Khelouyene, where the burned-out Tala Ilane school had been repaired, the council decided to build a large reservoir and to bring the water right to the village through a pipe.

What Ait Braham wanted most was a school building. When Derradji found out from the Préfecture that no money was available for it, he decided to build one anyway. He called a meeting of the villagers and requested that each family provide every week a man day of work or its equivalent in money. They all approved. The school was built very simply according to Kabyle masonry techniques, with stones held together by compressed clay. Lt. Bauer* juggled his accounts and gave Derradji money to buy the tiles, the windows, and the doors. The story became known at Tizi Ouzou, and M. Vignon came by helicopter to inaugurate the school and congratulate the villagers. The total cost amounted to 800,000 francs for a large three-room building, and it was displayed by the Préfecture as the model for emergency school houses in Kabylia.

Aside from construction projects, we persuaded the councils to adopt and enforce simple rules for cleanliness in the villages. The streets were regularly cleaned, a garbage pit was dug in every village, and each family built latrines. ("If you had not told us, we would never have done it," said a villager to the officer in charge at Ait Braham, "yet look how clean our village now is.")

One day 2d Lt. Robert,* who succeeded Dubois* in Bou Souar, suggested to the council that every house be whitewashed. Some people protested on the ground that it was too much work. Robert,* a newcomer in the company, would hear no objection, and he gave the villagers twenty-four hours to do it under penalty of a heavy fine. I visited Bou Souar by accident the next day and saw all the villagers, including Bekri,* busy whitewashing houses and shacks. I returned to see the results and was amazed at the change. Bou Souar had been a slum; now it was a poor but decent village. And the change was not just physical. The mood of the villagers had improved too, and they visibly felt like new men, self-respecting and worthy of consideration. I called all the other mayors and took them to Bou Souar to see for themselves. In a week, and this time without orders from us, my entire *sous-quartier* was transformed. As a matter of fact, so great had been the sudden demand for limewash in Tizi Ouzou that the local dealers abusively raised their prices; but a phone call to the Préfecture settled the matter. My colleagues in the *quartier* promptly imitated me, and now the whole Djebel Aissa Mimoun stood out conspicuously as the neatest area in Kabylia; the white houses were visible for miles, from beyond Tizi Ouzou. When I returned to the place for a short visit in May 1959, the process had been extended to the whole of Kabylia.

I now had five schools, one in each *commune* plus a smaller one at Grand Remblai for the children from Oumlil and Agouni Taga, with a total of about 1,100 boys and girls—40 per cent of the school-age population. Twelve soldiers were employed full-time as teachers. One of them was a regular teacher who had just finished his training in France when he was drafted. I used him as inspector of the Aissa Mimoun Education Department. He visited the schools, checked the teaching, trained the improvised teachers, and took special charge of five bright young boys aged 12 to 14, whom I had selected as possible teachers. For I did not know how long the Army would stay in the area and I did not want to see our foundations go to waste once we were gone. These five children were able to double as secretaries for the municipal councils.

The abundant supply of water at Tala Ilane allowed us to give the children showers once a week. The girls enjoyed it particularly (under the surveillance of a matron). A minor revolution occurred when the girls were asked to discard once and for all their dirty head scarves, and to clip their hair and wash it; it was contrary to local customs and superstitions. But once the change was made, everybody approved heartily. "They now look like French girls," was the general comment.

During the summer recess, we organized games and outdoor activities for the children twice a week. When they kept gathering near the schools all the time, the organized activity was extended to the full week, on a voluntary basis.

In 1957 private and state organizations invited Algerian children to summer camps in France. We proposed one hundred children on the basis of their achievement in school, and the councils finally selected thirty children from the list. The SAS gave them new clothes and pocket money, and off they went to Algiers, where they boarded a plane. They returned enthusiastic at the end of the summer, and they had to repeat the story of their trip so often that we had them address meetings of the assembled villages. What impressed them most was the wealth of France, the old feudal chateaux, and the Renault factory. What impressed their parents most was the fact that they had been mixed with French children and treated exactly like them.

The children being well taken care of, my other main concern was the 15-to-20-year-old group, probably the most important politically. There was unfortunately little I could do for them with my own means. They all worked in their fields and did some odd jobs such as gathering wood. I organized volleyball teams, the only sport requiring only a modestly small flat area, the hardest thing to find in Aissa Mimoun. Lt.-Col. Lemoine* opened at Tigzirt a vocational school staffed by soldiers, to which I sent several boys from my *sous-quartier*. They were fed and taught carpentry, masonry, driving, and mechanics. These vocational schools were later greatly expanded by the Army, and they filled an enormous gap between the needs of the masses and the output of the regular civilian vocational schools, all well staffed and well equipped but necessarily highly selective.

I needed female help for the work I intended to do on Kabyle women, and I persuaded the WAC lieutenant in charge of the zone's social affairs to lend me a hand. She talked to an Army nurse, and they both came one afternoon to Igonane Ameur to meet the local women and make a demonstration of baby care.

The success exceeded all our expectations. Nearly 500 women came to the meeting, about 200 of whom managed to crowd into the small schoolhouse while the others peeked through the windows. They giggled, pointed to the two French women, and discussed their dress and their manners. With great difficulty mayor Haddad* imposed some degree of silence, and the nurse started showing how to wash a baby. In the front row sat an old woman who, I learned afterwards, was the village midwife. She watched intently and made various comments which, from the expression on her face, I took to be disparaging. When the nurse proceeded to wash the baby's hair, the audience shrieked. Through the interpreter the midwife indignantly said that babies' hair is never washed, for it is very bad for their health. Some women booed the midwife, and she turned on them furiously, supported by the older generation. When calm was restored, the nurse explained the advantages of the modern technique.

The midwife's attitude was typical of the older generation. It was not so much that they protested against progress itself. No. But they had endured the old system all their life, and they saw no reason why the younger women should escape the slavery and the misery they had known. It was unfair.

Another day, while I was away, the WAC and the nurse visited Ait Braham escorted by Lt. Gerbaut,* my new deputy. As soon as they dismounted from their horses, they were assailed by the local ladies who undressed them above the waist to check if these French women really had breasts like the Kabyle women.

"You should have seen, *mon Capitaine*," reported Gerbaut,* "how a young Kabyle girl described approvingly with her hands the small breasts of the nurse. Then she pointed at an old Kabyle woman and explained with gestures how her breasts reached the navel!"

My benevolent helpers could not devote much time to my *sous-quartier*, for they had their own work at Tizi Ouzou. The situation was fortunately much improved in the latter part of 1958, when specially trained teams of French and progressive Algerian women arrived to take charge of feminine activities. This new corps had been organized on the basis of a report I wrote in November 1956, in which I had stressed that Algerian women were our largest group of potential supporters provided we took the lead in their emancipation (see Appendix 2).[3] I had learned this from the Chinese Communists.

---

[3] The very report that brought me the honor of being condemned by *Le Monde* and *L'Humanité*. (See footnote 1, p. 150.)

V. Mobilizing the Population

What constitutes victory in this sort of war? When does pacification end? My personal answer can be stated this way: victory is won and pacification ends when most of the counterinsurgent forces can safely be withdrawn, leaving the population to take care of itself with the help of a normal contingent of police and Army forces. It is therefore necessary to make the population participate actively in the counter-insurgent effort, to mobilize it in the struggle. Winning over the population through the various steps I have just described had no other purpose than to create the right climate for this mobilization.

I had in mind four specific objectives:

(1) organizing self-defense units in each *commune*;
(2) levying a *harka*;
(3) getting the population to police the area itself;
(4) preparing the local leaders to take over the propaganda work.

If running village affairs was a valid way for me to assess the worth of the local leaders, the amount of help they were willing to give me in these tasks was surely an even better test.

My first attempts at raising self-defense units were made in the fall of 1956, when I was carrying out the 13-point program at Igonane Ameur. Four to six villagers reported every day to the Army post, each picked up a shotgun and a counted number of cartridges, stood guard, and sometimes went along with my men on patrols or even ambushes. They received no salary; they were merely fed while on duty. The system was accepted, but it had been imposed on the population, which was its major flaw. Irrespective of these militiamen's outward attitude, my policy was not to trust them as long as they had not given positive proof of their loyalty. They would behave properly so long as they were mixed with my soldiers, but I had no guarantee of what they would do when left to themselves. Still, I was confident that loyalty would ultimately develop with the general improvement of the situation in my *sous-quartier.*

The system was extended to Bou Souar when the village was occupied. I gave the militiamen responsibility for protecting the schoolchildren and the teachers during classes; they stood outside the school and watched. This was a mission I could safely entrust them with because their own children were in school.

In March 1957, when I was about to raise a militia at Khelouyene and Ait Braham, the *préfet* publicly promised the villagers that militia duty would be paid. He unfortunately discovered later that he had no appropriation for it. I was thus obliged to disband the existing militia and to abandon the idea for the other *communes.*

The militia in Aissa Mimoun was recreated spontaneously, and in a big way, in the wake of the May 13, 1958, revolution in Algiers. (See below, Part 4, II.)

The word came in April 1957 that I could raise a *harka.* The *harkis* would serve full time with my company, as I saw fit, operating within the *sous-quartier* or outside. They would be paid 900 francs a day, armed and clothed by us but not fed. I was authorized to recruit up to twenty-five volunteers.

I wanted to have five *harkis* from Bou Souar, five from Igonane Ameur, seven from Khelouyene, and eight from Ait Braham. I was debating whether they would serve principally in their own *communes,* or, on the contrary, in alien ones. The question was settled when both Asli and Derradji refused categorically to have *harkis* from Bou Souar and Igonane Ameur acting as policemen in their *communes.* "We have no confidence in these people!" The recruiting was entrusted to the mayors. More volunteers than needed came from Khelouyene and Ait Braham. Igonane Ameur furnished just the number asked. At Bou Souar, Bekri* again proved his inadequacy and, after several meetings with the population, two volunteers appeared, and later three more.

When I had all the names, I met with my confidants, Asli, Boukrou, and Scheik.* The last of these was a World War I veteran from Ait Braham, a lionhearted old man, who had previously volunteered to accompany us on operations and had given us much useful information before the purge of his village. We went over the list and eliminated all those in whom they did not have full confidence, except for the Bou Souar contingent whom they did not know well enough. I named Boukrou sergeant and Scheik* corporal. I assigned the command and the training of the *harka* to my assistant, Lt. Gerbaut,* and gave him Master Sergeant Ben Ali,* my regular Moslem NCO, Marty, one of my best sergeants, who had commanded a group of one hundred auxiliaries in Indochina, and two French corporals.

One month was devoted to their training. They would report at Tala Ilane every morning and receive technical and tactical instruction. At night they returned to their posts, except when there was a night exercise. I insisted that they be trained as propagandists. Two or three times a week we would develop to them various propaganda points to be repeated to the villagers they met. They were all illiterate, so my education inspector took charge of them for one or two hours every day. Most of them learned the alphabet in a month, and some even learned how to write, though with many mistakes in spelling. Several *harkis* thanked me spontaneously for educating them. "I am 45," said one, "and now for the first time I can write my name. You are my father!"

A few days after the *harka* had come into existence, I sent Lt. Gerbaut* on a night patrol to the house of a *harki* living in Khelouyene. Gerbaut* threw a small stone on the roof, but nothing moved inside; he threw a bigger stone and heard some stirring in the house; he whistled softly as the rebels used to do; there was more stirring, but the door remained closed. The next morning, when the *harka* met as usual at my command post, Lt.-Col. Lemoine* and a major in charge of G-3 at the zone headquarters arrived unannounced to inspect it. We all met afterward in the classroom, and I asked the *harkis* whether they understood that their task was not simply to act as ordinary soldiers but to track the rebels in every way, notably by collecting intelligence on them. A chorus of "yes" answered my question. Then I told them what had happened the night before. Why didn't the *harki* report the incident? He claimed he had heard nothing. Sergeant Boukrou scoffed at him. The man then said he thought the incident was not important enough to report. I fired him on the spot as a lesson to the others. He was so terrified at not belonging to the *harka* any more that he asked me for a visa for France, which I gave him, and he left the village.

When the training period was over, I used the *harkis* in three different ways:

1. They served in their own *communes* under the orders of my local commanders. They patrolled alone or with my soldiers, took part in ambushes, and stood guard at the post or at the school. They spread information and propaganda. They controlled the population, watching particularly for and reporting alien visitors. To check on them in this last activity, I occasionally sent villagers from small remote hamlets near Ait Braham to Bou Souar and Igonane Ameurj along paths on which I knew the local *harkis* were patrolling. Invariably the decoys (who did not know they were being used as such) were spotted and brought to the nearest post. My expulsion of a deficient *harki* was paying off.

2. Integrated in the company, they participated in operations inside and outside the *sous-quartier*. I used them as scouts, a function in which their mountaineering attitude, their endurance, and their speed made them invaluable. They were uncanny at finding caches; during an operation 8 miles north of our *quartier*, one *harki* discovered a pistol with ammunition hidden under a rock, another found a shotgun in a bush, and each received a 2,000-franc award. They also had a knack for spotting lookout men for the rebels; being Kabyle farmers themselves and well acquainted with the local habits and customs, they knew when a civilian had no business sitting on top of a ridge and enjoying the scenery. When we were searching a village, I used them to calm the population and to enter the houses ahead of my soldiers, and they would thus notice immediately anything abnormal. I had warned them that if I ever caught one of them stealing from the population or abusing his power, I would subject him immediately to a court-martial composed of myself and his peers. No incident of this sort ever happened.

When we took part in outside operations, we always had to leave my command post at night, generally just before dawn. Consequently, I had to give some advance notice to the *harkis* so that they could get their gear from home and assemble at Tala Ilane the night before our departure. Any villager could easily observe the departure of the *harkis* from their village and pass a warning to the rebels. I tried several ways to shorten the notice, but feint, I believe, was again the best system: we staged numerous false sorties, and sometimes deployed simultaneous ambushes around the villages in the hope of catching tbe rebels' informants, if any.

During these outside operations the *harkis* were given combat rations for which we withheld money out of their salary.

3. When my *sous-quartier* was further extended to cover the entire south slope of Aissa Mimoun and the plain up to Oued Sebaou (see below), I used the *harka* extensively to operate as a body in my territory under Sergeant Marty. They would go out for two or three consecutive days, sometimes disguised as civilians, hiding during the day and ambushing at night. They kept liaison with me through an S.C.R. 300.

Late one afternoon in May 1957, a *harki* was ambushed and killed as he left his isolated house south of Ait Braham. The rebels took away his shotgun and ammunition. My garrison in the village gave the alert on hearing the shots and rushed to the spot. I arrived there very shortly afterward with all my available men. Civilians told us the six or seven *fellaghas* had taken the direction of Tikobain, and we pursued them in vain until nightfall. I arranged with my Tikobain colleague to establish that night a series of ambushes on both sides of our boundary line.

At 4 a.m. a group of *fellaghas* ran into an ambush set by my neighbors in the Chaba Bou Aradou ravine. Two were killed, including the chief, and one was wounded and captured. The wounded man admitted that his group had killed the *harki*; they had come especially for that purpose from their usual area near Abizar, about 3 miles northeast of Tikobain. Was this part of Aissa Mimoun within their normal sphere of operation? No, it was in fact the first time they had penetrated into it. They obviously had an accomplice in my *sous-quartier*.

The *harkis*, particularly those from Ait Braham, were naturally incensed by the incident. Some of them remembered that, just before the murder, a villager from the small hamlet near Hill 194, south of Tala Ou Abba, had spent several hours two days in a row around our post at Ait Braham. Asked what he was doing there, he had said he was thinking about joining the *harka* and asked questions about the *harkis*, their salary, the nature of their work, etc. We went after the man. He had just left his house, villagers told us, carrying a bundle of clothes. We caught him on the road to Tikobain.

He denied he had been spying. He even denied having talked to the *harkis*, which raised my suspicions still higher. I confronted him with the wounded *fellagha*, who recognized him as the man who had planned the murder and guided the rebel group to the *harki*'s house. We searched the suspect's house thoroughly and found the missing shotgun. I phoned my battalion commander and asked him if he agreed that the man should be shot on the spot. He did. The *harkis* executed him.

I was left with a problem: the murdered *harki* had five children. I decided to keep paying his salary to his widow until the SAS could arrange for a pension. (When I left my area in April 1958, the affair was still pending in spite of all promises. Another case of red tape.)

I lost another *harki* from Khelouyene one night in June 1957. Returning from an ambush position near Dar Mohammed El Makkour in the low land at the foot of the Djebel, a patrol met some *fellaghas*, who fired first and killed the *harki* walking behind the sergeant. A *fellagha* was killed in the exchange. This was our only night encounter with the guerrillas in my *sous-quartier* during my time.

For the policing of my area by the population itself, I took the direct approach and called a meeting of all the mayors and councilmen.

"We are now enjoying a large degree of peace in our small area. You are not disturbed in your work or in your homes, and I am doing my best with my soldiers and the *harkis* to protect you and your family.

But you can see for yourself that we are here an island of peace. Watch the Djebel opposite us across Oued Sebaou, and you will see military operations going on practically every day and every night with bombing, strafing, and villages being encircled and searched. None of this happens here. You are free to tend your fields and take care of your families with no hindrance and no hardship. You must help me maintain this situation. The *fellaghas* outside our island cannot operate here unless they first send spies or receive information from the supporters they may still have among the population. I urge you, therefore, to ask the population to report to you, to the *harkis*, or to any of my soldiers any visit by an outsider and any suspicious event."

The population responded so well at Khelouyene and Ait Braham that, whenever a strange face was seen in the *communes*, the wives would alert their husbands, who in turn stopped the visitor and called the *harkis*, who brought him to the nearest post even when the poor visitor had already been given a pass by us. I remember one day a visitor being brought to me twice by different villagers. I finally had to give him an escort so that he could reach his destination on top of the ridge. The population of Igonane Ameur was also vigilant but not so virulent; they reported having seen strangers, but did not stop them.

Asli, the mayor of Khelouyene, was so vigilant that he often walked down to Grand Remblai and waited for the bus from Tizi Ouzou. He would examine the passengers as they disembarked and bring the newcomers to me, generally Kabyles who were returning from France. Asli had given them the oral treatment on the way and, when they appeared at my office, they would often spill out all they knew about the FLN organization in France. I passed the information on to the Sûreté, to be forwarded home. Asli also knew that a certain number of rascals from my *sous-quartier* had prudently taken refuge at Tizi Ouzou. He requested that I furnish him with a group of soldiers and *harkis*. He went to Tizi Ouzou, grabbed the suspects, and brought them back to me. Among them was the father of Oudiai, the former bandit chief in Aissa Mimoun, a man who had spent several years at hard labor in French Guiana for having raped a 10-year-old Kabyle girl in the 1920s.

The response was well below par at Bou Souar. The crop of local leaders was not living up to my expectations. They did, of course, what they were specifically asked to do, but their co-operation did not extend beyond that point. Were they doublecrossing me? Had a new, though inactive, cell been rebuilt, and was it threatening the population by its mere existence? I tried every trick I knew to check on this. I sent provocateurs; I gave delicate missions to the local *harkis*; I repeated my money-checking process when the villagers went to the Saturday market at Tizi Ouzou; I let ammunition loose in the post; I set up ambushes just after I had given notice to the Bou Souar *harkis* to report at Tala Ilane for an operation. All in vain. On the basis of unchecked information, I strongly suspected cousin Oudiai's father of stirring up opposition. I was, however, reluctant to arrest him because of his age (he was 74). I warned him privately and publicly that I would expel him from the village at the first sign of hostile activity.

I had been unlucky with my crop of local leaders at Bou Souar. In the lottery—for it was a lottery—I had drawn the bad ticket. We just could not find a man worth anything except the farmer who lived at Azib Djalout, too far, and Cheurfa,* the priest, whom I did not want to support. I approached the *préfet* with a proposal to dismiss Bekri,* but M. Vignon was reluctant to do it; he asked me to put up with him as long as the situation did not deteriorate.

Propaganda conducted by the Kabyles themselves was the last item in my mobilization program. But propaganda to whom? The population in the *sous-quartier* was already kept well informed by my soldiers and *harkis* either during regular mass meetings (which, though attendance was no longer compulsory, were well attended) or through individual contacts. The men who attended the meetings usually repeated at home what they had heard; we had checked that fact with the women when they came to the dispensaries.

I scrapped the item, keeping the idea open in case I ever needed my Aissa Mimoun villagers to convince the population outside the *sous-quartier*. The opportunity presented itself in May 1958 (see below).

VI. Limits to Local Efforts

No matter how much effort was devoted to pacification locally, we would find sooner or later that we had reached a plateau above which we could not rise. Two factors kept limiting our local achievements: the same old political instability in France, and the same old lack of a standard operational procedure in Algeria.

I shall never be able to insist enough on these two points, for they were the key to our success and failure in the Algerian War.

We were all trying to get a definite commitment from the Moslem population. We had every reason to believe that only a minority actively supported the rebels. A small amount of co-operation from the majority, and the FLN's fate would have been sealed rapidly. Yet we could not get it except in a few isolated spots. Even in my *sous-quartier*, where improvements in the population's attitude were spectacular, I could not vouch for their real depth because they had not been submitted to a hard test by the rebels.

Why was the population stubbornly sitting on the fence? Very simply because the Moslems were no fools. They realized perfectly well that the ultimate issue depended on Paris, not on whatever was said and done in Algeria. Just as they were beginning to be impressed by the firmness (still relative) of M. Mollet's government, the cabinet fell on May 21, 1957; the whole French policy in Algeria was brought in question once again. A cabinet presided over by M. Bourges-Maunoury took over on June 12; it fell on September 30. After a 36-day crisis, the longest on record, another cabinet was organized under M. Gaillard. The Algerian Moslems had every incentive to avoid commitment, and who could really blame them? The entire burden of the counterinsurgency in Algeria fell on the French Army, for the civil administration, even after its expansion in 1956, was still far short of the demands. The officers in the field who remembered the fate of those Vietnamese in Tonking who had fought the Vietminh with us wondered if they had any moral right, under the circumstances, to press a commitment on the Algerians. Yet the government's instructions and directives to the Army were explicit: defeat the rebellion and restore peace. This we tried to accomplish. When the Moslems found our pressure too strong, they bowed to it but carefully took out a counter insurance policy with the rebels; the obscure farmer kept paying his dues to the nationalist movement; the more exposed mayor or councilman betrayed us.

If there was nothing we could do in regard to political instability at home, there was a wide margin for possible improvement concerning our tactics in Algeria. By no means had most units reached the plateau I have mentioned above. Perhaps if they had, victory could have been achieved in spite of the political handicap.

Unfortunately, the lack of a concrete, precise doctrine resulted in a mosaic pattern of pacification in the field. To give a real example, my battalion's *quartier*, where my methods had been more or less adopted by my colleagues, could be considered as well advanced. Immediately to the north of us, the II/404 R.A.A.'s *quartier* was grey; rebels still controlled the population, still operated permanently in the *quartier* in groups of five to ten men, and larger groups crossed it almost at will at night. South of us, the I/93 R.A.M.'s *quartier* was definitely black; our troops had scant contacts with the population, operations occurred practically every day, units were not deployed below company strength, and no unit of less than a platoon could move with any degree of safety. I remember attending a joint civil-military meeting presided over by the *sous-préfet* of the Tizi Ouzou *arrondissement* in June 1957, when a proposition was seriously made to create a forbidden zone in this *quartier*; any civilian seen in it would be shot on sight. Yet it was the same terrain, the same Kabyles, the same guerrillas, the same French soldiers in all of these *quartiers*. Local factors could not account for such differences in the situation. In the absence of a doctrine, each piece of the mosaic merely reflected the personality of the local commander, his success or his failure. The Kabyles in my *sous-quartier*, who certainly appreciated the peace we had imposed, could not fail to realize that their safety was at stake as soon as they reached the market at Tizi

Ouzou. They perceived that they lived on a small island surrounded by the turmoil of the war, and they felt conspicuous.

I complained as early as November 1956 about the lack of systematic action on our part. In this sort of war, I pointed out, the insurgent must be confronted with a concerted, solid front. Without it, he will always find room to maneuver; pressed here, he will concentrate and develop there. My report was apparently found judicious, for General Gouraud forwarded it to Algiers. When I was in Paris during my New Year's leave, an officer from the office of General Ely, then Chief of Staff of the French Armed Forces, who had heard of the report, asked me to comment on it. My talk was tape-recorded, and later General Ely had the Minister of Defense, M. Bourges-Maunoury, listen to it. Yet none of my recommendations seems to have been put into effect at the time; their results did not appear until much later, in 1959.

In March 1957 I decided to synthesize my experience and to draft a step-by-step process for the pacification of Kabylia. This document (see Appendix 3) was approved by every officer to whom it was shown. General Lacomme agreed with my formula, General Guerin, the new zone commander, concurred, and the *préfet* was enthusiastic except for very minor points. I was asked to take it myself to General Dulac, General Salan's Chief of Staff in Algiers. Once more it had no effect. I only convinced Major Renard,* my battalion commander, and my fellow officers in the battalion. Yet everybody realized I was not talking theoretically; the situation in my *sous-quartier* was proof that my process worked. Indeed, whenever the zone commander, the *préfet*, or even Algiers wanted to show visitors that pacification was no dream, they sent them to my area. Thus I received General Salan (twice), General Ely, the then Minister of Defense M. Morice, plus any number of lower officials and foreign journalists.

I am not writing all this to show what a genius I was, but to point out how difficult it is to convince people, especially the military, to change traditional ways and to adapt themselves to new conditions. I have no doubt that General Guerin was sincere when he approved my methods. He cordially gave me direct access to his office and supported my action in every way. Nevertheless, he was more interested in military operations. That was his trade, and the famous "score" was his essential concern, for he was judged by the number of *fellaghas* killed or captured, not by the number of schools opened by the Army in his zone. I remember the visit in late 1957 of a General Nogues, Inspector of Infantry. Algiers was complaining more loudly than usual about the shortage of combat soldiers in Algeria, and General Nogues had been dispatched to investigate the situation. I briefed him on the disposition of my company, then spread over six posts with ten to fifteen men each, and spoke to him about the local councils, the *harka*, the schools, and the economic development. He was horrified:

"With your forces spread out as they are, you have lost all military value. Your posts are utterly useless, their strength is too small to allow any serious sortie against the guerrillas!"

Lt.-Col. Blanchet,* the zone G-3, tried to explain that the very fact that I could disperse my company so much was proof of my success. General Nogues would not be convinced.

One last significant example. General Guerin proposed me for exceptional promotion in June 1957. Algiers turned it down: how could I be proposed when I had been given no combat citation? How many rebels did I kill? General Guerin waited two months, and with General Salan's connivance gave me a drummed-up citation "for having brilliantly participated in numerous operations and contributed decisively to the destruction of so many rebels and the capture of so many weapons."(!) The proposal came too late, for I was already on the regular promotion list.

VII. Prisoners and Suspects

The rebels' ALN (National Liberation Army) reached its peak in Algeria during the spring of 1957. Hastening to smuggle weapons and equipment from Morocco, and particularly from Tunisia, before our fences were completed, the rebel organization abroad succeeded in sending convoys loaded with automatic rifles, radio sets, light mortars, and ammunition. The convoys moved only at night, across the most difficult terrain, preceded days ahead by scouts who checked the paths and, with the help of the local OPA, organized feeding and hiding facilities for the men and the mules. A few of these convoys managed to reach Kabylia. I remember taking part in December 1956 in a large operation, involving our zone and the Zone Ouest Constantinois in the Djurdjura Range, to intercept a convoy reported by our intelligence. We did not find it, either because we missed it or, more likely, because the intelligence was faulty. An important convoy was caught in February 1957 near Fort National; the weapons seized were U.S.-made Browning automatic rifles, German submachine guns, and British hand grenades. Simultaneously with sending arms in, the rebels sent groups of unarmed recruits out to Tunisia to be equipped and trained there. Many of them were intercepted by us at great loss to the rebels. All this traffic ceased for all practical purposes by the spring of 1958, when the borders were effectively sealed. Only dribbles of men and arms succeeded in getting across, in such insignificant numbers that when, by chance, a crate of twenty-four hand grenades (enough to keep terrorism alive in a large town for several months) did get smuggled in, the Commander-in-Chief felt enough concern to send special reports on the case to Paris.

The ALN forces now became more formally organized. The rebels obliged us by committing the mistake of creating units of a larger size than they could handle. In some areas, notably in the Constantine region, they attempted to operate at battalion strength, but at such heavy cost that they renounced the idea, and the *katiba* (company) remained for a long time, until 1959, their largest operational unit.

The most striking feature of the rebels' operations was their inability to co-ordinate action at any level. When, for instance, most of our zone's units had left their static positions, leaving behind a skeleton garrison, and were engaged in a several-day-long operation elsewhere, the rebels never attempted to move into the depleted area to wreak havoc. Seldom was a convoy harassed more than once at widely separated spots. This could be attributed, of course, to a lack of signal equipment in the rebel camp; only the *Wilayas* (regions) had efficient radio sets to communicate with each other and with the ALN command abroad. (By the end of 1959, the *Wilayas* had been reduced so much that only one was still in touch with the ALN headquarters in Tunisia.) Yet even in Tunisia, where they had every facility, the rebels very seldom attempted to create diversions along the border fences, thus occupying our reserves while crossing at a weak point. There is no question that Algerians are good individual fighters, but they do not make an army unless officered by European cadres.

We often seized documents and orders from the *Wilaya* to lower levels prescribing general attack here or intensified harassment there. Our zone headquarters invariably issued a warning to all units, and invariably nothing happened. Some of the rebels' orders insisted that every small guerrilla unit set up at least one ambush a week; even this low figure proved unrealistic. The guerrillas were essentially concerned with their survival and avoided as a rule any show of aggressiveness. Their main activity consisted in terrorism against civilians, more often than not just blind terrorism.

The ALN attrition began to overtake the input of volunteers and weapons during the summer of 1957. The average ratio of loss, which remained constant throughout the war, was ten *fellaghas* for every French soldier killed or wounded.[4]

Most of the rebels were killed. We captured perhaps one or two out of ten, and these generally because they had been wounded. Surrenders

---

[4] When the seven-year war ended in 1962, we had no more than 300 missing, of whom the rebels returned only 20.

were extremely rare. I have already explained why so few prisoners were taken. Encounters were generally sudden, marked by brief exchanges of fire at close range, with the rebels generally firing first from their hiding position. On our part, we understandably preferred not to take undue risks with our draftees if we could avoid it. We used dogs, not because they were any good in sniffing rebels out, but because hidden rebels often lost their nerve, fired at the poor beasts, and gave themselves away, thus saving a soldier from the murderous buckshot.

On the rebels' part, the reason why they did not surrender, even when hopelessly cornered in a cave, could be attributed to fear of us and of their own leaders. If their high losses were due mostly to the nature of the combat and only partly to our own error, the result was nevertheless evident, and the rebel propaganda made capital out of it. The *fellaghas* were told that it was futile to surrender; they would be killed anyway. In addition, they were kept under a system of mutual suspicion that made individual desertion difficult and group desertion almost impossible. They were warned that their families would pay for treason on their part. Discipline in their ranks was kept by a simple system of punishment: death, often preceded by torture. It was not rare for us to find bodies of *fellaghas*, often horribly mutilated, in areas where we had not recently conducted any operations. As for the guerrilla leaders, why should they surrender when they feared we might treat them similarly and when the best we could offer them was a return to their previous obscure condition in their villages after they had tasted the excitement of power? Most of them had committed crimes in their villages, and they knew that if the French could perhaps forgive, the families of those they had assassinated would not.

The only case of a large group of *fellaghas* coming over to our side occurred in the summer of 1957, when a rebel chieftain, Bellounis, broke with the movement.

How to increase the number of surrenders preoccupied the French authorities, and M. Lacoste came out with an offer widely publicized by newspapers, radio, and pamphlets. Every *fellagha* who surrendered would be given a safe conduct; his case would be examined, and if, to our knowledge, he had committed no crime against civilians, he would be free to return to his village or to join our forces; if there was a charge against him, he still had a choice between accepting trial and going back to the maquis. The offer had little or no effect.

We had another problem in interrogating captured *fellaghas* and OPA members. The former were our main source of operational intelligence. Sometimes they spoke readily, often giving false or obsolete information. Prisoners were interrogated on the spot by the first officer who happened to be there and was not too busy leading his troops, unless an intelligence officer was available, as was the case when the operation involved at least one battalion. As we were in a hurry to get exploitable information, the interrogation techniques were crude and the results poor. In the spring of 1957, a new policy came into force in our zone and lasted until late that year: prisoners were flown by helicopter to the zone headquarters to be interrogated by better-trained intelligence officers. Results were appreciably better, but the method involved delays, and opportunities were missed.

OPA members, because of the large number of arrests among them, were a permanent headache. For a long time, in fact until late 1957, no provisions were made at *quartier* and sector level to house, feed, and interrogate them. The burden fell on the *sous-quartier* commander. Methods, as usual, varied greatly from one *sous-quartier* to the next. In most, the policy was to interrogate suspects summarily and to dismiss rapidly those (the great majority) who had not readily confessed; in some *sous-quartiers*, it was "talk or else." The companies were not organized, and their cadres generally not qualified, for this sort of work; every company had a contingent of Moslem draftees from whom it was impossible to hide any mistreatment of civilian prisoners. The picture was altogether unpleasant, and a number of officers refused to have anything to do with it.

Under the pressure of a press campaign against "tortures" (in my view 90 percent nonsense and 10 percent truth), a special unit was created in the fall of 1957 under the name of D.O.P. (Détachement Operationnel de Protection). The lowest D.O.P. unit was the section attached to a zone. It was a mixed group of Army and police officers under a captain, with secretaries and Kabyle interpreters, most of them former *fellaghas*. The section operated under a dual chain of command: it reported directly to the D.O.P. at the Army Corps (and hence to Algiers) and to the zone's G-2. D.O.P. teams went along with every large-scale operation. Other teams were permanently or temporarily attached to some sectors; sometimes the duality of command led to conflicts with the sector commander. The D.O.P. in my zone was stationed in the brick factory with my battalion command post, close enough to Tizi Ouzou for fast liaison yet far enough from civilian eyes. A wall topped with barbed wire was promptly built to enclose a courtyard, inside of which a small prison was erected with ten individual cells; German shepherd dogs helped keep the prisoners in and the curious out.

If I were to state now which was our single most important improvement in our counterinsurgency operations in Algeria, I would flatly put the D.O.P. first. D.O.P.s took over from amateurs all the handling of prisoners, guerrilla and civilian. They eliminated the frightful bottleneck we had with the OPA prisoners. They relieved the *sous-quartier* commanders of a time-consuming and unpleasant task. In my case, all I had to do henceforth was to telephone the D.O.P. captain and find out if he was free, in which case I made my arrests, gave him all the relevant information and guidance, and waited for the results.

I had only one strong objection to the system as we put it into practice. I may sound hypocritical, but I maintain that, instead of making the D.O.P. an Army unit and camouflaging civilian police officers with uniforms, it would have been much wiser to do it the other way round and to set up the D.O.P. as a police force distinctly apart from the Army. How our Army bosses ever accepted such a deal escapes me.

I have shown earlier how our judicial system, unsuited to the situation, became bogged down. The Special Powers Act granted by the Parliament, however, provided a way out. The *préfet* could and did assign any suspicious person to forced residence. This meant either that the person would be obliged to move to a specified town or village, and there, although free, would have to report to the police every day, or that he would be interned in what was called officially and euphemistically a *"camp d'herbergement."* In Kabylia, rebel VIPs whom the *préfet* hoped to convert were assigned to live in comfort and luxury, at government expense, in a first-class hotel formerly managed by the French Transatlantic Company at Michelet, which in better days had been a ski resort situated high in the Djurdjura Range. I don't know how many FLN supporters were converted in this way. Many people criticized the *préfet* for this unegalitarian extravagance, but I personally think he was entirely right. Unnecessary harshness never pays.

Two *"camps d'herbergement"* were built for the small fry in Kabylia in 1957. One was located near Mirabeau west of Tizi Ouzou and had a capacity of 500 prisoners; it was under civilian responsibility and guarded by gendarmes. The other, smaller, was located at Tigzirt and was run by the Army under the responsibility of the sector commander. In both camps the prisoners were given technical training as in a vocational school.

Throughout the war our prisoner camps were open for unannounced inspection by the International Red Cross, the reports of which were made public. As was the case with every one of our activities, for a long time no standard pattern governed our conduct toward the prisoners, and the atmosphere varied greatly from camp to camp. In tbe best camps, efforts were made to sift the tough prisoners from the soft; where it was not done, the camps became schools for rebel cadres. Tigzirt was a liberal camp, where prisoners even got passes to visit their families. (None ever failed to return. Lt.-Col. Lemoine* told me of a case in which two prisoners on leave missed the Army convoy from Tizi Ouzou to Tigzirt. They hired a cab for 2,000 francs in order not to be late.) In some camps, by contrast, psychological experts thought they could convert prisoners by having them repeat regularly certain slogans and songs.

The *préfet* released groups of prisoners on the occasion of national or Islamic holidays. Individual cases came under review regularly, with proposals by the camp commander being passed upon by a board presided over by the *préfet*. SAS officers were always consulted, but their advice was not always taken into consideration. I had no difficulty on this score. The few OPA members arrested in my *sous-quartier* were kept in camps as long as was needed.

When things were regularized, i.e., in the latter part of 1957, the rules concerning arrests of civilians by Army units were as follows: a report of the arrest was forwarded within forty-eight hours to the local SAS officer, who sent it to the civilian authorities; a civilian could not be kept more than ten days by the Army; if he had not been released by that time, the *préfet* made the decision to free him or to assign him to a camp.

VIII. Further Expansion of the *Sous-Quartier*

The level of pacification reached in my *sous-quartier* by the summer of 1957 may be measured by the following signs:

1. The only times that my soldiers had occasion to spend ammunition otherwise than in firing practice were in the two cases when a small rebel party harassed Igonane Ameur from a safe distance at night, and in the one encounter in which a *harki* and a *fellagha* were killed.

2. A severe epidemic of flu affected most of my men in the fall of 1957. In some of my posts, no more than four or five soldiers were well enough to stand watch. I spent a nervous week, but no rebel attempt was made to exploit the situation, which I could not hide.

3. So peaceful was the *sous-quartier* that I moved from post to post in complete safety, riding on my horse and escorted only by my bodyguard mounted on our second horse.

4. Kabyle workers were returning from France in larger numbers. When asked why, they showed me letters they received in France from villagers in Algeria telling them how quiet the situation was now.

5. In July 1957 all my mayors received threatening letters from the rebels ordering them to resign, or they would be killed. They all brought their letters to me, even Bekri* from Bou Souar. I offered them additional protection, but they refused. Asli and Derradji, to whom I had already given a pistol, accepted protection only when they went to Tizi Ouzou.

6. Now that we had a complete census of the population, with even the missing Kabyles accounted for, our check showed only three men as having joined the rebels since my arrival in the area: the young man from Igonane Ameur in the fall of 1956, and the two from Mendja who had already deserted from the maquis.

7. Villagers from Tikobain and nearby hamlets petitioned the *préfet* for permission to be included in my *sous-quartier*, "where one knew where one stood."

Ironically, the rebels were so isolated from the population that I could get no information on them. The only case where I did receive information was one in which villagers from Igonane Ameur told me that a young *fellagha* from the village had written a note to his father saying he was on a short leave and wanted to see him. I visited the father and gave him a pass: "Tell your boy he can return any time." The father denied the story, of course, and did not move from his house. Just in case, I borrowed the sound truck from Tizi Ouzou and broadcast an appeal to the young *fellagha* urging him to come back. No result.

In September 1957 the sectors of Tigzirt and Tizi Ouzou were merged, and in the reorganization described below, my battalion was given a lion's share of the territory, taking over the Boudjima *quartier*. Specifically,

1. The battalion command post moved to Boudjima, leaving in the old command post the supply and service platoons of the C.C.A.S. (Command, Support, & Service Company).

2. The 1st Company was released from its Kasbah duty and stationed in three posts around Afir (5 km north of Tikobain).

3. The 4th Company moved from its position on the Aissa Mimoun ridge, occupied Tikobain, the hamlet near Hill 700 (2 km west of Tikobain) and Djebla (3 km southeast).

4. The 2d Company took charge of the north slope of Aissa Mimoun and occupied Imkecheren, Hill 801, and Tahanouts in addition to its previous position at Akaoudj.

5. I took over the entire south slope of Aissa Mimoun plus the flat area up to the Sebaou River (see Figure 8).

Two important villages were located in my new territory, Timizar Laghbar at the southwest tip of Aissa Mimoun, and Tala Atmane at the southeast end of the plain. Reorganizing my company once more and reducing still further the size of my detachments, I found I had only enough means to garrison one more village. I chose Timizar because of its location at the entrance of the Oued Sebaou gorge, because of its large population (about 1,800), and because it was still considered a bad village with an active OPA. I assigned to it W/O Pierre,* leaving

Figure 8
Final Deployment of the 45th B.I.C. (September 1957)

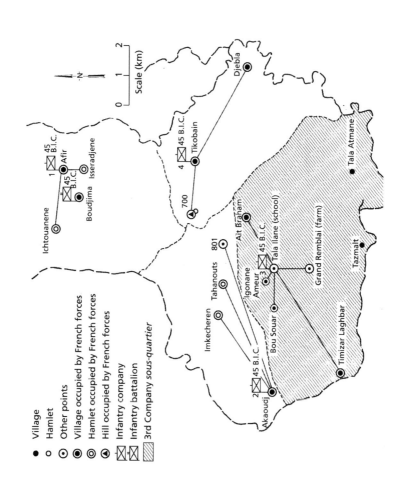

Igonane Ameur, close to my command post at Tala Ilane, in the hands of Sergeant Marceau* and ten men.

Timizar had a bad name for several reasons: a large number of its people worked in Tizi Ouzou, where they came under constant pressure from the FLN; it had contributed many guerrillas to Oudiai's band in the early days; it was the home of rebel Sergeant Ben Smail, who had succeeded Oudiai; and Ben Smail had several brothers in the village, one of whom managed the local grocery store. A further complication for me came from the fact that Timizar and the lowland called Douar Sikkh Ou Meddour was administratively dependent on the Tizi Ouzou SAS and not on mine at Aissa Mimoun.

Within a short period we applied our familiar pacification process, our task greatly helped by our use of the D.O.P.

Our post was established in the highest house in the village. I had no fear that the rebels would ever attack it, but I expected that they would harass it often. They could easily approach it through the narrow lanes in the village or fire from the other side of the gorges. I wanted to prevent this, and therefore asked Pierre* to call a meeting of the entire population at 3 p.m. one Sunday. I went there with the SAS officer from Tizi Ouzou. Villagers were milling around, but none had come to the meeting place. I sent patrols to bring them in and collected a 500-franc fine from every family head. I warned the population that we would naturally fire back with every weapon at our disposal, including, artillery, if the post was ever harassed. To show them that I meant it, an artillery liaison officer from the I/93 R.A.M. made a registration fire with smoke shells on a point a few hundred yards north of Timizar. The population watched with great interest and more curiosity than fear. To our great confusion, the rebels did indeed harass the post a month after our demonstration. We frantically called the I/93 R.A.M., but the 105mm battery had been moved away for an operation. Pierre* saved my face by firing bazookas and 60mm mortar flares.

The purge of Timizar was the result of precise information given by an old widow who lived in a shack near the post. Sergeant Marty had befriended her by giving her food. She became our best undercover agent in the village, getting her information from other, unsuspecting women. We contacted her only at night, one of my most reliable *harki* serving as interpreter. During the day, we pretended to treat her roughly; Pierre* even ordered her to leave her shack, saying that he wanted to destroy it because it obstructed our line of fire. The old woman (what a comedian!) asked neighbors to intercede in her favor, and Pierre* pretended to relent.

She warned us one day that Ben Smail and his gang had a rendezvous the following night with *mousseblines* near a *café maure* below the village on the highway. How did she know? She had seen a twig placed in a certain fashion at the door of Ben Smail's brother's grocery; that was the signal for the rendezvous. We went to the spot and caught two rebel auxiliaries from Azib Seklaoui, one of whom had a shotgun. An ambush set by the artillerymen on the left bank of Oued Sebaou not far from the bridge saw a group of men walking, one of them carrying a lantern. They thought these were our men and did not open fire. Nor did they challenge the group for fear of giving away their ambush. It was Ben Smail and his gang.

On another occasion, the widow told us that a farmer at Azib Seklaoui had a shotgun hidden in a shack under a pile of wood. We found the gun and arrested the man. The rebels were demoralized to see us acting on precise information; they knew they were being betrayed, but they never found out by whom.

This information made it unnecessary for us to purge the village by my two-step process. We instead arrested the OPA members directly, one of whom was Ben Smail's brother, and turned them over to the D.O.P.

The mayor of Timizar elected after the purge was a well-educated Kabyle who had been a *conseiller général* (county councilman) before the rebellion. He told me freely that he had co-operated with the rebels, but what else could he have done when they might have assassinated him at any time? The test of his new loyalty was passed when he secretly asked me to give him a pistol. He passed easily all the efficiency tests, and it did not take more than two months for the village to have reached the pacification level of my other *communes*. The school at Timizar, incidentally, was attended by 250 children and kept five soldiers busy.

Tala Atmane, with a population of about 1,200, was the largest village in the flat area of my *sous-quartier* and rather prosperous. I was much annoyed at not being able to garrison it, for its population had given me unmistakable signs of its readiness to co-operate with us. I had received three anonymous letters through the post office telling me all about the OPA. Several villagers had confirmed this information. Yet when asked if they would accept weapons to defend themselves, the villagers refused; they would do it only if I could station a core of my own soldiers, and this I could not do. My *harka* operated in the flat area most of the time, but I needed it as a mobile unit; it was my only reserve in case of trouble.

I pleaded for a reinforcement of my company, if necessary by transferring a few soldiers from the other companies. Why should we stick so rigidly to our Table of Organization? My own platoons as such did not exist any more; the same thing could be done with companies. I was promised a G.M.P.R. (Groupe Mobile de Protection Rurale), a unit made up of Moslem volunteers[5] with a small core of French cadres, paid by the civilian administration, and operating like a *harka*, but not in its native territory. But I never got it. After waiting two months, I reluctantly purged Tala Atmane. I learned soon afterward with no surprise that a rebel cell had been rebuilt. I repeated the purge.

The man who was elected mayor was courageous. He could not persuade his fellow villagers to accept arms, but he nevertheless undertook the job with energy. I never asked him for more than he could safely do. I even hinted to him that he could pretend to play both sides until I could station a garrison in the village. He was assassinated in September 1958.

During October 1957, my telephone line to the old battalion command post was cut on three occasions on the highway between Grand Remblai and Timizar Laghbar. We set many one-man ambushes during

---

5   Officially all Algerians, many G.M.P.R. Moslems were in fact Moroccans.

the day and larger ones at night, with no effect. With the agreement of the *préfet*, I inflicted a collective fine of five sheep on the inhabitants of Dar Mohammed El Makhour, the small hamlet south of Azib Djalout. They may have been perfectly innocent, but in any case the sabotage ended. Either the saboteur came from the hamlet, or its population had links with those who did it. The Kabyles in this hamlet were all related to Challal,* the OPA boss from Igonane Ameur who had fled to France on the eve of his arrest. I received information that a man from the hamlet was acting as liaison agent for Ben Smail's guerrilla group. I arrested him with three other suspected villagers, but he managed to escape from my command post (see page 27).

IX. An Operation in the Mizrana Forest

The Mizrana Forest is a natural forest of corktrees and thick under-growth, starting right on the coast and extending 7 km inland. It comprises two clumps of wood, the larger one triangular in shape with a base measuring about 0.5 km. The forest covers a hilly, rocky ground with sharp changes in level. Oued Taxibt cuts a deep north-south ravine and provides the only clear landmark. The forest is surrounded by a cluster of hamlets.

This setting has always offered a natural refuge for bandits. With the rebellion, the Mizrana Forest became a haven for the guerrillas, a real base where they felt safe enough to establish crude permanent camps and command posts. Controlling the population in the sur-rounding hamlets, they received supplies and ample warning of our every move. The forest was one of the places in Kabylia where any operation on our part was certain to meet rebels. Their strength in 1957 could easily be estimated at one hundred to two hundred men, representing one or two *katibas* plus the rebels' sector commando. They were armed with automatic rifles, submachine guns, army rifles, and shotguns.

Policing the forest was the unhappy lot of our 15th B.C.A. (Battalion de Chasseurs Alpins). Its command post was located at Tigzirt, one company at Tizi N'Bou Ali, another at Agouni Goughrane, the two remaining companies being stationed east of the Tizi Ouzou–Tigzirt highway. A single battalion was, of course, utterly unable to cope with the problem. Even supposing that we could once clear the forest of guerrillas, preventing their return was a task that could be solved only at the zone level by strictly controlling the entire cleared area from the coast to Oued Sebaou. All the Chasseurs could do, and did, was to harass the rebels in the forest by mining certain paths, by laying ambushes, and by surprise (?) incursions and occasional opera-tions involving a battalion or two.

In the latter case, other units from the sector were invited to par-ticipate, and it was not the most welcome assignment, for the ratio of losses between the rebels and us, instead of being 10 to 1, was usually closer to 1 to 1. Exploiting our manpower and firepower superiority was impossible. The only possible formation was a line slowly advancing through the underbrush, with the soldiers a yard apart trying to scan the ground a few steps ahead. Whoever moves in this situation is sure to lose against an enemy who is waiting for him. Rebel snipers used to climb trees, fire a burst of submachine gun on our advancing line, and vanish before we had even determined the direction of the fire. Support from heavy weapons was out. Tanks could operate only along the one track crossing the forest. Air cover was equally futile.

So irritating was the Mizrana problem that, with Algiers' agreement, it was decided to burn the forest. We dropped napalm during a week in August 1957 when a hot sirocco wind was blowing, but for some reason the forest did not burn. Experts said that the burning undergrowth used up the oxygen in the air and thus prevented the fire from spreading to the corktrees. I suggested once that the forest be officially made an Army testing area; with the population properly forewarned, we could then use gas. Preliminary studies concluded that the amount of gas needed to achieve anything would be enormous. My suggestion was finally rejected on the ground that our use of gas would give the FLN supporters in France and abroad a good argument for a powerful psychological campaign against us.

I amended my idea and suggested that (1) we spread rumors that we were determined to clear the forest once and for all; (2) we issue gas masks to a few units in the area and ostentatiously move in a number of drums manipulated by soldiers wearing masks; (3) on D-Day, we set up rings of ambushes around the forest and invite newspapermen to watch the operation; (4) we evacuate the population from the hamlets; and (5) we spread DDT by air over the forest and catch what came out. General Guerin found the plan imaginative, but nothing came of it.

When M. Morice, our Minister of Defense, visited my *sous-quartier* in September 1957, I told him my problems and mentioned that one of my fears was a possible raid in force by guerrillas from the Mizrana in my otherwise quiet *sous-quartier*. The Minister questioned me about the rebel strength in the forest. Then he turned to General Salan with raised eyebrows, and Salan turned to General Guerin and asked him how it was possible that we tolerated such a concentration of rebel forces.

"Sir, you ought to see the place. We have tried everything. Operations are very costly in this forest, and I hate to lose draftees in an operation that would not pay off."

"I'll give you all the support you ask," replied Salan, "you can have all the Theater Air Force at your disposal if you want."

The operation, postponed twice because of the weather, took place in October 1957. The plan was to make a feint on D-Minus-1 in the Port-Gueydon area. On D-Day a *bouclage* would be established under Colonel Bertrand* from the 9th R.I.C. of Bordj Menaiel:

(a) along National Road No. 24 on the coast (one cavalry, one infantry company);
(b) along the motor track in the western part of the forest from the coast to Hill 601 (three infantry battalions);
(c) along the same track from Hill 601 to Hill 679 (commando battalion from the Theater General Reserves).

The *ratissage* units (six infantry battalions) under Lt.-Col. Lemoine,* starting from the line Hill 76–Hill 142–Hill 220–Attouri–Tizi N'Bou Ali–Hill 621–Hill 803–Hill 744 (see map and Figure 9) would move west to the ridge Hill 215–Tala Mimoun–Hill 627–Hill 664, and would spend the night there. This move would be accompanied by a preplanned bombing of Oued Taxibt by B-26s and of Oued Smela by Vampires. T-6s would give air support on request and strafe any moving target ahead of the *ratissage*. On D-Plus-1, the *ratissage* units would comb the rest of the forest up to Oued Taxibt, where the *bouclage* units would meet them. A paratroop battalion was held in reserve. General Guerin himself took command of the operation and established his command post near the Maison Forestiere d'Adrar Tourmast. The word to the troops was to proceed slowly but thoroughly, to look over every tree and every rock, and to avoid any gap in the line.

Figure 9
Operation Mizrana Forest (October 1957)

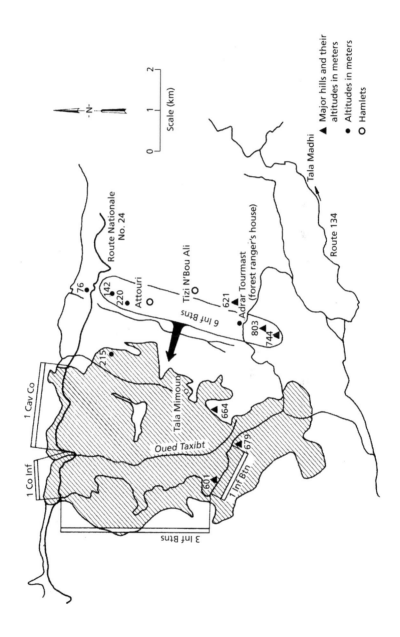

The operation went as planned. I commanded a company of my battalion, with 60 men from my company and 60 drawn equally from the 1st and 2d Companies. In the afternoon of D-Minus-1, my battalion was transported to the area of Tala Madhi on Road D-134 east of the Mizrana. We deployed, combed the area noisily for a distance of 2 km southward, spent the night there, and boarded the trucks the next morning at 7. We detrucked in the forest near Adrar Tourmast and took up position around Hill 621. The front given to my battalion was 1 km wide.

At 9 a.m. a flight of twelve B-26s flew over us and dropped a carpet of bombs on Oued Taxibt. At 9:30 we received the "go" signal. Three of my platoons started the move across the denuded terrain, and I followed with the last platoon 300 yards behind. Just as my reserve platoon had reached the bottom of the valley, a Vampire made a dive on us and released a bomb; when the smoke cleared, nobody was found hurt, but what a concert on the air-ground radio channel! We resumed our march, one eye on the terrain ahead and the other on the planes above. As we reached the edge of the forest on the other slope of the valley, T-6s were strafing 100 yards ahead of us, probably over my scouts. I switched again onto the air force channel and told them to stop. We settled in our positions for the night, near Hill 627 outside Tala Mimoun, arranging for liaison, closing gaps, and assigning firing positions.

At about 10 p.m. a strong wind rose and made it impossible to listen for noises. We heard several bursts of submachine-gun fire close by, shortly after 10. The rest of the night passed uneventfully. At dawn the body of a *fellagha* was carried to my battalion command post; he was later identified as the political commissar for the rebels' sector; he had been killed by the Chasseurs on our right while trying to force our cordon; a German submachine gun was seized.

We started moving again across the forest. Once more, I deployed three platoons in line, with a platoon in reserve 20 to 50 yards behind. Each platoon in front had a team of two dogs accompanied by their masters. We advanced very slowly, stopping every fifteen minutes to reset the line and check the direction on the compass. I used a whistle to order stops and advances. We searched every foot of the forest. To give an idea of how meticulous our search was: the move started at 7 a.m. and we reached Oued Taxibt near 12 noon—five hours for a distance of 2 km on the map. We found a dump with about 100 pairs of shoes, a cache with medicines, and some old radio batteries. So thorough had been our advance that, when we met the *bouclage* units, we saw five wild boars being barbecued. With the exception of the political commissar, the boars were the only victims of the whole operation. General Guerin was understandably furious and puzzled. He thought that we had not searched the forest with enough attention and he ordered the search repeated the following day. So we went around once more, with no better result.

We learned much later from a captured rebel lieutenant what had gone wrong. The whole group of rebels, about 160 strong, had made its escape on D-Day night by crossing the northern *bouclage* on the coastal highway and moving east along the coast. They had luckily been helped by the gale-force wind which drowned out all noise.

Lest I give the impression that every one of our operations was a fiasco, I must state that I participated in April 1958 in a similar large affair southwest of Tizi Ouzou, where we killed or captured seventy-six *fellaghas* at the cost of three killed and seven wounded.

X. The Manpower Crisis in the French Army

The manpower problem in the French forces in Algeria, partly alleviated in 1956 by the recall of reservists for a short period, returned to plague us with a vengeance in the second half of 1957. The yearly levy of draftees, to begin with, was unusually small owing to the low birthrate in France during the 1930s. Military service, already extended to twenty-eight months, could not reasonably be lengthened at a time when we faced such a serious labor shortage at home that coal miners drafted in the Army had to be released immediately after their basic training in order to relieve the industry. French civil and military officials in Algeria, under constant attack by the opposition press, had often publicly emphasized how much the situation had improved in Algeria. Consequently, when the Gaillard Cabinet found itself caught between recriminations and opposition at home and the Army's needs in Algeria, the latter were sacrificed. Not only was further reinforcement ruled out, but it was decided to cut down the existing strength.

It remained for our command in Algeria to comply with the reduction at a minimum cost to our operational effectiveness. One of the solutions consisted in disbanding several battalions; the personnel from their C.C.A.S. (Command, Support & Service Company) would serve to replenish the combat companies, which would be attached to other battalions. In the winter of 1958, my battalion in Kabylia became the first victim of this decision, although it was regarded as one of the best in the zone. The selection had been made in Paris, not on tactical grounds but on purely administrative ones: as the newest unit in the Colonial Army, having no past or tradition, the 45th Colonial Infantry Battalion was doomed.

The reorganization took about two months. Our 1st, 2d, and 3d Companies were assigned respectively—for administrative purposes—to the 1st, 2d, and 3d battalions of the 9th R.I.C. of the Bordj Menaiel sector; our 4th Company was transferred to a battalion of the 6th Senegalese Rifles at Fort National. For operational purposes, the 1st Company, and shortly afterward the 2d, moved into the expanded

Bordj Menaiel sector and took *sous-quartiers* at Sidi Namane and Tala Mokkor west of Tizi Ouzou. I alone remained in my original area. The former Aissa Mimoun *quartier* was split now between the *quartier* of the I/93 R.A.M. in the south and the II/404 R.A.A. in the north, the dividing line being the crest of the Djebel. A company from the II/404 R.A.A. was now my neighbor on the other slope of Aissa Mimoun.

The change brought me a whole set of logistical and command problems. I had to get my supplies now at Camp du Maréchal instead of at our old command post near Tizi Ouzou. Medical assistance to the population by our 45th B.I.C. doctor, an important and regular feature of our civic action, was seriously cut down, because my new operational boss claimed it was a logistical matter, which should therefore be provided by the III/9th R.I.C., while the commander of this battalion insisted it was an operational task. To be frank, the situation had advantages in some cases, for I managed occasionally to play both sides and get help for operational reasons and the same help for logistic ones. But on the whole it greatly complicated my work. As for the command situation, I had no direct telephone line with the I/93 R.A.M.; I had to pass through the zone switchboard. Major Gambier,* the I/93 R.A.M. commander, was naturally more interested in his own original *quartier* than in his new acquisition, and he left me mostly to my own devices.

These were minor problems, however, compared to the deterioration of the situation on the north slope of Aissa Mimoun. Under the best of circumstances, if all the sectors, *quartiers*, and *sous-quartiers* in Kabylia had reached more or less the same stage in pacification, the replacement of one unit by another would have brought troubles; it would have taken at least two months for the newcomers to become well acquainted with the area and the population. But such a uniformity did not exist. In the absence of a well-observed counterinsurgency doctrine, my new neighbors acted as they were used to in their former *quartier*, not as we and as the population in Aissa Mimoun were accustomed. For instance, instead of constantly ambushing every night even though all seemed peaceful, they contented themselves with laying an average of four ambushes a week, not four a day as we did. Having ignored the population in their former area, they continued to ignore it here. Whenever something happened on the north slope of Aissa

Mimoun, as for instance when a *harki* was assassinated at the fountain near Tahanouts, they reported first to their own chain of command before remembering me. (The delay in this case was fifteen minutes, enough to allow the terrorist to escape.) Yet for the rebels as well as for the population, Aissa Mimoun was a single entity; cutting it into two different *quartiers* could only favor the rebels. Indeed, I soon learned from my Timizar Laghbar informant that Ben Smail was now operating most of the time on the north slope and was increasing his pressure on the villages there.

The island of peace created by the 45th B.I.C. had shrunk now to my *sous-quartier.*

In February 1958, I passed command of my company to Captain Simon,* our 45th B.I.C. intelligence officer. The transfer took two weeks, in which Simon* visited with me every village and hamlet, and met every soldier and most of the population. I left him our census in good order, our intelligence records, a note on the history of the pacification of the *sous-quartier*, a note on the current local military problems, and a note on the political prospects which was, so to speak, my testament (see pp. 206–207). Waiting for another assignment in the Bordj Menaiel sector, I joined Major Renard* at our old battalion command post and helped him liquidate the 45th B.I.C.

While we still had our C.C.A.S. personnel and could count on the 3d Company, I suggested to Major Renard* a last effort to catch Ben Smail, our remaining opponent, before leaving the area forever. I wanted to set up a co-ordinated series of ambushes for several nights in succession. Renard* agreed, and I organized the operation with Captain Simon* and Captain Gauthier* from the C.C.A.S.

At 8 a.m. following the third night, Lt. Gerbaut* telephoned me from Tala Ilane and announced that Captain Simon* had been killed. I rushed there. Simon* had left Tala Ilane at 10 p.m. with a 30-man ambush party; reaching the Tizi Ouzou–Tikobain highway at the crossroad with the Tala Atmane highway, the party split in two, one going to Tazmalt, the other with Simon* toward Tala Atmane. Near Hill 127, about 500 yards north of this village, Simon's* patrol was crossing the small Tacift Guilmania river when they were shot at suddenly from the other bank. Simon* and Ali Asli (one of the two sons of our Kbelouyene mayor serving in the *harka*) were killed instantly. Their bodies were carried to Tala Atmane at dawn by the rest of the patrol, and the villagers offered a truck to bring them to Tala Ilane.

Luck—good or bad—plays its large part in war, and Simon* had been unlucky. Nevertheless, after-the-fact criticism shows that he made two mistakes: (1) there was no need to go out at night with such a large party, the size of which was bound to make noise; (2) Simon* compounded it by leading his patrol himself and working as a scout instead of commanding in his proper place. Once he was dead, confusion overtook his soldiers, and the rebels managed to escape without loss.

His death was a psychological blow to us, for it reminded the population, if they had ever forgotten it, that the rebels were still alive. General Guerin ordered me to resume command of the company, to revive the spirit of our soldiers and the villagers.

We soon discovered that the rebels who had killed Simon* were part of a band operating generally on the south side of Oued Sebaou valley. The I/93 R.A.M. caught a liaison *fellagha* in an ambush; he carried a letter addressed to his boss by the rebel sector's chief:

"You requested a medal for having killed a colonialist captain. The medal cannot be granted unless you provide us first with the following information: What is the name of this captain? His unit? When, where, and how was he killed? I expect your report."[6]

If rebels were operating in the vicinity of Tala Atmane, they certainly had a purpose, and no doubt they had a cell working in the village. I knew this from informants, who reported that the cell I had previously destroyed had been replaced. I pleaded again for reinforcement of my company so that I could garrison the village, and I was again promised a G.M.P.R. which I did not get. Once more I reluctantly purged a village in which, right from the beginning, the population had shown its willingness to co-operate with us. Four villagers were

---

[6]   One more example of the truly extraordinary influence of French bureaucratic ways on the FLN.

arrested, turned over to the D.O.P., and subsequently sent to prisoner camps.

I now turned my attention to Timizar Laghbar. Letters from the rebels had recently reached the mayor asking him to resign or else. The mayor was sure the letters had been sent by Ben Smail. My old lady informer told us Ben Smail was staying in Aissa Mimoun. Partly on the basis of tenuous indications, and mostly on a hunch, I decided to search a ravine starting between Hill 450 and 512 (500 yards east of Akaoudj). I set H-Hour for 10 a.m., in broad daylight, and I believe the choice was decisive in the outcome of the operation. Barely fifteen minutes after the *ratissage* company had deployed from Akaoudj and started working down the ravine, they surprised a group of five or six *fellaghas*, three of whom were killed in a brief exchange of fire. Among the dead was Ben Smail. We freed a Kabyle draftee still wearing his French Army uniform; he had been on leave in his village of Akaoudj and abducted from his house the night before.

XI. Attempts at Organizing a Party

Assuming that by following my pacification technique we would identify friendly elements among the population, test them, and eventually establish them locally in positions of power, the fact remains that
these leaders would still be politically isolated, each in his small area,
yet facing an enemy politically and militarily organized on a national
scale. As long as our forces stayed, we could control the situation with
the help of the local leaders; but if we had to leave or if our forces were
greatly reduced, the local leaders might be swept away by the rebels
unless they were backed on a national scale by an organization of their
own at least equal in scope and size to the rebels'. In other words,
local leaders had to be grouped in a political party. Thus provided with
political goal, guidance, and support, they would be able to consolidate
their ties with the population, broaden the base of their local support,
and consolidate the pacification.

This was the last item in the program I had developed in my
March 1957 study of a pacification technique (see Appendix 3). I considered the task a purely political one and as such devolving on our
civilian authority. The Army's role, in my view, was over when the
potential local leaders had been identified and tested.

M. Vignon, the *préfet* of Kabylia, entirely agreed with me. He
wanted me to accompany him to Algiers, see M. Lacoste, the Minister-
Resident, and sell him the idea. On the day set for the meeting, in June
1957, M. Lacoste unfortunately was obliged to fly once more to Paris
for a cabinet meeting. M. Vignon agreed to discuss the project with M.
Maisonneuve, Lacoste's first assistant. The meeting took place not in
Maisonneuve's office but over lunch at the Yacht Club, in the presence
of four other guests. The atmosphere was not conducive to serious talk,
if only because incredibly pretty girls—for which Algiers is famous—
were sunbathing in bikinis on the terrace just below our table. When
cheese was served, M. Vignon tried to steer the general chat toward our
subject. M. Maisonneuve was visibly cold to the idea.

"A political party is fine, of course, but which party do you have in mind, the Radical-Socialists, the Mouvement Républicain Populaire, the S.F.I.O., or what?"

"It need not be an existing French political party," I replied. "If I am to believe our official platform according to which we want to build a new Algeria, why shouldn't we organize a 'Party for a New Algeria' with those Algerians who also believe in it?"

"With both Moslem and European members?"

"Certainly, why not? I do not pretend that it would be an easy task, that the party could be created overnight. As things stand today, I do not believe we have yet found enough Algerians willing to stake their future on it, so we still have some time ahead. But we must not waste it. Suppose the FLN were to take us at our word and accept today our ceasefire-elections proposals, aren't you afraid they might sweep the elections unless we have a strong pro-French party to oppose them?"

This was all I managed to say before our host looked at his watch and remembered his appointments for the afternoon. I never heard anything more on the subject.

Back in Aissa Mimoun and far from girls in bikinis, I wondered if I could not at least initiate a nucleus of a party in my own *sous-quartier*. The conclusion I reached was negative. Because of the small size of my area, my pool of local leaders was too minute to offer enough people who combined loyalty, energy, and brains. How could I organize a party when not a single adult Kabyle was literate?

What I did, however—and this just before I passed my command to Captain Simon* in February 1958—was to gather together my most trustworthy Kabyle supporters. In the final analysis, the basis of my strength in Aissa Mimoun, the degree of control I exerted over the population, and the amount of support I received from it all rested on an inner circle of six Kabyles, of whom I was absolutely sure because they had given me proof of their commitment when it was still dangerous for them to do so. In this group figured Asli, the *harki* sergeant, Boukrou, Scheik* the *harki* corporal, and three other *harkis* from Ait

Braham and Tala Ou Abba. On the basis of loyalty and opposition to the rebels, I could also add the young veteran from Igonane Ameur who had been wounded in a terrorist attempt. Around this core was a larger group of about twenty men who had committed themselves firmly to our side, but they had done so only after the purge, when the danger had diminished. In this group were people who had clearly both brains and ability, notably Derradji, the mayor of Ait Braham. Should I include this second group in my projected organization? I decided to play it safe and to deal only with my seven faithfuls, leaving the decision to expand to my successor.

I gathered the seven men. I told them I had entire confidence in every one of them, and I explained why. If they trusted me, they should therefore trust each other entirely; united, they would represent a strong force for rallying the population and thus keeping the area free of rebel agents. The help they would give my successor as a united group, particularly in the period when Captain Simon* was still not well acquainted with the area, would be invaluable and would probably be the best guaranty against possible troubles. Consequently I invited them to elect a president among them, to meet frequently with him in order to discuss any problem in the area, to settle problems with Captain Simon,* and to strive to expand their group. They agreed enthusiastically, and unanimously chose Asli as their leader.

When I returned to the *sous-quartier* after Simon's* death, I inquired whether the group had met during the two weeks I was away. No, they had found no time for it yet. I was too busy purging Tala Atmane and tracking Ben Smail to press the matter further. On April 1, 1958, I again handed over my command, and strongly urged my successor, Captain Hermann,* to keep pushing Asli and the inner group and to give them guidance.

A month later, the May 13 revolution in Algiers suddenly changed for the better the atmosphere in all Algeria, and my small political nucleus had mushroomed to such an extent that it covered every village and hamlet in the *sous-quartier*. "Comités de Salut Public" had sprung up everywhere, hundreds of villagers had requested and received arms, and a new feeling of confidence swept the entire population.

●　●　●　●

I visited Aissa Mimoun for the last time in May 1959. Captain Hermann* was no longer there; he had been killed in December 1958 by a strong rebel commando sent from the Mizrana Forest just for the purpose. His successor had shown no imagination and no understanding for the peculiar nature of this war; contenting himself with military activity, he let the SAS officer, also a newcomer, handle all the work with the population. Marty, my best sergeant, and three *harkis* had been killed in a surprise encounter with a strong rebel group in the Bou Souar ravine, in which the *fellaghas* lost seventeen killed, wounded, or captured. My area had visibly retrogressed to the average level of most of Kabylia in 1959, clearly above the situation as I had found it when I arrived in 1956, but below the one I had left.

"Where is my friend Asli?" I asked. Dead also, killed accidentally by our troops near Timizar Laghbar. A small group of rebels had been spotted there one day and an operation immediately launched. Asli, always spoiling for a fight with the *fellaghas*, rushed there wearing his usual civilian clothes, holding a pistol in his hand. Soldiers from the II/404 R.A.A. mistook him for a rebel on the run, fired, and killed him.

I inquired also about our political nucleus. Captain Hermann's* successor shrugged his shoulders. "Worthless, they distrusted each other, they kept bickering among themselves, they were incapable of agreeing on anybody and anything." Of this I had no doubt. Moslems are Moslems, and even the rebels, with their strong motivation and their ferocious ways of settling differences, had had a hard time keeping their followers in line. Yet I could not help but feel that the result would have been far different if Hermann's* successor had not lost sight of his strategic goal. (I am using the word "strategic" not in its conventional military meaning but in its political one, the only one that makes sense in insurgency and counterinsurgency warfare.)

But how could I blame some captain from *sous-quartier* such-and-such? To build, to nurse, to steer a political organization, to guide it with experienced political workers on leave from their own party in

Metropolitan France, this was not a responsibility for a captain in the field. The guilt lay elsewhere.

PART FOUR

War in the Bordj Menaiel Sector

I. The Spring of 1958

The net result of my promotion was loss of direct command. While the French Army in the postwar period suffered from a severe shortage of lieutenants and captains owing to the attrition in Indochina and to the decrease in the number of applicants to our military academies, there was a large surplus of officers with the rank of major and above. Command of a battalion was hard to get; it was given directly by the Bureau of Personnel in Paris on the basis of seniority, the idea being that each major should have a chance to comply with the peacetime rule of having exercised two years of effective command before being considered for further promotion. As battalions were far less numerous than majors, the waiting list was long. When I finally received my promotion on April 2, 1958, all I could hope for, and all I got, was an assignment as deputy commander of the II/9th R.I.C. in the Bordj Menaiel sector.

The units in the sector consisted of the three battalions of the 9th Colonial Infantry Regiment,[1] plus a company of Gendarmes Mobiles and two G.M.P.R.s. It was, I believe, the only case in Kabylia where a colonel concurrently commanding a sector and a regiment had all his subordinate battalions with him.

The sector (see map and Figure 10) covered the westernmost part of Kabylia and comprised two areas strikingly different in terms of terrain and population.

1. In more than two-thirds of the sector in the north and west, the terrain was low, relatively flat, denuded of cover (a characteristic of almost every Arab-occupied area). The Mizrana Forest on its east-

---

[1]   The French colonial troops, from the seventeenth century to the end of the nineteenth, were Marines, employed and supported by the Navy. As our colonial empire grew, so did they, until the Navy complained that the Marines were using too large a share of appropriations. At the turn of the century, the Marines were separated from the Navy, attached to the Army as an independent force, and called the Colonial Army. The government realized recently that "colonial" had become a bad word, and in May 1958 we were given back our old name of "Marines," and the 9th R.I.C. became the 9th R.I.M. (Regiment d'Infanterie de Marine).

Figure 10
Bordj Menaiel Sector (April 1958)

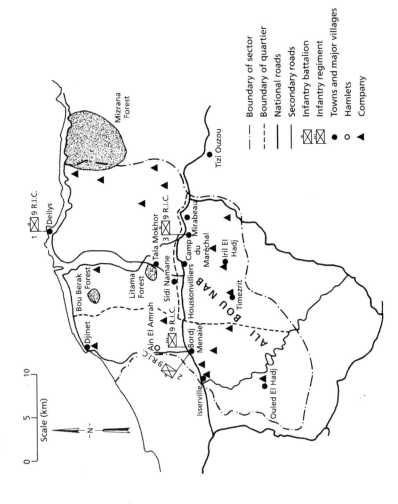

ern limit and the two small Litama and Bou Berak forests were the only natural troublespots. The nature of the terrain was such that small rebel bands could not maintain themselves in the area for long, and large bands could only cross it at night. It was easy ground for us, perfect for a mounted unit.[2]

The population gave us two more advantages: we had the tactical benefit of the presence of European settlers (which was not always a political blessing), and the native population was largely Arab.

Along the Oued Sebaou and Oued Isser valleys, European settlers, many having come from Alsace after the 1870/71 Franco-Prussian War, had transformed malaria-ridden swamps into rich farms producing vegetables and wine. None of the farms was abandoned, but most required some sort of protection from the Army in addition to the farmers' self-defense organization. A sizable number of Europeans lived in western-type villages surrounded by Moslem quarters, such as Bordj Menaiel, Camp du Maréchal, Mirabeau, and Isserville. We could count on them to take over some of the village defense chores. Yet only at Bordj Menaiel were they organized into *Unités Territoriales*.

The fact that the majority of the Moslems were Arabs did not help the Kabyle rebels; this was for them a *terra alienensis*. The Arabs either worked for the French farmers (vegetable and wine-farming requires a large ratio of workers per acre), or they cultivated their own land, growing tobacco as their main cash crop. The French administration had long organized rural co-operatives for them, staffed with competent rural engineers, and the Arab farmers were relatively prosperous and dependent on the smooth working of the French administration.

2. South of this area, Djebel Ali Bou Nab occupied the last third of the sector. It was a ridge similar in extent and height to the Aissa Mimoun, entirely populated with Kabyles, who were dispersed in an incredible number of small hamlets. In a single square kilometer south of Haussonvilliers, for instance, the map showed nine separate ham-

---

[2] We did convert some motorized cavalry units into horse cavalry, with good results. The chief difficulty was in finding NCOs who remembered how to take care of a horse. Several *harkas* were also mounted.

lets, and this was not the total number. The usual trees, covers, bushes, ravines, and caves made it natural guerrilla country.

The Djebel was particularly important for the rebels because it was the Kabyle mountain range nearest to Algiers; bands moving to and from the Mitidja Plain had to pass through it. In the same way, it served as a stepping stone for bands on their way to and from the Mizrana Forest. It also had the distinction of being the birthplace of Krim Belkacem, one of the top FLN leaders. Ali Bou Nab was thus the focal point of the sector and should have required the most careful handling on our part.

In 1958 the sector coincided almost exactly with the administrative limits of an *arrondissement* headed by a young *sous-préfet* at Bordj Menaiel. The northern part was administered, as in France, by long-established elected communal councils, all the members of which were French because the Arabs had resigned under FLN pressure. The Kabyle area in the south came under direct (but theoretical) administration by SAS officers, attempts at organizing new Kabyle *communes* having failed in 1957. The military situation was such that the SAS officers were unable to play their role.

The result of our efforts in the sector since 1956 could be aptly summed up in a single word: fiasco. It was due essentially to the personality of the two successive sector commanders. The first one had been blind to the peculiar nature of this war and had wasted the critical years of 1956 and early 1957 when the rebels, although large in number, were actually weak in both their military and their political organization. He operated there as he had in Indochina, where we were confronted with a powerful Vietminh army. He concerned himself with purely military operations, ignored the population, thus allowing the rebels a chance to build up a tight OPA. As a result, the guerrillas he killed—and he killed many—were immediately replaced, not necessarily by local people but often by volunteers from other sectors. Moreover, since he did not control the population, he did not control the terrain either, in spite of having companies stationed in so-called strategic positions on the ridge. Taking advantage of the organized support from the population, guerrillas from other areas came to reinforce the local ones, and the number of the rebels grew, as well as the size of their units and the quality of their armament. When I joined the sector, a rebel *katiba* (company) and a special commando were permanently based in the Djebel, sometimes reinforced by as much as two other *katibas*. I do not remember a single operation during my stay when we did not encounter *fellaghas* in numbers.

In other words, a real war was going on in this sector, aggravated because the rebels had managed to grow in political and military strength.

The second sector commander, Colonel Bertrand,* a man for whom I have the greatest admiration and respect and with whom I have been closely associated for most of my military career, also concentrated on military activity, not out of blindness but for moral reasons. He felt we had no right to deny the Algerians their independence even if only a small minority demanded it. He believed Algeria would sooner or later get its independence anyway. There was no point, therefore, in trying to involve the population on our side and prepare nasty morrows for the poor chaps we might have attracted.[3] Besides, he con-

---

[3] Following is part of a letter, published in *Le Monde* (January 26, 1963), from General F. Cazenave, one of the commanders who did comply with official orders to win over the population, and came to regret deeply having misled the Algerian Moslems with promises of French protection that went unfulfilled.

"In your 11 January issue, reporting that I have been placed in the reserves at my request, you have added the following comment: 'General Cazenave, whose testimony during Challe's trial in 1961 was a strong attack on the government policy in Algeria, had no assignment.'

I cannot concur in a wording which might lead people who do not know me well enough to think that I would have left the Army before my due time simply because I had no assignment; in brief, because I was in disgrace.

From my return from Algeria at the end of March 1961 until last July 3, when I asked to be retired, a request that was granted six months later, I have never ceased to be on duty in various study groups in the Army general staff; in order to retire, I was obliged to refuse the direction of the preparation of our national war games for 1962, to which I had just been assigned.

In any case, when one has served, like me, with passion for forty years, it takes other motives than a disgrace to leave the Army before the time is due. Here are my motives:

In my various commands in Algeria, and notably, from April 1960 to May 1961 when I commanded the 9th Division and the Orléansville Zone, I made multiple efforts, in accordance with the orders I received, to commit Moslems on our side, and promised

sidered action on the population as being the responsibility of the civil administration; if the civil administration was wanting, he would not substitute for it unless specifically ordered to do so.

I took advantage of our long friendship to plead with him for a change in our tactics. I pointed at the results I had painlessly achieved in Aissa Mimoun both for our troops and for the population. Even in this sector there were two bright spots. In the difficult *sous-quartier* bordering on the Mizrana Forest, a young captain, who was subsequently killed by a sniper, had managed to gain the confidence of the population and had turned his territory into a safe one. Another captain was achieving the same result in the Ouled El Hadj *sous-quartier* on the western fringe of Ali Bou Nab. Didn't the colonel appreciate these results? "Yes, but I am a soldier and I refuse to be anything else. Let the Government take its full responsibility."

No unit had any real contact with the population except in the two isolated cases above. We were caught in the classic vicious circle of an insurgency: because of the repeated and costly operations, the Kabyle population was solidly against us; because of the attitude of the population, our soldiers tended to treat every civilian as an enemy. Most of the adult Kabyle males had disappeared, having either joined the maquis or fled to safer places in Algeria or to France. Entering a village, we would find only old men, women, and children. The following story will give an idea of the attitude of the population. One day during a sortie by the 3d Battalion, the doctor offered medical assistance to the villagers. A Kabyle woman told him:

"We are not sick, we are sick only when you come. So go away, we don't need doctors."

As for our troops, a man seen running was automatically a rebel, hence a target. During an operation I commanded, I heard an automatic rifle burst ahead. The company commander reported having shot a *fellagha*. I went to the spot and saw a dead Kabyle, a man about 30,

---

that France would see to their protection whatever happened.

On July 3 last, all that I had thus said and promised had been scoffed at for good or disavowed. A wound remains in me which denies me rest.

I have not been able to bear it, and I took recourse in the ultimate action open to a soldier when what is called "*la servitude militaire*" has become unbearable: I resigned."

dressed like any other villager. No weapon, no compromising paper on him. He may have been a *fellagha* or he may not. In any case he was dead. Another time, in a large operation where we were in *bouclage* positions, a company commander reported via radio that he had spotted a group of suspicious men one kilometer in front of him, and he was going to open fire on them.

"Have you been fired upon?" I asked.

"No."

"Do you see any man in uniform or carrying a weapon?"

"No."

"Then send a patrol to check and report."

As I expected, the suspicious group was just a bunch of scared villagers. During the same operation I heard a paratroop battalion commander in the *ratissage* asking for artillery fire registration on a village he was approaching, just in case he met with opposition. I could see with my binoculars a crowd of inhabitants, mostly women and children, assembled in a small open ground in the village. I intervened with the operation commander for the fire registration to be made only with harmless smokeshells and on a target away from the village.

The deployment of our units (see Figure 10) did not reflect the demands of the situation nor the relative difficulty of the terrain. The flat area north of the Tizi Ouzou–Algiers highway had a certain geographic, demographic, economic, and political unity. Although it was large—25 km by 16—the terrain was easy, communications were good, the presence of Europeans, if properly exploited, facilitated our military task, and its Arab population, more pliable than the Kabyles, would have been easy to win over. It should have been made into a single *quartier* and entrusted to a single battalion. As it was, the area was divided between the 1st Battalion, entirely stationed on its eastern part, and the 2d Battalion, whose *quartier* extended to its western part. In spite of its size, this area could almost have taken care of itself with a minimum of military protection and civic action. But this would have required (1) a small, fast-moving reserve, (2) dispersing the companies over a number of posts located in the villages, and having them live with the population. The risk was very small, since the rebels, as a rule, avoided encounters with us in this terrain. Yet all the companies were kept together in Army-built camps located in "strategic" positions away from the population.

In the Ali Bou Nab, on the other hand, we were understrength and our forces were badly utilized. Four companies (three from the 3d Battalion and one from the 2d) were stationed on the crest. They were never attacked in their positions. When they were harassed, which was seldom, they replied with a heavy volume of fire. They were each below the critical size for independent offensive operation. With the ever-present possibility of meeting 100 or 200 *fellaghas*, a long-range sortie of less than a full company was dangerous, particularly in this terrain. The ridge being narrow and sharp, a company could not maneuver by itself without being engulfed in the ravines and the steep slopes on both sides; it could only meet rebels head on. Obliged to leave half his company to guard the post with its large store of ammunition and equipment, the company commander could not muster more than two platoons for a sortie. Thus, these four companies were wasted in this situation. They enjoyed a wonderful scenery but could do very little besides rest between large operations.

I remember my shock when, reading the sector's daily situation report, I realized that my former company in Aissa Mimoun was conducting more ambushes a night than a battalion here, sometimes indeed more than the whole regiment.

Supplying the Ali Bou Nab companies was no small affair. The only access was an Army-built road leading from Afir, south of Haussonvilliers, up to Iril el Had on the crest, then to Timezrit farther west, and finally down to Ouled el Hadj. The road from Iril el Had toward the east on the crest had been made unusable by the rebels. Every convoy was an operation in itself, carried out twice a week and immobilizing most of our forces for the entire day. To give an indication of how ineffective we were, our company at Timezrit had recruited ten *harkis* from a nearby hamlet, but the *harkis* and their families had to live within the company barracks, for they would not have been safe at night in their hamlet.

The obvious solution for this part of the sector was:

1. To move the command post of the 3d Battalion from Camp
   du Maréchal, in the plain below, up to the ridge in order to
   allow the battalion commander the possibility of co-ordinating the actions of the companies every day and thus operate
   as a battalion.
2. To relieve the 2d Battalion almost entirely of its static duty
   and to keep it operating as a mobile unit in the Ali Bou Nab
   until the rebel forces were reduced to more manageable size or
   expelled.

Then we would be able to start doing more constructive work with the
population, spreading the static companies in the villages and, if necessary, regrouping the population that we could not easily control.

I submitted a plan for the reorganization of the sector along these
lines, but it was turned down. The zone, it was objected, had a permanent option on a battalion from the sector (not any specific battalion
but a force of battalion size made up from units drawn from the sector),
and it would not relinquish it. I was vindicated in 1959, when a new
colonel took over the sector and adopted my suggestions. His achievement made headlines in the French newspapers, which spoke of "a new
look in pacification." The situation in Ali Bou Nab, already miracu-
lously changed after the May 13 revolution (see below), improved so
much that the father of Krim Belkacem himself came out of hiding
and joined our side.

Unfortunately, because of the constant demands of the zone, our
sector contributed forces for outside operations so often that our plans
were always upset and our officers complained that they could not
fulfill tasks at hand. In my 2d Battalion, I spent half my time away
on operations, most of them futile, and always the same sort of *bouclage* and *ratissage*; I stayed half the time at the base in Bordj Menaiel,
alternating in this work with the battalion commander. Operations
were fun, exciting, and healthy, but we saw no end to them, and the
"warriors" who used to ridicule the "pacifiers" were beginning to have
second thoughts. Our troops were psychologically ripe for a radical
change in tactics; I could feel it from the reactions of the officers when
I explained my methods to them. The proof that my success was not

due to luck or to special circumstances was provided when the former 1st and 2d Companies of my old battalion repeated the process in their new *sous-quartiers*.

I will now add some details to this general picture of the situation in the Bordj Menaiel sector.

Military Activity of the Rebels

Rebel activity was near zero. Either because they needed peace in the Ali Bou Nab and avoided provoking us in order to cross the Djebel safely, or because they were incompetent and concerned only with their survival, they undertook very little besides terrorism and arson. Occasionally, they spread automatic fire from a considerable distance at Bordj Menaiel or at our posts at night, or they fired before sunset at isolated cars on the Tizi Ouzou–Algiers highway.

Only one successful rebel ambush occurred during the three months I was in the sector. One night our neighbors from the Menerville sector sent an ambulance escorted by a scout car to Algiers for an emergency case. As the cars were passing under a railroad bridge, they were fired upon by rebels stationed on the bridge. A doctor and two soldiers were killed. The rebels did not even attempt to finish the job and to take arms and ammunition.

The Algiers–Tizi Ouzou railroad crosses several viaducts between Haussonvilliers and Mirabeau, which would have been very easy to sabotage, particularly since, for some reason, they were not guarded. Yet no attempt was ever made by the rebels.

Operations

In the northern part of the sector, there was seldom any need for operations involving more than a battalion; this happened only when rebels were thought to be hidden in the Bou Berak forest. The usual activity consisted of sorties by platoons and companies.

Encounters with rebels were extremely rare. One morning while most of my battalion was away, I learned that the G.M.P.R. from Djinet had made contact with a group of rebels in the hamlet of Ain

El Amrah (6 km north of Bordj Menaiel). I alerted the Gendarmes Mobiles Company at Les Issers and rushed to the place. Captain Victor,* the G.M.P.R. commander, told me that, while patrolling the area at night with part of his unit, he had been fired at from inside the hamlet at about 2 a.m. He had encircled the place and waited until daylight to search it. His radio had broken down, which explained why he had not reported the incident at once.

When the Gendarmes Mobiles arrived, I organized the search in the usual *bouclage*-and-*ratissage* fashion. An L-19 observation plane placed at my disposal by the sector reached me, and I ordered the pilot to watch for rebels who might have escaped through the G.M.P.R. ring and might be spotted in the denuded terrain. The Gendarmes Mobiles, moving from Hill 195 southeast of the hamlet, started combing toward the Djinet–Bordj Menaiel highway. They had almost reached the road when shots were heard.

Within a few minutes two gendarmes were dead, and another was heavily wounded (he died while we called a helicopter to pick him up). The first gendarme had been killed at point-blank range from behind a thick screen of reeds covering the banks of a small *wadi*; the second gendarme had rushed up to help his comrade and was hit in the same way, and so also the third. The gendarmes captain and I arrived just in time to prevent another fool from exposing himself in the same way. We laid a heavy blanket of fire over the reeds and thus retrieved safely the bodies of our men.

The *wadi*, I could see now, was in fact a deep trench; a man posted in it would be well protected and could fire with much safety against any comer. I had lost enough valuable men. I radioed for a light tank and a sound truck, which arrived after half an hour. I massed two platoons on the north side of the *wadi*. With the sound truck I asked the rebels to give up, promising them life; to give them an idea of what they faced otherwise, the tank, the gendarmes' half tracks, and all our automatic weapons fired into the reeds. Nothing happened. I repeated the appeal, with no better result. Then, firing as they advanced and throwing grenades into the *wadi*, my men reached the reeds and killed three *fellaghas*, one of whom was identified later as a sergeant.

We found only two weapons. A gendarme swore he had seen a *fellagha* armed with a U.S. carbine when his colleagues had been hit. We looked everywhere for the carbine, going over the ground inch by inch. We did not find it. I left the G.M.P.R. to continue the search; they were equally unsuccessful.

Gendarmes Mobiles are an elite troop meant for the maintenance of order. Each gendarme is a carefully selected NCO. How wasteful, I felt, to use them as ordinary infantry when we were all so short of NCOs.

Operations in the Ali Bou Nab part of the sector were naturally different in scope and nature. There were two types of operations:

1. From the crest down on either side, combing one or more ravines. This was rather easy and required no more than a battalion, including the *bouclage* party at the bottom. But since troops had to be sent up the ridge by truck prior to the operation, surprise was seldom achieved. Nonetheless, operations rarely ended with a blank score, so numerous were the *fellaghas* in the area.

2. Along the crest, eastward or westward. This required considerably more than a battalion because of the *bouclage* demands. The *ratissage* units had to watch out against being fired upon by rebels stationed on the lateral branches of the ridge; they often waited until our column was well engaged and then fired from the rear if we had not been cautious. We proceeded generally by echelons, each covering the one ahead.

One day I was making a feint with my battalion in order to prepare the area for a much larger operation organized by the zone. Advancing along the crest, we met a full *katiba* armed with automatic rifles. The rebels shot at my scouts from less than 200 yards and by chance did not hit. Also by chance, my artillery liaison officer brought his first salvo right onto them. Most of the *fellaghas* retreated precipitously toward the bottoms on both slopes, where I could not follow them without widely dispersing the battalion and losing control of our intended maneuver.

At that point, our air force (one L-19 directing and T-6s attacking) took over, and either strafed the *fellaghas* with rockets and machine guns or directed the artillery fire. We spent that day 500 shells (105mm) and I don't know how many rockets. We found the bodies of three rebels. In my report on the operation I compared the price of our ammunition with the result and suggested that perhaps offering 500,000 francs (1,000 dollars) to each *fellagha* who surrendered with his weapon might be a cheaper and more effective way. The idea was forwarded to Algiers, examined, and rejected for the following reason: if we gave a premium to *fellaghas* who surrendered, what would we give to the Moslems fighting on our side?

The rebels were generally sparing with their ammunition, particularly with their automatic weapons. After a brief initial burst, the rebel carrying the automatic rifle usually withdrew under the protection of the others. The effect of the border fences was beginning to tell, and in May 1958 we found for the first time an automatic rifle hidden in a cache. We learned from prisoners that the *katiba* was very short of cartridges and had to hide many weapons.

The Struggle Against the OPA

Captured guerrillas and seized documents were the main sources of intelligence on the OPA in the sector. They always led to the arrest of a large number of FLN supporters, who were kept in extremely decent conditions in a small camp organized and managed by the sector intelligence officer on a farm north of Bordj Menaiel. However, since there was no follow-through on our part to prevent the cells from being rebuilt, the stream of arrested rebel agents never ceased. The sector intelligence officer claimed that the quality of the rebel agents deteriorated, and that the second-generation cell was never as efficient as the original one. He admitted, however, that the level of efficiency of the third- and fourth-generation cells, although low, was sufficient to keep the population under the rebels' control.

Identifying the OPA members in the north area of the sector was a difficult matter simply because guerrillas were not very active there and we consequently had few opportunities to catch prisoners. I had long wanted to try an idea which could not be put to the test in my

Aissa Mimoun *sous-quartier* because of its small size. One night, just after an operation conducted by the zone south of Ali Bou Nab, in which we had killed or captured about sixty rebels, I sent a group of pseudo-*fellaghas* all the way from Bordj Menaiel to Djinet. I used for the purpose a team of *harkis* from Ouled El Hadj under a Corsican sergeant who could pass for a Kabyle (as long as he kept his mouth shut); they wore *fellagha* clothes and badges and carried captured weapons. On reaching a village, they were to claim that their band had just been dispersed with heavy losses and they were trying to regroup by contacting the local guerrilla leader.

This raid proved to me how weak was the OPA in the north part of our sector. The villagers were very lukewarm in their attitude toward my pseudo-*fellaghas*, and those who showed the most enthusiasm did not know how to contact the local guerrilla gang. How easy it would have been to pacify solidly this Arab-populated area.

I was planning to repeat the performance in the Ali Bou Nab, using this time my Aissa Mimoun *harkis*, when I was transferred to Paris.

The 2d Company of my II/9th R.I.C. battalion was concentrated at that time on a farm near Bordj Menaiel, undergoing a training period to become the sector's *"commando de chasse."* By order of Algiers, each sector was to organize one such commando, which was supposed to be constantly on the move tracking the *fellaghas*, destroying the small bands when they could, or reporting their movements if they felt they could not do the job alone. This order came as a result of a successful experiment conducted in another part of Algeria.

I studied the training manual and found that its main concern was military technique; once more the population aspect was ignored. In order to impress on the company the necessity of not antagonizing the civilian population, and if possible winning it over, I organized a four-day operation in the easy part of the sector in conjunction with the 1st Company already stationed there. I also wanted to stress the need for surprise and feints.

On the afternoon of D-Day, which was Joan of Arc Day (a legal holiday in France), the 2d Company went to Djinet, where the G.M.P.R. had organized a feast for the population. The soldiers paraded in their dress uniforms and went to the beach for a swim. Just before sunset the men boarded the trucks, changed rapidly on the way into their combat fatigues, and were dropped truck by truck along the road to Bordj Menaiel. They laid ambushes during that night at various spots in the low hills between Ouled Ali and Douar Raicha; the G.M.P.R. and the 1st Company also set up ambushes in their *sous-quartiers*.

At dawn on D-Plus-1, we combed the bed of Oued Aoudja, the G.M.P.R. closing the north, the 1st Company the south and west, and the 2d Company doing the *ratissage* from the head of the ravine down. The units were ostensibly disbanded after the operation and returned to their camps.

The 2d Company went back to the area just before sunset and settled by platoons in four hamlets. They remained there for three days, carrying out a program of contact with the population: they conducted the first census, spread information and propaganda, cleaned the hamlets, fixed the wells, and helped the farmers.

I expected no result from this one-shot affair other than training the 2d Company for its future tasks. And this, I believe, I achieved; for the French soldiers, once in contact with the population, gave way to their normal fraternizing tendencies and easily fell in with the game. To my surprise, however, the zone looked on the operation as a model of how to win over the population, and gave wide and—to my view— misleading publicity to my experiment. No, a population cannot be pacified in three days. I don't know of any shortcut.

The Problem of the European Settlers

There had not been a single European in my former Aissa Mimoun area. Here in the Bordj Menaiel sector lived several thousands of them, who, by their mere presence, complicated the situation.

All shades of opinions existed among them in regard to the basic colonial dispute with the Moslems, from ultra-conservative to advanced liberal. Within limits, of course; for, while I never met the kick-the-native type of *colon*, neither did I meet one who contemplated the possibility of an Algeria entirely controlled by Arabs. They all made a distinction between the masses of Moslems, with whom they got along reasonably well, and the minority of rebels to whom they were unanimously opposed, at least outwardly. (Some *colons*, among them the most vociferous anti-rebels, were caught in 1959 paying money to the FLN to protect their farms. If a terrorist organization can achieve such results against its basic enemy, one can easily imagine how much more it can achieve against people who are in theory its basic allies.)

Being the political, economic, and cultural leaders in their townships, the Europeans exerted a great deal of influence over the Moslems, if only because they were the largest employers. The wages they paid were considerably higher than what native farmers gave to their workers. And they paid regularly. The two most influential men at Bordj Menaiel were two Europeans, the mayor and the veterinarian. The mayor, an old man in his sixties, lived very simply with an old sister. It was rumored that his farm brought him an annual income of 40,000 dollars. He spent most of it building his political machine among Arab voters. He knew a lot but kept his information to himself. The veterinarian was used by the rural Moslems as an unofficial referee in their frequent squabbles. He also knew a lot and at first co-operated with the intelligence officer; but when he found that his tips were not used or that we bungled in their exploitation, he clammed up.

The Europeans participated in the defense system. Those living on their farms had been armed with submachine guns and grenades in addition to their own shotguns. They were authorized to arm some of the Moslem workers who were their responsibility. They were provided with flares for signaling attacks at night. Some of the strategically located farms had special radio sets monitored constantly at Bordj Menaiel. In case of attack, the *colon* had only to press a button on his set; a bell would ring and a red light flash at the monitoring station, and the intervention platoon that was on duty every night would rush to the scene on half tracks. This never happened while I was in the sector. The rebels never attacked farms, they only infiltrated at night, cut fruit trees or grapevines, and burned haystacks and farm equipment. The losses were often extensive and the *colons* screamed for more protection; they complained loudly about the inefficiency of the army.

They all wanted army units stationed on their farms at harvest time, which was impossible for us to do.

At Bordj Menaiel, all the European males between 25 and 40 belonged to the *Unité Territoriale*. The chief of the U.T. was a school-teacher, a lieutenant in the reserves. Every day he made a list of about ten men who took duty at night. They collected their weapons (army rifles and obsolete submachine guns) from the local police station and manned an observatory on top of the water tower; they also patrolled the town at night. Bordj Menaiel being the command post of both the 9th R.I.C. and its 2d Battalion with their command, support, and service companies, soldiers were not lacking for the immediate security of the town; the U.T. was useless under these conditions. It would have been wiser on our part to move some of the service units out of Bordj Menaiel to less well-garrisoned villages and to use the U.T. to its full potential. This reform had to wait until a new colonel took over the sector in 1959.

Terrorism

The level of terrorist activity in Bordj Menaiel had been low and irregular until the spring of 1958. The shape of the town, spread as it was along the main highway and a parallel road to the south, did not lend itself to easy escape. Every perpendicular street leading to the Moslem quarters was barred with barbed wire or mobile obstructions. Most terrorists so far had been caught in the act, a fact which did not fan the ardor of the others. But, as in Tizi Ouzou, the rebels still managed occasionally to persuade some fool from a remote village who did not know about this to try his luck at the game. The attempt consisted almost invariably at throwing a grenade at random, preferably into a European shop.

Two weeks after the May 13 revolution, the local rebels, who had been stunned by the event and by the reaction of the Moslem population, began to realize that control of the masses was definitely slipping away from their grip. Terrorism was the normal remedy, and this time the rebels were determined to use it at any cost, with their own *fellaghas* if necessary. The terrorist wave lasted a month, with a total of twelve to fifteen attempts. Some were perfunctory, as when grenades were twice thrown from the street across the wall into the stadium where some of our soldiers were billeted. An offensive grenade in a crowded café fortunately failed to explode. The small hotel where I was staying at the time with my wife received a grenade causing extensive damage but no injury. In two cases the terrorists resorted to murdering isolated Europeans. Thus the caretaker of the cemetery, an old man of more than seventy, was found dead one morning among the graves, his head bashed in and his throat cut. The European population was particularly incensed, as we all were. In order to impress the Moslem population, the sector psychological officer announced all over town that he was willing to meet alone any rebel who would take up his challenge. "If they are not all cowards, let them come. I will wait for them at the cemetery every morning between 6 and 8." And so he did. The gesture was theatrical and rather reminiscent of "High Noon," but it did impress the Moslems.

Preventing terrorism, as opposed to catching the terrorist *after the act*, is no doubt the most difficult task in counterinsurgency. Even with the full co-operation of the population, spotting and catching the insurgent before he commits a terrorist act is almost impossible. I therefore can see no alternative to a certain degree of regimentation, until the population can be counted on to report immediately every unfamiliar face in the village and every suspicious move by a neighbor. Lest the term be misconstrued, "regimenting" in this context means the setting up of organizations such as the "Dispositif de Protection Urbaine" (see p. 152), with committees and leaders for every district, street, and even building.

But we were far from having reached this stage at Bordj Menaiel; a reliable census of the population did not even exist. We could do nothing beyond the elementary precautions such as constant patrolling, checking systematically or at random people in the streets, and searching the Moslems who came to town.

The local Sûreté, in charge of intelligence work in the town, succeeded, but only after these events, in dismantling the terrorist cell in Bordj Menaiel, whose members were given away by spontaneous informers, a good sign that the climate had changed in our favor.

Successful Operations by the Former 45th B.I.C. Companies

In January 1958, when Captain Peretti* and his 2d Company moved from Akaoudj in the Aissa Mimoun to his new *sous-quartier* around Tala Mokhor (just south of the Litama Forest), which now was included in the Bordj Menaiel sector, he was assured by his predecessors that it was an easy *sous-quartier*, well pacified, very quiet. Peretti* began to entertain some doubts when he discovered that the population census was practically nonexistent. Doubts gave way to certainty when he set up numerous night ambushes, as he was used to doing in his former area. He soon had one, two, three clashes with *fellaghas*. He decided to concentrate his efforts on military operations for a while, and thus he upset the status quo. As he told me later, a tacit agreement must have been in force between his predecessors and the rebels, unconsciously on the part of the former, consciously on the part of the latter. For the rebels the Litama Forest was an important stepping stone between the Djebels in the south and the large Mizrana Forest in the north; they had no interest in stirring up trouble there. Peretti's* predecessors had mistaken the apparent quiet for a serious achievement in pacification.

Peretti* succeeded, within a month, in killing a dozen *fellaghas*, losing in the process one NCO and one soldier and having three others wounded. He discovered a depot of brand-new German-made surgical equipment; in a swampy island 3 km north of Guynemer, he found a large cache of food and shoes; in the reeds, barely 100 yards from the much-travelled Tizi Ouzou–Algiers highway, he seized a stock of cartridges and grenades.

He proceeded next to impose his will on the population by ordering various tasks done in the villages; he rapidly took a thorough census; he eliminated the OPA by using the methods I have already described. Simultaneously he opened schools and dispensaries, got money from the local SAS, and had the villagers build a motor road from Sidi Namane to Tala Mokhor. Elections of *commune* officials were under way when the May 13 revolution radically improved the situation. Late in May 1958, the new mayor of Tala Mokhor assembled on his own initiative the entire population of the *commune*, invited Captain Peretti* to the meeting, and delivered the most stirring speech I ever heard or read in all my years in Algeria. I deeply regret having lost its text, but I can give the substance of the mayor's speech:

> We were told, and we believed, that the French were colonialist oppressors. We have seen with our own eyes what you have done for us here. You never molested us. None of your soldiers ever cast an eye on our women. Far from stealing from us, they shared their food with the poor. Our sick are taken care of, our children are educated, schools and roads are being built. Recently you had the people elect freely their own leaders and we are now planning with you how to improve our life. If this is colonial oppression, then in the name of all the people here I want to thank the French Army for it. Speaking for all of us, I want to tell you that we will help you finish with the criminals who misled us. Just give us the weapons.

"He said it so plainly, it was so obvious that it came from the depth of his heart, that many of my soldiers had tears in their eyes," said Peretti.* "The war is won now; with de Gaulle back in power it will be only a matter of a short time before it's all over."

Late in 1958 Peretti* was moved again with his company, to a new *sous-quartier* east of Ouled El Hadj in the Ali Bou Nab. Once more he had to start from scratch. He was exhausted from a recurrent amoebic dysentery he had caught in Indochina. His cadres were discouraged at being moved from one area to another just as they had become deeply attached to the local people and were reaping the benefit of their hard work. When Peretti's* time was up (30 months in Algeria for a captain), he did not apply for an extension of his tour and went home.

What I have just described for Captain Peretti* also fits Lieutenant Bravard* of our former 1st Company at Sidi Namane. Only Bravard* did not return home; he was assassinated by an obscure terrorist in Tizi Ouzou.

II. The Revolution of May 13 and Its Aftermath

On May 9, 1958, I was sent to attend a short course in air support given in Algiers, a welcome assignment because it meant that my wife could join me there from Paris. I was billeted at the officers club, which had been an old Janissary barracks under the Turks, with walls so thick that the rooms were pleasantly cool and soundproof.

The air-support course was supposedly designed for majors and lieutenant-colonels, yet it differed in no way from the elementary course given to junior officers. This caused some initial grumblings, but we were all set to enjoy this break from Djebel life.

Algiers was boiling at the time. The manner in which Prime Minister Felix Gaillard had handled the Sakiet Sidi Youssef incident with Tunisia (first supporting and then disavowing the French Command in Algeria), another long cabinet crisis with the same old agonizing reappraisal of our policy in Algeria, the announcement by the FLN organization abroad that four French prisoners held in Tunisia had been condemned to death and executed, all this had raised to a high pitch the irritation of the population. M. Robert Lacoste had warned against a possible "diplomatic Dien Bien Phu."

To us officers in the field, popular agitation was so much nonsense. We all realized that the system was rotten, and we deplored it freely and openly in our mess talks. But long traditions of political aloofness and our more pressing tasks at hand kept us from active meddling in politics. I remember a lunch one day at my 45th Battalion command post when a captain said:

"How long are we going to bear this? I am going to do something if nobody does. Who wants to join me in plotting a coup d'état?"

Major Renard* stopped him cold:

"If you are joking, I think it's a bad joke. If you are not, then you have eight days of house arrest. Which is it?"

Looking at a group of European shopkeepers closing their stores after a strike order in Algiers, Major Le Guen,* an old friend I had met at the course, exclaimed:

"These bastards who scream so much, why don't they come and fight with us in the Djebels instead? What do they hope to achieve with strikes and demonstrations?"

"You never know what may happen," I replied, "remember how ripe tomatoes and rotten eggs once changed the government's policy."

Le Guen* was furious because the announced general strike had spoiled our plan for a family dinner at his home in the outskirts of Algiers.

At around 6 that evening, my wife and I were sitting on the terrace of the club, overlooking the Place du Gouvernement, chatting with another couple, when we saw a procession of civilians following a flag and a civilian brass band and marching back to Bab El Oued, the "*pieds-noirs*" stronghold. Young men riding motor scooters were darting around sounding Ti Ti Ti Ta Ta (Algérie Française) with their horn. We went to bed early in the soundproof Janissary rooms.

When I ordered my breakfast in the dining room the next morning, my eyes fell on the huge headline in *Le Journal d'Alger*: "Revolution in Algiers," "Population Storms Government Building," "Salan Heads Committee of Public Welfare." How mortifying to have slept bourgeois-fashion through a revolution!

A feeling of intense jubilation seized Algiers instantly. No one had a clear idea of where the event would lead us, but at least we were heading somewhere. Every night huge crowds, mostly Europeans, converged on the "Forum," a square in front of the Government Building, and listened to passionate oratory. On May 16, if I remember well, a major event took place. Out of the Kasbah marched tens of thousands of Moslems, the veterans in front with flags and all medals showing on their chest. They marched to the Forum shouting "Algérie Française," "Long Live the Army," "Long Live France." On the way, European men and women joined the column, hugging the Moslems and fraternally mixing with them. The enthusiasm was indescribable. It was as if a long nightmare had suddenly ended. At the Forum, Moslem women tore off their veils, proclaiming their determination hereafter to live like French women.

Lt. Bauer,* the SAS officer in Aissa Mimoun, had for some months been head of an SAS in Algiers' Kasbah.

"This looks terribly impressive, but how sincere, how genuine is it?" I asked him the next day.

"Do you believe we could have organized such a demonstration? Last week it would have taken a whole division to move the Moslems from the Kasbah. Today they have understood, rightly or wrongly, that the Army has assumed power, and that's enough for them. They know that, for a change, we are going to follow a straight line and finish with the FLN once and for all. They are more interested in peace than in anything else. Since they sense that now we can bring peace soon, they have rejected fence-sitting and committed themselves on our side."

When General Salan one day shouted "Long Live de Gaulle" from the balcony of the Government Building, almost as an afterthought, enthusiasm rose still higher among the Moslems. For what would de Gaulle's policy be if not to keep Algeria French and to guarantee a fair deal to the Moslems?

My air-support course went on as usual. A bombing demonstration was cancelled solely in order to save ammunition, for Algeria was now cut off from France. I returned to Bordj Menaiel with my wife, who was now stranded in Algeria. I found most of my battalion gone; it had been sent to the outskirts of Algiers, officially to help maintain order in case of need, in reality, as I learned later, to watch a paratrooper unit and prevent any coup on its part. For in fact, and contrary to later legends, Salan's main concern was to maintain republican legality in Algeria and to keep his links with whatever government ruled in Paris. It was with the government's approval that he had agreed to lead Algeria's Committee of Public Welfare, "the only way to prevent bloodshed with the European masses." Indeed, he had thrown into confinement several political agitators who had rushed to Algiers from France at the news of the revolution.

M. Vignon was the only *préfet* in Algeria who opposed the coup. His courage and resolution won him, however, the grudging admiration of the Army. He called upon a company of Gendarmes Mobiles to protect the Préfecture at Tizi Ouzou. Seeing that even the gendarmes, the defenders of legality, sided with the revolution, he succeeded in foxing General Guerin and escaped in his car toward the Djurdjura Mountains. He was finally caught after an epic chase which lasted several days, and was sent to Algiers under escort and finally shipped home. General Guerin was now the military and civilian chief of Kabylia.

Committees of Public Welfare sprang up everywhere. Every village in Aissa Mimoun had one, and among their first decisions was to march to Tizi Ouzou and demonstrate for my immediate appointment as *préfet* of Kabylia! I felt greatly honored, but asked my successor, Hermann,* to stop them.

The sector commander designated me as his representative to the Bordj Menaiel C.S.P. (Committee of Public Welfare). The committee was born spontaneously in the early hours of May 14. One of the local schoolteachers heard on the radio the news of the events in Algiers; he woke up his colleagues and they went to the *mairie*. A group of Europeans and Moslems had had the same idea, and soon the committee was in business with eight Europeans and four Moslems.

The first days were spent drafting motions and sending cables to the C.S.P.s of Algeria, to General Salan, and to the President of the Republic. The European members of the committee also engaged in a feud with the town's mayor, and they tried to drag me into it. I slowly channeled the energy toward more practical matters. Order was prevailing all over Algeria, normal authorities were in place everywhere, and there was no point in trying to substitute for them. The C.P.S., to me, was a heaven-sent device through which we could link more closely the authorities and the population on the one hand, and the Europeans and the Moslems on the other. It could be used as the core for a Dispositif de Protection Urbaine against terrorism. The sector commander was skeptical, but he agreed to give me a free hand (under his control, of course).

I enlarged the number of Moslems in the committee to parity with the Europeans. French women were persuaded to hold open house for the Moslem ones. Civilians of both races visited our Army posts and invited soldiers to their homes. This may seem little, but it was in fact an extraordinary change.

My main concern, however, was to make the population participate effectively in the struggle against the FLN and, first of all, against the terrorists. Some Moslems, not many, had already volunteered to join the U.T. What I wanted was an extensive street organization with a net of reliable informants able to spot immediately any suspicious activities. For that I was dependent on a great deal of support from the Moslem population.

The psychological impact of the revolution in Algiers had been slow in reaching the town of Bordj Menaiel, more so than in the countryside around it. Although rebel activity had stopped almost entirely, the bulk of the Moslems in the town was still not budging. Perhaps, if they could see how people had reacted in other areas, they would abandon their noncommittal attitude. Through the C.P.S. I organized a mass meeting at the local stadium. I called on my Aissa Mimoun supporters to help. They came in huge numbers with their new self-defense corps, the mayors wearing their official insignia, they brought all the schoolchildren and even some women (something unheard-of before). The committee had planned to have the crowd in the stadium and the official people in the stands, but a gay disorder upset all the arrangements, and soon everybody was mingling with everybody. General Guerin, who had come for the occasion, was lost in a sea of Kabyles, the *sous-préfet* was hopelessly trying to make his way, my wife and other French women were surrounded by hosts of Arabs.

Kabyle mayors, the president of the C.P.S., and General Guerin made speeches. One of the Kabyle orators (they have an innate gift for rhetoric) said:

> If colonialism means that people from one country go to another country to make money and bring it home, then who is colonizing whom? Not only do the French bring money here, as you all know, but hundreds of thousands of us go to France to make money to send home.

And another, Azem Ouali, a worker who had educated himself in France and became a member of the French Parliament in 1958:

> The Seine River cuts across Paris, the Mediterranean Sea cuts across France.

Just before General Guerin's speech, twenty rebel political agents were set free in front of the crowd. They had had no idea of what we were planning to do with them when we loaded them in a truck to bring them to the stadium, and their happy surprise was not faked.

After the speeches somebody grabbed the microphone and shouted: "Let's go to the War Memorial." We went there in the same euphorious mood.

It was difficult to judge the effect of the show. During the speeches at the stadium I kept my eyes on the local Moslems to watch their reactions. Some were visibly impressed, but most of them looked simply curious.

It was announced a week later that General Salan and M. Soustelle would preside at a mass meeting at Tizi Ouzou. It was then that I began to feel the concrete effects of my own mass meeting. Moslem employers in Bordj Menaiel came to the C.P.S. and said they would give a paid holiday to their workers so that they could go to Tizi Ouzou. All the Moslem truck and bus owners offered free transportation. The Army also provided trucks. I had insisted, and won my point, that under no circumstances would Moslems be forced to attend the meeting. This was the only way to assess their feelings objectively. It turned out that our transport provisions were largely inadequate. There was such a monstrous traffic jam around Tizi Ouzou that people had to disembark and walk several kilometers to reach the town.

The crowd was so dense in the Place de la Mairie that policemen could not make way for General Salan and M. Soustelle, who had to dive into the crowd, pushed here and there by Kabyles anxious to touch them and shake hands with them. When Salan finally reached the *mairie* and started speaking from the balcony, a grenade exploded in the crowd. I could see from my vantage point on the steps of the *mairie* where the grenade had exploded. A panic would have been terrible, but nobody moved, there was no stampede. Salan stigmatized the terrorists and promised stern measures against them. A roar of approval greeted his words.

I was invited after the meeting to attend a reception in the *mairie* with the C.P.S. members. General Allard, the Algiers Army Corps commander, spotted me:

"Look here, Galula, what's this story about your going to the Psychological Warfare Bureau in Algiers?"

"First I've heard of it, Sir."

"They want you there, but I won't let you go. You have a more useful job here."

A cable arrived from Paris in the middle of June 1958. I was assigned to the Psychological Action Branch, Ministry of Defense, and was to take up my new post immediately. "Nothing doing," fulminated my new sector commander, "there is a rule that says an officer in the field in Algeria cannot leave until his replacement has arrived."

General Guerin called me the same week. Now that he was both zone commander and *préfet*, he wanted me to take over the civilian part of his job. My title would be Secretary General of the Préfecture. It was very tempting, but I decided to let my superiors fight it out among themselves. Paris finally won.

When I took leave of Colonel Giraud,* the new Bordj Menaiel sector commander, he told me:

"All this excitement about French Algeria and integration is very interesting, but I don't believe anything serious will ever come out of it. Sure, for the first time four *fellaghas* surrendered this month in the sector, but I do not see the masses of Kabyles here moving any closer to us. It's all bluff."

In September 1958, a referendum on the subject of the new Constitution took place in France and in every French territory overseas, including Algeria. The referendum had a special meaning in the colonial territories, for de Gaulle had already indicated that a negative vote would be interpreted as a vote for independence, which would be immediately granted. (Only Guinea voted "no.") In Algeria, which technically was not a colony, the issue was nevertheless the same. A "yes" vote would mean a French Algeria, a "no" vote an FLN Algeria.

The FLN had threatened death to any Moslem who voted. They later amended their order and requested that every Moslem vote "no" and keep a "yes" bulletin as a proof. Because of the FLN threat and the possibility of sabotage on the part of the rebels, the voting in Algeria was spread over three days and took place area by area, so that the French forces could give protection to the rural voters.

After the referendum I received a letter from the sector commander. He was flabbergasted, he wrote. He had expected few voters to show up at the polls, and in any case had foreseen a massive "no." But all the voters came. He had the largest turnout in the zone. Even Krim Belkacem's father had come out of hiding to vote, and he publicly voted "yes." "I'll be damned," concluded Colonel Giraud.*

What an irony that one of the least pacified sectors of Kabylia had so catapulted itself into the forefront. And what a lesson, for what ultimately counted most was not the tenacious, dedicated effort of officers in the field but a sudden political change at the top. This battle for the minds of the people, which I believe I had won in my Aissa Mimoun area when the situation was black or grey everywhere else in Kabylia, a revolution in Algiers won in a single stroke.

What happened thereafter in Algeria is another story, which I will not attempt to relate.

PART FIVE

Conclusions

I. Major Factors in the Algerian War

Every war is a special case, and the Algerian rebellion does not escape this rule even though it belongs in the general category of post–World War II revolutionary war. The important geographic factors, for one thing, are different in every instance. Thus, the proximity of Algeria to France (five hours by plane, thirty hours by ship) was in our favor: psychologically, because French public opinion was obviously more interested in events there than it had been in so remote a theater as Indochina; physically, because Algeria was so close to the center of France's power and resources (it was possible to airlift units of Gendarmes Mobiles on very short notice). On the other hand, the size of the territory, the density and the dispersion of the rural population, the long borders with Tunisia and Morocco, and in some parts the difficult terrain, all worked against us.

In drawing general conclusions from my experience, therefore, one has to note what was specific to the Algerian case, singling out the factors that influenced the struggle one way or the other. The following, though by no means all, are among the most important of these factors:

1. **The political instability in France and the absence of a firm, continuing, clear cut policy on the part of the various French governments all through the war.**

2. **Our truly enormous material superiority over the rebels.** Once it began to bear upon the struggle, i.e., after 1956, its sheer weight was bound to produce results in spite of all our political, ideological, and tactical handicaps. It compensated largely for any of our errors in command at the bottom and at the top levels. When the period of muddling through was over, that is, when the Challe Plan (actually drawn up by Salan) was implemented in 1959, our strength was such that the war had been won for all practical purposes, especially if the impact of the May 13 revolution on the Moslem population is taken into account.

I realize this sounds odd when one looks at the situation of Algeria today. Yet if experts such as Hanson Baldwin (who asserts flatly that the French lost the war in Algeria) took the trouble of comparing our results in the first six years of the war—from the end of 1954 to the end of 1960—with the British achievements in Malaya—a successful counterinsurgency in their judgment and mine—during the same lapse of time, they would perhaps see my point. When General de Gaulle decided publicly in 1960 to "disengage France from Algeria," the rebel forces had been cut down to between eight and nine thousand men with 6,500 weapons, most of which were buried. Not a single *Wilaya* was in contact with the FLN headquarters in Tunisia, not even by radio. The rate of rebel actions had fallen to two a day for the entire Oran Army Corps area, purges were devastating the depleted ranks of the rebels, and some of the high-ranking FLN chiefs in Algeria made overtures to surrender (and were spurned by General de Gaulle). There was no limit to the number of Moslems we could have recruited for our forces; we had already more than 100,000 at the time, not counting village self-defense groups. The borders were absolutely closed to infiltration. All that remained to do was to eliminate the die-hard rebel remnants, who were cut off from the population and largely ineffective but still at large because of the size of Algeria and its terrain. In Malaya, this final phase of the counterinsurgency lasted at least five years, and even today, I am told, thirty communist rebels are still surviving in the jungle, not counting those on the Thai border. A counterinsurgency seldom ends with a ceasefire and a triumphal parade.

3. **The enormous psychological superiority of the rebels.** This was basically a colonial war on our part and a war for independence on the part of the FLN. What with the "tide of history," the scales were tipped against us.

4. **The legacy of conventional warfare thinking in our camp.** The majority of us realized that the population was the objective, but it took a rather long time to adapt our tactics to the fact.

5. **The poor leadership at all echelons in the rebel camp.** An example: in 1959, Amirouche, the chief of *Wilaya* III (Kabylia) and another *Wilaya* chief were killed in an ambush while on their way to Tunisia. Amirouche carried an important document listing all that was

wrong with the FLN's conduct of the war. He complained in particular about the fact that, five years after the beginning of the rebellion, the FLN had been unable to come out with a postwar political platform. (It still hasn't.) Amirouche was entirely right, so right that we put a top-secret label on the document and kept it safely locked. Amirouche was also complaining that guerrilla warfare and terrorism would never bring a victory, and he recommended the creation of a powerful regular army in Algeria by merging the existing small units. He was entirely wrong, and this was a part of his recommendations that we leaked to the FLN because it suited us so well.

II. Basic Principles of Counterinsurgent Warfare

Nevertheless, the fact remains that the war in Algeria broadly conformed to the characteristics of revolutionary war, and the essential "laws" of counterinsurgent warfare, as I see them, had to be respected by us. In all probability these laws will apply to counterinsurgencies elsewhere.

The first law. The objective is the population. The population is at the same time the real terrain of the war. (Destruction of the rebel forces and occupation of the geographic terrain led us nowhere as long as we did not control and get the support of the population.) This is where the real fighting takes place, where the insurgent challenges the counterinsurgent, who cannot but accept the challenge.

The second law. The support from the population is not spontaneous, and in any case must be organized. It can be obtained only through the efforts of the minority among the population that favors the counterinsurgent.

The third law. This minority will emerge, and will be followed by the majority, only if the counterinsurgent is seen as the ultimate victor. If his leadership is irresolute and incompetent, he will never find a significant number of supporters. The necessity for an early partial success by the counterinsurgent is obvious.

The fourth law. Seldom is the material superiority of the counterinsurgent so great that he can literally saturate the entire territory. The means required to destroy or expel the main guerrilla forces, to control the population, and to win its support are such that, in most cases, the counterinsurgent will be obliged to concentrate his efforts area by area.

As the war lasts, the war itself becomes the central issue and the ideological advantage of the insurgent decreases considerably. The population's attitude is dictated not by the intrinsic merits of the contending causes, but by the answer to these two simple questions:

Which side is going to win?

Which side threatens the most, and which offers the most protection?

This is the reason why a counterinsurgency is never lost *a priori* because of a supposedly unpopular regime.

As for me, I set out to prove a theory of counterinsurgency warfare, and I am satisfied that it worked in my small area. What I achieved in my first six or eight months in the Djebel Aissa Mimoun was not due to magic and could have been applied much earlier throughout Algeria.

Appendixes

Appendix 1

Mohamed Boudiaf's Statement to *Le Monde*
November 2, 1962

As a co-founder of the CRDA (Revolutionary Committee for Unity and Action), which provided the spark for the rebellion in Algeria, Mohamed Boudiaf is one of the so-called historic leaders of the FLN.

He was captured with Ben Bella and three other top rebel leaders at the end of 1956, treated as a political prisoner, and finally released in the spring of 1963 following the conclusion of the Evian agreement between France and the FLN.

When Ben Bella, whose star was already waning when he was captured, successfully seized power after Algeria became independent, Boudiaf broke openly with him and went to Paris to stir up opposition among the Algerian workers in France.

His statement to *Le Monde* gives a clear picture—from the horse's mouth, so to speak—of how sketchy was the rebels' plan and how small their means. Although Boudiaf obviously minimizes the role of Ben Bella and the Egyptians in the early days of the rebellion, the substance of his statement fits with the actual facts. It shows how much can be achieved by terrorism and the accompanying publicity when a revolutionary situation exists.

The FLN Plan for the Rebellion

One of the survivors of the "revolutionary committee for unity and action," M. Boudiaf, recalls the conditions under which the insurrection was launched on November 1, 1954.

[*Le Monde* writes: On November 1, 1954, the launching of the rebellion appeared as a "suicidal operation" in the eyes of the great majority of Algerian nationalists. Those who openly clamored for their country's independence condemned an action which, in their opinion, had no chance to succeed. We know the different views that at the time opposed M. Messali Hadj, president of the MTLD (Movement for the Triumph of Democratic Liberties), and those who, hostile to what they called "his dictatorship," are known as "centralists" (favorable to a central committee). We also recall the creation in 1948–49 of the OS (Special Organization) and, in the following years, the arrest of many of its members including Ben Bella, Ait Ahmed, and Khider. More secret remain the reasons that prompted the CRUA (Revolutionary Committee for Unity and Action) to start the insurrection on the morning of All Saints' Day.

One of the survivors of this Committee, and also one of the most notorious, M. Mohamed Boudiaf, former vice-president of the Algerian Republic Provisional Government and former member of the FLN political bureau—today in the opposition—is at present in Paris. During an interview with us, he related as follows the conditions under which the decision was taken by him and by his former friends. He assumes, of course, full responsibility for his assertions, which on various points are at variance with commonly accepted versions.]

"When the CRUA was created in March 1954 [he told us], there was no question for one second of creating a new movement; we were obsessed with the idea that the unity of the party (MTLD) had to be preserved at all cost; in order to rid it of its bureaucracy and impotence, we had to throw it into action; it was the only way to bring to the base a truer conception of things. We requested as an immediate step the meeting of a broad, free, and democratic congress."

"Who took part in this first CRUA?"

"Two former members of the OS—Ben Boulaid and myself, who was then a member of the Federation of France Secretariat—and two centralists—Dakhli, now a member of the FLN organization committee, and Moussa. We could not hold Messali's dictatorship in check without support from some centralists. They were indeed in control of the permanent members of the organization. Now, among these permanent members, very few joined our side then. The first practical initiative of the CRUA was to publish a bulletin, *The Patriot*, which was disseminated in a limited way in Algeria and not at all in France."

[*Le Monde:* During a meeting of twenty-two militant nationalists in Algiers at the end of May and the beginning of June 1954, it was decided to establish a collective leadership. On the second ballot and with a two-thirds majority, M. Boudiaf was chosen to select the members; he called on Didouche, Ben Boulaid, and Ben M'Hidi—all killed since—and on M. Bitat Rabah. It was only in August that the leadership committee members decided to include M. Belkacem Krim, who was already in the maquis in Kabylia. And M. Boudiaf, whose statements we have thus condensed, continues:]

"If I tell you all this, it is because this is the truth and not because I want to appear more 'historical' than others. The very reason why we had created the CRUA was to struggle against the idea of an 'historical' or legitimate leader. As far as 'historical leaders' are concerned, we were then young militant men, perfectly unknown. Ben Boulaid alone was a member of the central committee."

"How was contact established with the exiled nationalists in Cairo: Ben Bella, Ait Ahmed, and Khider?"

"This group, too, wanted to glue together the pieces of the party. They made contact, with no result, with Mezerna and Filali from the Messalist group, and with M. M'Hamed Yazid and Hocine Lahouel, both centralists. In July 1954, I saw Ben Bella at Berne. Things were beginning to become clearer; either we would constitute a third faction, which we did not want, or we had to start the action. The Cairo group gave its agreement, and I insisted on the fact that the leadership would, in any case, be collective. . . ."

Leaks Force Postponement of Target Date

"How and at what time was it decided to start the insurrection?"

"A first date was set, October 15, but there were leaks; some Moroccans and centralists learned about our intentions and we were forced to postpone our projects. The final date was selected on October 22. In order to safeguard secrecy, it was agreed that regional structures would be set up only two days before the start of the operations and that zone chiefs would receive the attack orders on the selected objectives only six hours before the action."

"Did the policy of M. Mendès-France's government, which was then in power, facilitate or hinder your action?"

"Without any doubt, it hindered us. Many among the militant pointed out that a peaceful solution was now possible. As far as we were concerned, this seemed to us a profound illusion, but this feeling existed nonetheless."

"What were your resources in men, weapons, and money?"

"Our resources were extraordinarily feeble. Our establishment was mediocre in the Oran region; in the Algiers region we had practically nothing south of Medea; the situation was better in Kabylia and in the south Constantine region. In France we did not exist. As for arms . . . , we had about four hundred fifty. Not a cent, not a weapon had been furnished from abroad, in spite of persistent efforts.* I had made contacts in Tunisia, in the Rif, in Tripoli, all in vain. We had even paid Moroccans for weapons which were never delivered. The situation was so desperate in some respects that a man responsible for the Oran region, Ben Abdel Malek, told us that there was nothing but to die fighting, which he did on November 1."

Three Steps Foreseen

"If such was the situation, why did you nevertheless make the decision to start the action?"

---

* This is a point on which M. Boudiaf's assertions are in flagrant contradiction to the most serious historians. There is no doubt whatsoever that during their stay in Cairo, M. Ben Bella, Ait Ahmed, and Khider received aid in money and equipment from Egypt where Nasser had just acceded to absolute power. (Note from *Le Monde*'s editor.)

"We hoped, without being certain of it, that the masses would enter into the game. One of two things: either they would do it and we would be justified; or they would not, and then our opponents from the MTLD, from the UDMA* and from the Algerian Communist Party would have been right. It would have been a suicidal operation. We firmly thought that the first hypothesis would be the right one.

"We foresaw three steps. The first one, purely military, would allow the creation of small groups, which would avoid frontal attacks and limit themselves to destruction and harassing operations. We would take advantage of this step to give military training to as large as possible a number of fellow citizens.

"The second step would see a general insecurity: attacks on public works and setting up of a clandestine organization—what was later called the OPA—the essential function of which would be to make the masses participate in the conduct of the insurrection.

"In the third step an embryo of a government would be established on a free base.

"You know that we were not able to adhere to this plan. We had no illusion anyway as far as the immediate future was concerned. In order to give the impression that we had an organization able to act anywhere at any time, we had planned a distribution of several pamphlets to be distributed at several days' interval. One announced the insurrection, another—the one published in Mandouze's work**—announced the creation of the FLN. In fact, both were distributed on November 1."

The Algerian Revolution and the Soummam Congress
"Did you on the eve of the insurrection have a precise idea of what should be the program for the Algerian revolution?"

"Frankly not, nothing precise outside of national independence and the will to make the masses participate in the insurrection. The word revolution, which is used in the pamphlet I was referring to, referred mostly to the way we wanted to conquer independence against a colonial apparatus, on the one hand through violence against the

---

* UDMA (Democratic Union for the Algerian Manifesto).

** *La Revolution Algerienne par les textes.* Francois Maspero, Editeur.

reformist and bureaucratic methods of the nationalist movement, on the other hand by exploding the old structures of this movement."

"What were the immediate results of the insurrection?"

"Disastrous in a large part of Algeria. In the Oran region, notably, the repression was extremely brutal and efficient. Boussouf at Marnia and Ben M'Hidi in the Nemours area alone were able to maintain themselves, but their coffers were empty and their weapons allotment was tragically insufficient. It was even impossible for me during the first two months to establish a liaison between the Rif [in Spanish Morocco] and the Oran region. In actual fact, in the Oran region, the Messalists rapidly regained control of the militant nationalists. The leadership of the insurrection was supposed to meet in Algiers on January 12, 1955; it could not do it. And yet, as you know, in spite of its setbacks, the movement kept going without interruption. But the masses joined only very gradually."

"Without going into the whole history of the FLN, and looking at the FLN of November 1, 1954, and the FLN of today, what do you think was the single most important event that affected it?"

"The real turn came during the Soummam Congress in August 1956. People have talked much about the 'platform' adopted at this Congress, which contains extremely positive elements. The real question, however, is not only to define a program, but to know who will implement it and how.

"One can say that, as of August 1956, roughly speaking, the FLN ceased to be a unitary organization and became a coalition, more precisely a 'front,' as its name indicates; the former members of the MTLD and the UDMA moved into the leadership organs without really renouncing their individuality. It was in 1956 that the Front of today, this magma, was constituted."

Appendix 2

Notes on Pacification in Greater Kabylia

This is a report that I wrote in November 1956 after three months of actual participation in counterinsurgent work in Algeria.

At the time, our large-scale military operations had achieved their aim, the rebel bands were shattered, and we were entering a new phase in the war. Yet the officers in the field were groping in the dark, with no instruction from above. I wanted to present a picture of the main problems as we were encountering them in the field.

The report was forwarded through regular channels and finally published in expurgated form in *Contact*, a restricted publication for the counterinsurgent cadres in Algeria.

Notes on Pacification in Greater Kabylia, November 1956

I have spent the past eleven years watching the Communists in action: in China, where I saw the triumph of their revolution, and in Greece, where I saw its failure. I have acquired in their school some theoretical experience of the so-called "revolutionary war." (I dislike that term because it automatically relegates us to the "counterrevolutionary" camp.)

As commander of a *sous-quartier* in Djebel Aissa Mimoun since the beginning of August this year, I have acquired some practical experience in this sort of war.

The following remarks are the result of both kinds of experience. In checking the locally gathered indications against the theory, I hope to be able to rise above the narrow framework of my *sous-quartier*, to analyze the causes of our success and failure, to give an overall judgment of our action in Greater Kabylia, and to offer, finally, a few concrete suggestions for improving our efficiency.

I. The Situation

I was pleasantly surprised, when I arrived in the Operational Zone of Kabylia (ZOK), to find that the principles of revolutionary warfare seemed to be generally understood and that considerable effort had been devoted to adapt our methods and our means to them. Thus:

- The ZOK, provided with a dense concentration of troops, was considered an experimental zone, which implies that we were planning to test in it a method, to revise this method according to the results, and, if successful, gradually to expand its application to other areas after having trained in Kabylia the necessary cadres.
- Our plan of action, as I reconstruct it, consisted in:
  1. destroying or expelling the large rebel bands.
  2. establishing ourselves in the villages in order to renew contacts with the population.
  3. controlling the population.
  4. winning it over.

What are the results today? I will deal mostly with my own *sous-quartier*, which I know very well, and with my battalion's *quartier* which I know well, using only a few pieces of outside information received from unimpeachable sources.

Point 1, requiring only purely military action, may be considered as entirely accomplished. Mere remnants of rebel bands remain in the area, incapable of action in strength. Within my *sous-quartier*, where I lay an average of four ambushes a night, only one of my patrols had the opportunity to fire a submachine gun burst at two shadows during the last three months. The fact remains, however, that these remnants, precisely because of their decreased size, are the most difficult to track, and their final elimination will have to wait until we reach the ultimate stage of our plan, when we will have the population co-operating with us.

Point 2 has been partially accomplished. Tactical and logistic difficulties have prevented us from establishing ourselves in every one of the villages, which are numerous and widely dispersed. But the main villages have been occupied. Thus, in my *sous-quartier* I have been able to install a platoon at Igonane Ameur and a squad at Agouni Taga, and I am closely watching Oumlil, another hamlet near my camp. Only Bou Souar and Azib Djalout escaped my authority, and they were naturally the rebels' favorite crossing and staying places. On November 10, I at last placed a platoon at Bou Souar.

Point 3 has been accomplished entirely in the two villages long occupied by me, and partially in the one that I am watching, and it is under way in the village I have just occupied. A census of the population has been made, and the movements of civilians are being kept under such close watch that repeated contacts with strangers are practically ruled out. Two dark spots remain, however: the delivery of mail and postal money orders is made by a man who has a post-office box at Tizi Ouzou and is sure to be a rebel agent. I have been unable to control the mail. Also I cannot prevent the population from contacting the rebels at the Saturday market in Tizi Ouzou. Cleaning up this town and especially its market is well outside the scope of my authority.

Point 4 needs to be more accurately defined. In my mind, to pacify the population means to identify the minority which is still favorable to us, then to use it to destroy the hostile minority and to control and rally the neutral majority. By this definition I am obliged to admit to total failure, with a single exception that happened in these very last days. I had been unable to receive the slightest tip on or denunciation of agents. All my efforts to identify friends and foes were in vain. Using the means of pressure at my disposal, I had implemented the "13-point process to rally the population," the population had made superficial gestures of bowing, but I had reached its main line of resistance, a line characterized by a stubborn wait-and-see attitude which I could not break. With a single exception, I repeat, to which I will come back later because it illustrates one of my principal points.

Certain local and purely fortuitous factors made me hope for better results. Six months ago, the villagers from Ighouna, where most of my company is stationed, had been forced to leave the place as a punishment for an ambush that had occurred there. With the coming of the olive season, several villagers asked my permission to return to the oil mills and the houses near our camp. I told them that only those who gave me concrete proof of their loyalty would receive the permission. Within twenty-four hours the people in Igonane Ameur elected a village chief and eight councilmen, an affair that before had dragged on for several weeks. Living under the threat of expulsion, these people do whatever administrative tasks I request of them, but no more. Are there rebel agents in their village? Of course not. Have they ever seen *fellaghas*? Never, they stay quietly at home, they take care of their women and children, they till their fields. Have they ever paid taxes to the rebels? No, everyone can see how poor they are. But what about the wealthiest villagers? Well, they don't know, they have seen nothing, they have heard nothing. A wall of silence with no crack.

What are the reasons for this attitude of the population? It stems to varying degrees from racial hatred, from the combination of terror and mutual suspicion instituted by the rebels, and from a lack of confidence in France. Here are some significant illustrations of this state of mind:

- Private Boyer*, schoolteacher at Igonane Ameur, jovially asks his boys: "How's everything today?" Answers young Mourad, eight, who surely repeats candidly what he has heard at home: "Fine, but if we had guns and cartridges, we would have thrown you out long ago."

- An officer and a gendarme from Makouda, accompanied by local auxiliaries, disguise themselves as *fellaghas* and visit one night a man suspected of being a rebel agent. The women greet them with "hysterical" show of joy, according to the gendarme. They kowtow, they kiss the *fellaghas'* feet....

- Time and again, Kabyles say to me: "*Mon Capitaine*, we are not afraid of you, we fear the *fellaghas*."

To sum up the situation, points 1, 2, and 3 have been totally or partially achieved. It would be easy to accomplish points 2 and 3, their implementation requiring only a simple mechanical action that depends solely on matters of equipment and matériel: huts or building material to house the soldiers in the villages where billet facilities are nonexistent, a few more mules to supply the posts, a few more pieces of signal equipment. It is hard to understand why, in this experimental zone where our command has not been stingy with personnel, our action should be hamstrung all the time by a lack of equipment and money.

As for point 4, the critical, indeed the decisive one, which depends on political action, there has been failure. Were our battalion to leave the ZOK today, things would soon revert to their previous state. Our goal, to be sure, is to leave, but the area must first be in the hands of the Kabyle elite able to keep it for us.

II. Causes of the Failure and Some Remedies

War is the continuation of politics by other means. Everybody knows that. Revolutionary war is no exception to this rule. One might even say that, in this sort of war, military action is but a minor factor of the conflict, a partial aspect of the operation. Give me good policy and I will give you good revolutionary war!

The Communists with their class warfare, with their agrarian reform, possess at the outset an ideological level of action which allows them *a priori* to find cleavages in the population, and thus clearly to identify friends, neutrals, and enemies. The Algerian nationalists have another formidable lever, nationalism.

As we have no such lever with which to inflame passions to the point where reason is smothered, we are suffering from an initial handicap. Is our cause necessarily lost then? Not at all, for in every situation, whatever the cause, there will always be a favorable minority, a neutral majority, and a hostile minority. And the better the situation and the cause of one side, the more favorable to it will be the ratio of these three groups.

Provided we have a firm and continuous policy in which our action in every field—military, economic, psychological, etc.—could be integrated, it is possible, by using the technique of revolutionary warfare, to win this Algerian war. Our initial handicap, against which we are powerless, will merely make this struggle longer and more costly.

The principal causes of our failure at the level of execution—the only one on which we could pretend to exert influence—seems to me to be:

- lack of adaptation of our units to their task.
- lack of systematism in our actions.
- lack of firmness toward the population.

A. Lack of Adaptation of Our Units to Their Tasks

My company, of a light type, consists of four combat platoons of thirty men each and one command platoon. It has no heavy weapons to drag. Food being managed directly by the battalion, I am relieved of the main administrative concern. The company's office entrusted to a corporal works perfectly well with a minimum of paperwork. I can thus state that my company is admirably adapted to the nature of the *military* operations to be faced in Algeria. But my main task today is a *political* one. I ask therefore: "Where are my political officer, my propaganda team, my intelligence and security team; where are my reams of paper, my mimeograph machine, my portable movie projector, my cans of glue and paint?" This kind of personnel and equipment are just as necessary to me in this phase of pacification as were combat soldiers and grenades when the task was to destroy the rebel bands. Does it mean that I want an increase in my Table of Organization strength? Not at all, I ask simply that my company be organized differently with the same people, and that it be well understood that in this political phase it will no longer be burdened with purely military offensive missions such as combing, etc. My company ought only to do what is needed to ensure its own safety and the protection of the inhabitants in the controlled villages. It can afford to take what risks are involved in penetrating more deeply into the villages, for its safety will be ensured by outside intervention units.

The company is without any doubt the "unit of pacification." The platoon is too small and too much glued to its village, the battalion too large and too remote from direct contact with the population. The company should therefore be provided with the modicum of means necessary to its mission. But the higher the unit in the scale, the larger must be the proportion of means devoted to political action compared with those earmarked for purely military action. Yet my battalion has but one intelligence officer. Whatever his personal qualities, he is bound to be snowed under in a battalion responsible for a population of more than 10,000. There is, of course, nobody in charge of propaganda, no mimeograph machine, no movie projector (with the appropriate movies), no public-address system. On the other hand, my battalion recently received halftracks and motorcycles that nobody requested and which make it heavier and needlessly use up personnel.

It is also at battalion level that there ought to be a small commando able to take charge of the minor operations called for at this stage: an ambush on receipt of information, a raid to arrest an agent, etc. Although I would hate to deprive myself of personnel when a fourth of my men are regularly absent for one reason or another, I am ready to sacrifice a sergeant and four soldiers for such a commando. With the same contribution by the other companies, the battalion's commando would be twenty men strong, enough for its future tasks.

Would it be possible for the company as it is organized today to fulfill its pacification task? It would surely be great progress if the following two conditions were met: (1) if the company commander were given an assistant so that he could devote his attention to pacification, for to study the situation in a village, to concoct a plan, and to implement it requires time and leisure; (2) if his work were predigested by the higher echelons (see point B).

B. Lack of Systematism

This fault is obvious in our every field of action and leads to incoherent, uneven, and inefficient work.

(1) Our cadres and soldiers are not indoctrinated uniformly and at the same time. Yet we all understand how necessary this is. The fact that one leader or one man in a unit is convinced of the usefulness of pacification tactics, which is an operation of a new type, and understands the methods to be used, will inevitably lead to individual action, which must ultimately end in failure. Only in collective action lies our chance of success.

(2) Propaganda in all its forms—collective, person-to-person, oral, visual—is too often left to the initiative of the executants. The only instructions received regularly are those notes from the Psychological Bureau in Algiers, sent out only twice a month and then only in insufficient numbers of copies. This is not often enough. The density of the troops stationed in our test area justifies our considering a more intense

effort, the more so since it seems in the light of international events*
that this density cannot be maintained much longer.

Besides, these notes are limited in scope to the exposition of propaganda themes. It is just as important to explain in detail to the executants how to conduct this propaganda. Private Larue meets Makour
Ben Mohamed in the village. Starting from the usual "How are you?"
how is he going to lead the conversation to the question of French
Moslem solidarity and provoke discussion? Left to his own devices,
Larue will see the talk dying in banalities and salutations.

We ought to receive three types of propaganda notes:

(a) Notes on general themes: for instance, France's will to stay in
    Algeria, the mistakes of our policy in Morocco and Tunisia,
    the economic and social development of Algeria through
    France, etc. (one such note every fortnight).
(b) Notes on important current events: seizure of the ship "Athos"
    carrying weapons for the rebels, capture of the FLN leaders,
    slaughter of French civilians in Morocco, our reaction, etc.
    (one note a week).
(c) Notes on events of immediate interest, which do not need to
    originate in Algiers and consequently could deal with local
    events (assassination of an SAS officer at Tikobain, destruc-
    tion of a rebel band near Azazga, elections of councilmen in a
    village, etc.) (one note every day).

An instructor would not think of teaching his men only the
characteristics of the 60mm mortar; he readily understands the need
to explain also its technical and tactical uses. The same goes for propaganda, and more so, for it is an infinitely more delicate weapon.
Trusting the company commander, the platoon leader, if not the NCO,
to invent and disseminate themes can only bring disaster in most cases,
particularly in this trial-and-error period in which we find ourselves
now. Later maybe, when we shall all have reached an acceptable level

---

* A reference to the Suez Campaign.

of practical experience in propaganda, we can allow a broader margin of initiative.

Those who see in propaganda a simple instrument for stuffing the brain underestimate dangerously the people's common sense. We are dealing in Kabylia not with naive virgin minds but with people who have been abroad many times. We will not convince them with mere talk, but only with truth. We are not obliged, of course, to tell them all the truth. How do we inform them properly when we have not a single newspaper specially designed for them? If we do not inform them, others will, and against us.

(3) Our successes are not systematically exploited in our propaganda. In the days following the capture of the FLN top leaders, we should have shown newsreels to the population. Every *fellagha* who comes over to our side should be shown in the villages, as well as the prisoners. Whenever a battle takes place, delegates from the population should be brought to the spot to see for themselves. What is the use of our successes if they remain largely unknown to the population or known only in the abstract?

The foregoing paragraph shows how necessary it is that at *quartier*, sector, and zone levels an officer be made responsible for propaganda, be aware of all the activities of his unit, and be inspired to use every opportunity, including even our defeats, to make propaganda.

(4) There is no concrete, precise program of action incorporated in a time schedule. Note that the only time such a program was imposed—the famous "13 points process"—it was easily carried out. Everyone knew exactly what to do and in what order.

(5) In the units stationed in villages, which consequently live a rather static life, there is no program for the day that would assign regular hours to studying the propaganda notes and to going out into the village street to make the census, and the like.

(6) Having refused the help of Communist technicians (thank God), the rebels are not shining with organizing talents. In particular, indications are that they have left the children out of politics. They will sooner or later see their mistake. Meanwhile they afford us an unhoped-for chance to win over the young minds. I am not suggesting that we regiment them or turn them into informers, but that we gather

them in schools and, outside the schools, keep them busy with games and sports, and teach them rudiments of civics and hygiene, in other words, that we spread scoutism in the villages. And what better cadres for this task than the scout leaders from France with their experience, their traditions, and their dedication?

The French who lived in Indochina through the last World War remember how the Vichy youth organizations captivated the young Vietnamese. It is not through the fault of these organizations that things turned out so badly later.

(7) We have opened schools in the villages. I have two schools now in my *sous-quartier*, with a total of 160 boys and girls. The teachers are soldiers, they are hot for their task, and they do their best to teach the kids how to read, write, and count. We ought to use these schools to implant a few civic germs in the young brains. But for that the teachers should at least receive specially prepared guidelines on civic matters. And since this is very long-term work, it cannot be improvised by amateurs.

(8) Individual successes or failures are not being exploited for the benefit of all. I apologize for giving a personal example. I have divided the Igonane Ameur village into as many parts as there are teams in the platoon stationed there, each team being responsible for its part. Each team leader carries a small notebook in which he writes down the propaganda theme of the day, the name of the villagers to whom he has expounded the theme, how long he talked, and the reaction of the listener. It is a mechanical and superficial method, of course, but I don't know of any other, and I would be happy to know if other methods have been tried elsewhere and with what result. This one affords me rapidly a rough and superficial idea—I have no illusion that it is more than that—on the state of mind of the villagers.

I would also be happy to know what have been the results of soft or harsh methods in other villages.

How to disseminate the individual experience? By holding frequent meetings of the *sous-quartier* commanders and the village detachment leaders.

(9) The absence of a summary code for infractions and fines is one of the most serious deficiencies in the execution of our mission. To

pacify my *sous-quartier* I must impose a certain policy on the inhabitants, by persuasion or by firmness. Thus, in order to control the population efficiently, I have been obliged to forbid villagers to leave the village for more than twenty-four hours without my permission and to receive strangers without my permission. I do not refuse permissions except for good reason; I only want to check the movements. When one day two Igonane Ameur villagers left for France without asking me, I was forced to react. I inflicted a fine of one sheep, which was immediately slaughtered and distributed to the poor in the village. Was this fine too heavy or too light? I have no idea. What kind of punishment was imposed elsewhere in a similar case? I don't know. Perhaps some kicks in the pants, or a sermon, or forced labor, but probably not the same sanction. As news spreads quickly through the bush telegraph, villagers cannot fail to notice that such and such a village is firmly handled, another harshly, a third weakly. Thus put together, our actions seem to them inspired by our mood of the moment, whereas we ought to impress on them that we are acting according to a well-thought-out plan that leaves them no room for maneuvering.

C. Lack of Firmness

So long as Kabyles say they fear the rebels more than they fear us, those among them who are favorable to us—and they surely exist—will never dare come out. So long as they avoid a commitment, we shall not succeed in pacifying Algeria. The problem is clear, and there is no way around it.

If we want the pro-French Kabyles to come out, it is necessary to punish in exemplary fashion the rebel criminals we have caught in order that the pro-French elements no longer fear reprisals. The rebels' flagrant crimes must be punished immediately, mercilessly, and on the very spot where they took place.

It will be objected that our judiciary apparatus is slow and rigid, that in our system the accused is moved to the tribunal and not the tribunal to the accused. Yet if no reforms are made, some counterinsurgent cadres will inevitably be induced to take matters into their own hands; they will be tempted to administer justice themselves, on the sly, thus losing the benefit of the example which is one of the chief props of justice. And what of the terrible side effect of hasty, illegal executions on the morale of our troops? After all, we have no professional killers in our companies.

Not all our opponents, fortunately, are candidates for the firing squad. Our interest commands that we isolate the masses of rebels from their leaders, and the only policy by which we can divorce them from each other is embodied in the formula: "punishment for the criminals and the unrepentant, leniency for those who repent sincerely." I feel it necessary to add that it is up to the rebel to provide the proof of his sincerity, and the easiest way consists in giving information on his leaders and accomplices.

To implement such a policy would require a minimum of facilities, namely camps where prisoners may be won over with the help of a serious program of information and propaganda. An enterprise of this sort cannot be carried out at the level of small units in the field, at least not at this stage in our pacification work. Later on, maybe, when all the villages will have been purged and when pro-French leaders will have been placed in positions of authority, it will be possible to win over the hostile elements locally without isolating them from the population.

It will be objected again that I am suggesting Communist methods. Not in the least, for I am well aware that we would be unable to implement such methods even if we wanted to, since we have no totalitarian state structure. But between total action and total inaction there is a wide margin where humanity and common sense can play a part compatible with the spirit of our institutions.

I have noticed that the mere mention of the word "pacification" to a group of soldiers, whatever their rank, usually brings forth deriding smiles. Many of them seem to think of pacification as the distribution of candies to the children and smiles to the old people. We certainly must show the carrot in our left hand, but only if we brandish the stick in our right hand. If skepticism about pacification is prevalent today, it is due to the fact that the stick has been too inconspicuous until now, or used too haphazardly and without a plan.

There are two ways to show the carrot. We can make the Algerians promises of magnificent progress, starting from what they have today. We can promise, for instance, that we will bring electricity to their villages or build a new reservoir. But I know enough to fear that we will not be able, in general, to make good on our promises, for we will always run up against the famous question of appropriations. Is it not better then to deprive the inhabitants of part of the material and social benefits we have already brought them, and to restore these progressively as they co-operate? Are not peace and the return to normal conditions the soundest of all promises?

Although I have already gone into considerable detail, I think it would be useful before ending to give an account of a concrete case of the destruction of a rebel political cell in a village, a success made possible because I resigned myself to using harsh methods, disregarding my own abhorrence of police work.* This case constitutes the exception mentioned at the beginning of this report.

> November 1956
> Captain Galula
> Commanding the 3d Company/45th B.I.C.
> S.P. 86.836 AFN

---

* The story of the purge in the village of Bou Souar is related in great detail in the body of the main report, pp. 115–124.

Appendix 3

The Technique of Pacification in Kabylia

By the spring of 1957, my ideas on counterinsurgent warfare had been sufficiently tested to have proved workable. As we were still being left to our own devices, with no clear instructions on how to pacify, I wrote the following report for the benefit of my colleagues.

The ideas contained in this report were embodied in the Challe Plan (actually drawn up by General Salan) and became the basis of our counterinsurgency doctrine in 1959–1961.

I.

The mechanics of subversive war—the war imposed on us in Algeria — have already been explained with enough accuracy so that it is not necessary to recall them here. What we intend to do is to outline a process by which we can smother the rebellion and thus achieve victory.

Principal Aims

1. Every conflict is above all a contest of will between two camps. Whatever the inequality of the contending means, a camp with no will to win is lost. We will then assume, for the sake of this study, that our camp wants victory.

2. Our main war goal—the one, in any case, which rallies the majority of French public opinion—is to keep Algeria French in one form or another.

3. Whatever the formula chosen to that end—assimilation, federation, etc.—it is perfectly obvious that it can be implemented only if France leans on the minority among the Algerian Moslems who, by sentiment or self-interest, favor the French presence. It will be up to this minority, selected, tested, organized by us, to help us, first, to rally the majority, which is neutral, and eliminate that minority which is hostile, and then to implement the chosen political formula.

4. The problem amounts to identifying this favorable minority and then gradually giving it a share of power and responsibility.

5. The most elementary analysis of the present situation in Algeria reveals that this pro minority, although it exists, does not show up; terrorized or influenced by the rebels, it has melted with the neutral masses. Thus, we may divide the Moslem population into two classes:

- a basically hostile active minority;
- a majority whose feeling extends from benevolent neutrality to hostile neutrality.

6. Under these conditions the pro minority will emerge only once it has been fully assured of the firmness of our intentions and once the con minority has been, if not destroyed, at least paralyzed.

7. This result can be achieved by a series of well-defined political-military operations, the implementation of which is within the reach of the executants, each operation being a step toward victory. Here is the general scheme:

   (a) in a selected area, concentrate enough means to destroy or expel the large rebel bands.
   (b) leave in the area enough troops to prevent a return of the large rebel bands.
   (c) establish these remaining units in the main localities.
   (d) establish contact with and control of the population.
   (e) destroy the rebels' political cells.
   (f) set up locally elected provisional authorities.
   (g) test them by imposing on them tasks which will compromise them seriously in the eyes of the rebels while linking them with us through substantial moral and material advantages. Create, in particular, self-defense units.
   (h) discard the "soft," and keep the "activists" who have emerged.
   (i) group and train the activists in a new political party.
   (j) while controlling them, give them all our moral and material support so as to enable them to win over to the common cause the neutral majority.
   (k) with the pro minority plus the neutral majority, eliminate the irreducible enemies while striving to win over the ordinary followers.
   (l) order having thus been restored in the selected area, repeat the scheme elsewhere. (It is not necessary for point (k) to have been achieved before starting in a new area.)

8. This method, spread out in time, can also be spread out in space. It thus offers the advantage of our being able to respect the economy-of-forces principle. While a major effort is made in the selected territory, we can count on our action in other areas to do no more than prevent

the rebels from developing. A look at the present situation in Algeria—except along the Tunisian and Moroccan borders which are special cases—shows that this objective is attainable.

9. Besides, once the selected area is pacified, it will be possible to withdraw from it an important share of our means and to assign them to neighboring areas, thus spreading like an oil slick on the water.

10. The method has a certain irreversibility. In particular, as soon as point (e) has been achieved, the rebels will not find it easy to rebuild their cells; and once the activists have emerged and are exerting their power, chances are that they will be permanently committed to us.

11. This step-by-step method allows control of its implementation at every step.

12. It is a concrete method, easy to understand and to make understood, easy to implement and to make others implement.

13. One final advantage derives from the fact that the method has been tested through point (f) in a certain area of Kabylia, and with obvious success. Since this area was selected at random, there is *a priori* no reason why the method could not be repeated elsewhere with as much success.

14. The experiment remains to be completed in its entirety. Given the fact that point (e) is the most important and the most difficult to carry out, and that it has been carried out, one can hope that the remaining points will not offer insuperable difficulty and that the rest of the experiment will only result in minor modifications of the method.

The Allocation of Missions

1. As indicated in paragraph 7 above, the proposed method consists in a series of political-military operations. Is that to say that some, like points (a), (b), and (c), must be entrusted solely to military authorities and the others to civilian authorities? Not at all. The implementation of the political points, from (d) to (l), requires manpower that only the Army can furnish, and material means that the civil administration

alone can supply. It follows that the entire task must be implemented by the Army, and that control and responsibility as of point (d) must eventually pass to the civil authorities. All along, army and administration efforts must be co-ordinated. Co-ordination will be the easier to achieve if civilian and military components are united by a single doctrine for action. In any case, there must be a rule that the territorial command has primacy over the operational one.

2. Experience shows that the company is the unit of political action directed at the population. The platoon, the elementary unit of implantation, is too small and too close to the village, the battalion too large and too remote from the population. It is the company, then, which will have to conduct the operations as of point (d).

3. The implementation of the plan involves a few police operations, particularly at point (e) (destruction of the rebel political cells). For obvious psychological reasons, these operations, with such unpleasant aspects as confining people, interrogating them, etc., must not take place in the *sous-quartier*,* but should be carried out at a place remote from the local population. The regiment, or sector, seems appropriate for the centralization of this activity (see paragraph 6 below).

4. Points (a), (b), and (c) are the responsibility of the Army Corps area or at least of the zone, depending on the size of the means to be needed, especially in the initial step (a) (destruction or expulsion of the main rebel bands).

Adaptation of the Units to Their Mission

1. The first three points are of a purely military nature. As one approaches point (d)—i.e., the political part of the program—an important part of the units must adapt themselves and their organization to their new task. The other part will be kept as it is and serve as a striking force specifically charged with preventing the return of the large rebel bands

---

* The *sous-quartier* is the area entrusted to a company, the *quartier* to a battalion, the sector to a regiment, the zone to a division. Algeria was divided into three Army Corps areas.

and, in liaison with the static units, with tracking the rebel remnants that are left after point (a) has been implemented.

2. The adaptation of the static units to their political role consists essentially in making them lighter in armament and military equipment in order that personnel so freed may be used, with the appropriate equipment, in such police and military tasks as controlling movements, census-taking, collecting intelligence, conducting propaganda, giving medical care, teaching, taking care of youth organizations, and providing economic aid.

3. The higher the unit in the military scale, the more important the proportion of personnel and means devoted to political missions compared with those earmarked for military action.

4. The company, elementary unit of political action, must be given an executive officer on whom the company commander can rely for all routine matters; it must have a propaganda team, an intelligence and security team, and a team of secretaries.

5. The battalion must have a commando charged with any raids that are spontaneously ordered, and with the important arrests within the *quartier*; it must have two intelligence officers instead of one, with the necessary secretarial staff; one propaganda officer with his secretaries, including an artist equipped with a mimeograph machine; two doctors rather than one, for the battalion doctor cannot at the same time devote himself to the soldiers and to the population.

6. At regimental level there should be a field-rank officer in charge of co-ordinating the political action in the sector; and an officer in charge of propaganda, who must have all necessary printing and public-address equipment, a photo lab, a team of photographers, a mobile movie projector, several designers or painters, several intelligence and security officers, and a detention center where suspects can be kept, interrogated and sifted in decent conditions. The battalion does not lend itself to this kind of work, and still less so the company; besides, the number of suspects arrested in a *quartier* is too small to justify the building of such a center at battalion level; since it is indispensable that

the suspects be interrogated by those who collected the intelligence on them and made the arrest, nothing prevents the interested company or battalion from assigning to the sector's center, for the time of the interrogation, an officer familiar with a given case.

7. In pacification work political action is a command prerogative. It is, therefore, the direct responsibility of the general commanding the zone. It is a great psychological mistake to have labeled it "psychological action," thus confusing it with propaganda, and to have dropped the responsibility into the lap of a bureau of psychological action. In classical warfare, the leader reaches his decision by studying logistical and tactical factors. In revolutionary warfare, the additional political factor enters into the picture, and with great force. It would seem logical, therefore, for the chief of a large unit to rely on a "political" bureau, which should be on the same level in the organization chart, and carry the same weight, as the other staff bureaus.

Propaganda would then come under such a political bureau. In this sort of conflict, propaganda is important enough to be entrusted to a high-ranking officer who would be aware of, and take part in, every decision and would operate very close to the zone commander. Only under these conditions will he be able to plan the propaganda, to seize and to exploit at once every opportunity—and most opportunities arise very suddenly—that our successes or the failures of our opponents may present.

8. Among the means needed at division level and above, we can list:

- a loudspeaker and pamphlet company.
- a squad of newspapermen, photographers, and cameramen, who would be in charge, among other things, of publishing a newspaper designed for the local population.
- an engineer company in charge of providing technicians and cadres for public works (road building, water works, construction of schools, agricultural co-operatives, sanitation works, etc.). Experience shows that private enterprise cannot be counted upon; on the other hand, the Algerian administration's technical services, having lived too long on normal,

peacetime appropriations, do not have the necessary personnel and equipment for the fast utilization of the money appropriations suddenly allotted to pacification work.

- a camp where prisoners can be rehabilitated.
- a group of female social-welfare employees who would work on the Moslem women, whom we have too long neglected.
- a field hospital to reinforce the existing medical facilities available to the population.
- a sport and youth activity unit.

This list is by no means exhaustive.

Adaptation of the Minds

1. Subversive war is a special kind of war. And equally special is pacification, which is its answer. Both require operations of a particular type that differ from conventional warfare. This is why, if the pacification units must be adapted to their new missions, so also must be the minds of cadres and troops.

2. In the same way that there exist among the Algerian population a pro minority (even if it dares not show its feelings), a neutral majority, and a hostile minority, we find among cadres and troops some who believe in new pacification techniques, a majority who ask to see before being convinced, and a minority who will never believe. One can identify these groups by merely disclosing to them the method which is the object of this study.

3. If we had all the time we wanted to pacify Algeria, we could think of convincing the majority of cadres and troops before going deeply into pacification work. It would obviously be better to do so. Unfortunately, the war in Algeria has already lasted too long, it is costing too much, and the French public may become tired of it while the rebels, in spite of their setbacks, can still endure.

4. These considerations prompt us to approach concurrently the work of pacification and the indoctrination of our cadres and soldiers, with

the help of the minority that is *a priori* partial to the new doctrine. The duty of the leaders is to identify the members of this minority at whatever echelons they may be, to support them by giving them responsibility and power; to punish those who sabotage the task; and to assign to the striking forces those unable to adapt themselves.

II.

We will now take up in detail the various points of the scheme suggested in Part I.

Selection of the Area

1. In classical warfare, the objective is either the destruction of the enemy's forces or the conquest of his territory. In the so-called "revolutionary" wars, **the objective is the conquest of the population.** This implies that the area of operations must be selected principally on the basis of demographic and social characteristics. Classical factors such as terrain, communications, etc., while still cogent, will not be taken into consideration here.

2. Of all factors related to the population, its density is the most important. The denser the population, the higher the stakes for both the rebels and us. To the extent that our means allow it, we must aim at the areas where the population has the greatest density.

3. Next to enter into the account is the foothold that the population offers to our action, particularly in the economic field. The more rustic and autarkic the local economy, the less well can we operate. For this reason, and contrary to what one might think looking at the rash of terrorism in Algerian towns, the towns are precisely the places which offer us the best foothold. The ideal would be a string of towns separated by desert.

4. The degree of infection would have importance only where our means were too weak to allow us to cope efficiently with the most infected areas. As this is not the case in Algeria today, it is well to start with those very areas, thus going from the difficult to the easy.

5. The smallest cleavage within the population facilitates our action, whether the line is real or artificial, whether it is ethnic, linguistic, religious, political, or otherwise. Age and sex are lines of cleavage, too: we can lean on the youth against the old, and vice versa; on women against men (and this seems promising considering the state of slavery in which Moslem women are kept in Algeria).

6. The population's access to our propaganda—not to be confused with its susceptibility to it—is a very important factor in the initial phase, the phase where we are operating alone because we have not yet found and used the local pro minority. The areas where knowledge of French is most widespread, therefore, offer us the best opportunities.

7. These factors combined point to Kabylia as the key to the rebellion problem in Algeria.

Size of the Area

1. There is an optimum for the size of the operational area as well as for that of its population. Below it, rebel influence could too easily continue to penetrate from the outside; also the population subjected to our efforts, conscious of not being numerous enough and therefore feeling too exposed, would never dare follow us all the way. And above the optimum size, our efforts would never be sufficiently concentrated.

2. *A priori*, and taking into account the lessons of the limited experience quoted above, the minimum diameter of the area should be from three to five days' march, that is, from 100 to 150 km. in mountainous terrain.

3. Among the customs of the Algerian rural population there is one that we must absolutely take into account: the weekly market, which is a natural focus of agitation and propaganda. It would be futile to expect decisive results in the countryside as long as these *souks* (markets) have not been purged and controlled. We must cope with them first.

Destruction or Expulsion of the Large Bands

1. The goal of this operation, although important in itself, is essentially to allow the development of further action. For the static units must be able to spread to the maximum without risking the loss of a small post or even the danger of repeated harassing, the psychological effects of which on the population would be disastrous.

2. If the large bands are destroyed, well and good. If they are merely expelled from the area, the result is still good. The difficulty to avoid

is the dislocation of the large bands within the area, with the rebels retaining their strength in diluted form.

3. The *bouclage* and *ratissage* technique, a purely military operation, is too well known in Algeria to deserve comment here.

4. During this step, our propaganda must aim:

(a) **at our units:** to limit the material and moral damages wrought on the population by the operations.
(b) **at the rebels:** to incite them to accept the fight or to leave.
(c) **at the population:** to persuade it to remain at least neutral, by pointing out that our success would mark the beginning of its liberation, while continuing rebel activity would mean more operations and consequently more suffering.

Implanting the Pacification Units

1. This step cannot be considered as long as the goal set for the preceding step has not been reached. It is obviously to our interest to concentrate the maximum of means and personnel on the destruction of the large rebel bands; if they are withdrawn prematurely from this mission, the overall task cannot be fulfilled efficiently and rapidly.

2. Once the bands have disappeared, armed remnants will be left. Their complete destruction requires active co-operation from the population, a co-operation which the population will give only in the final stages of pacification. This does not mean, of course, that the static units shall not hunt and track the remnants through small-scale operations and ambushes, but these operations must never distract them from their primary mission, which is and remains pacification.

3. The large bands must not be allowed to return or to make incursions into the area. To prevent this is the job of part of the units participating in step 1 above; they will be kept in the area as striking forces. The personality of their leaders, especially their reactions to the proposed pacification policy, shall be the decisive factor in selecting the striking units.

4. Pacification is about to begin now. Let us evaluate roughly the density of troops necessary. The effort, started at the center of the selected area, will naturally decrease toward its periphery. In a region as mountainous and as heavily populated as Greater Kabylia, for instance, a company, which must ultimately be spread over five posts, can cover an area with a diameter of 3 to 5 km. and three to four thousand inhabitants; a battalion can cope with a diameter of 10 to 15 km. and ten to fifteen thousand inhabitants. A town of five to ten thousand people will require no more than a company, it being understood that the company will not be responsible for dealing with any general uprisings, which would obviously exceed its capacity. Toward the periphery the troop density can be reduced by half to three-fourths.

5. Because of the high degree of co-operation needed between civil and military authorities, the boundaries of the *quartiers*, sectors, etc., must coincide at all cost with the administrative ones, even if militarily it makes no sense. In the center of the area, there should be an S.A.S. officer for every *quartier*, a *commune mixte* administrator or *sous-préfet* for every sector. We must avoid a situation that has arisen too often, in which the population of a village subjected to the pacification work of a company comes under the jurisdiction of S.A.S. from a different area.

6. Until the purging of the political cells has been completed, it is neither necessary nor even useful to distribute the company's platoons throughout the *sous-quartier*. For as complete and precise as might be the orders received by the *sous-quartier* commander, nothing will teach him as much as practical experience acquired through action in the field. He will inevitably make mistakes at the beginning. Better to make them on a limited number of villages and inhabitants. To start with, one village with most of the company and another village under a detached platoon will be quite enough.

7. The units must be stationed, not in positions having a military value, but where the population lives, be it in valleys or on counterslopes that afford limited views.

8. The deployment must not be made according to a set and systematic pattern, with a set and unalterable strength (such as a platoon) for

every village. It must tend toward the ultimate solution: one gendarme and his four men. In no case must land or localities be left belonging to nobody.

9. Every territorial commander whose units are deployed in posts must organize his own reserves. These reserves, however, should not be allowed to remain idle when they are not militarily engaged. For a reserve without territorial mission is a dead weight, except at such high levels as in the zone or army corps area. The reserves, therefore, must be employed in pacification work, with the proviso that the territorial commander is free at any moment to draw on up to 50 percent of their strength.

10. During the initial stage of deployment, propaganda must be directed as follows:

(a) **at cadres and soldiers:** to explain the broad lines of the new form of warfare, insisting on the reasons for our actions, on the necessity of a systematic and concerted effort, on the usefulness of drawing lessons from everyone's experience. The leader at each echelon can begin to select the most apt among his subordinates.

(b) **at the population:** to convince the people that, while our deployment causes difficulties and some hardship because of our requisitioning houses and billets (though the requisitions will be compensated for by rental), the purpose of our deployment is to protect them from the rebels as well as from the damage they would suffer from large-scale operations, which are no longer necessary now. Our deployment testifies also to our will to stay; we would not spread out further if we were contemplating leaving.

(c) **at the rebel remnants:** to convince them—through pamphlets and rumors and by way of their families—that they are lost because they have been cut off from the population. If they want to give up, we are ready to accept them back on the conditions already publicized in Algeria.

Establishing Contact with the Population

1. What is to be done here is not to "chat" idly with the population or to distribute candies to the kids. The goal is to impose firmly our will on the people so that they fully understand that might, order, and bread are on our side; to control their activity and movements so as to cut them off from the rebels; and finally to obtain a modicum of intelligence for the purge that comes next.

2. During this step our action must be concentrated on the village or villages already occupied; action on the others will be conducted at a distance, but always with the same personnel, the personnel who will occupy them later. Stability is indeed a powerful asset.

3. See in Annex 1 a process for establishing contact which has been tested with success in a sector of Kabylia.* Implemented blindly, to the letter, it has changed within weeks the climate in thoroughly infected villages. This 13-point program can easily be carried out in two or three weeks. Take advantage of the program to note who among the villagers shows hostility and who shows good will. Beware of him who offers help to the counterinsurgent forces; he may very well be the chief of the rebel cell, for such a man alone would dare show himself.

4. Open a school in every occupied village with one or two soldiers as teachers. Ask the villagers to send at least one 8- to 12-year-old boy from each family; next, ask that girls attend school in the same way (if room is lacking, the boys in the morning, the girls in the afternoon). Every absence must be justified.

5. Open a dispensary. The battalion's doctor can train a medic in two weeks. Initially the villagers will not dare to come for treatment. Locate the sick and force them to come, except the women.

Control of the Population

1. Control of the population is established in the course of establishing contact with the population.

---

* Quoted in the main study, pp. 92–93.

2. Every occupied village will be divided into two, three, or four parts. Each is placed under the responsibility of a team, which will speed up the acquaintance process.

3. A census will be carried out in this way:

(a) A number will be painted on every house.

(b) All males above fifteen will be counted individually. They will be called to the post, where census forms are filled out.

(c) Families will be counted at home. Every family head will be given a census booklet with the name, birthdate, and sex of every family member, and the indication "present" or "absent." The result, as well as the name of the family, will be painted on the outside wall. Example:

No. 54 (house number)
ABBOUD (family name)
8/7 (total no. of persons/no. actually present)

(d) Using the individual census form and the family booklets, a general list will be established for the village (one copy for the local S.A.S). The census will provide statistical information such as the number of school-age children, the destitute, workers away in France, veterans, etc.

4. Keeping a census up to date is a never-ending job, but it must be done, checked, and amended. Villagers who have given false information will be punished.

5. On the very day that the village is occupied, the two following rules must be announced to the population:

(a) Nobody will be allowed to leave the village for more than twenty-four hours without permission.

(b) Nobody will receive a stranger, whatever the reason, without permission.

When announcing these rules, the population must be told that they are precautions taken in the very interest of the villagers.

Permissions will be granted as a rule, unless there are specific reasons to the contrary. The idea is merely to keep informed about movement in and out of the village. Permissions will always be issued in written form, with duplicate copies that are kept at the post. It will be easy after a while to detect suspicious movements and visits.

6. Every rule is bound to lead to violations and consequently to punishment. This is an imperative law: better to issue no order than not to punish a violation. Experience shows that the most effective punishment is the heavy one, and the one which bears no relation to the actual offense; provided it is given with a certain amount of fanfare, experience proves that it will not be necessary to inflict the same punishment twice in the same village. The one that has succeeded best is the fine of a sheep, or 8,000 francs, or fifteen days of labor. The sheep will immediately be slaughtered and distributed to the destitute in the village; the money received in lieu of the sheep will serve to buy medicines or schoolbooks. Fines must in no case be of benefit to the troops.

7. Collective punishment is to be avoided at all cost. It only serves to unite the population against the authorities, more often than not without benefit. It is different, however, when the population as a whole has to suffer indirect hindrance and harassment on account of this or that rebel or agent; then the blame is laid on a specific person.

8. At night, in addition to the classical ambushes, it pays to set up this type of ambush: three soldiers with submachine guns will enter a house, any house, check the identity of the dwellers against the family booklet, and remain in ambush inside the house for two or three hours. Probabilities are that they never will catch any rebel, but the story will spread and will contribute to cooling off the eagerness of the villagers to supply billets for the rebels. Houses located at the outskirts of the villages are best suited to this type of ambush.

9. On the occasion of a weekly market, make a check in the following way: send a team of soldiers from the village near the market to a road that the villagers have to pass through; stop all villagers, check the amount of money they are carrying to the market; when they return, check again. If they cannot explain what they have done with their

288 Pacification in Algeria, 1956–1958

money, chances are that they are tax collectors for the rebels. If the method does not always succeed, it will at least complicate things for rebel agents.

Gathering Intelligence

1. As the population is still under the rebels' influence and grip, it would be futile at this stage to count on getting a mine of intelligence that would lead to the destruction of the local cell, although, of course, a lucky strike can always happen.

2. The period of intelligence-gathering can be considered as completed when information has been received on a number of suspects, no fewer than three, not more than five. A month, at the most, is the time usually needed for it.

3. There are two ways to collect this information:

(a) Systematically give as much consideration as possible to the veterans and those who receive pensions from the government, invite them for lunch or dinner, give them rides in Army vehicles, consult them, etc. However, do not take their loyalty for granted; Ben Bella, to give one example, is a veteran who fought very well with us in Italy in 1944. There always will be one or two men in the group who will finally talk.

(b) Except for the veterans, do not grant any favor to anyone without counterservice. Suppose, for instance, that a villager wants to open a grocery store; nothing is wrong with that on economic grounds, but grocery stores are generally a source of supply to the rebels. Consequently, permission to open the store can be granted only if the villager is trustworthy; and we can be sure of his loyalty only if he proves it by giving information on the rebels. The same goes for the villager who requests permission to go to France.

These two approaches do not pay off the first day. They must be applied with patience. They have been tested with substantial results.

Propaganda During This Period

This stage is the most delicate of all because of the demands it makes on the energy, the imagination, and the perception of all, leaders as well as soldiers. After it, the other stages of the pacification process will seem easy and mechanical. Propaganda will here play a primary role.

1. **Cadres and soldiers** must be persuaded to make propaganda, more propaganda, constant propaganda through their behavior and through their words. The local events will provide enough examples (successes and setbacks) to illustrate the necessity for it.

2. **Propaganda directed at the population** will be conducted in visual and oral form.

   (a) **Visual propaganda:** In addition to the various posters affixed at random on the houses, set up two propaganda panels, one at the door of the army post where many visitors will come, the other at the liveliest spot in the village, such as the *djemaa* or the fountain. Post on these panels the daily paper, the posters issued by the Psychological Warfare Branch, and the pictures taken by the soldiers in the village itself. Since the villagers are, or claim to be, illiterate, admit no visitor to the post until the sentry has read and explained to him the contents of the panel.

   (b) **Collective oral propaganda:** Assemble the male population once a week, on the day and hour that cause the least hindrance to them in their work. Take a roll call and note the names of the absent, who must subsequently be interrogated. Read and comment on the important articles in the week's newspapers. Then develop the main theme of the meeting. Comment on local events. Answer one or two questions, if any. Finally, announce the time for the next meeting. These meetings must be carefully prepared; beware of the sudden inspiration. Speak loudly so that the women in the nearby houses can hear what the talk is about; they can be counted upon to spread the news to the other women. Always be frank or say nothing; never lie, otherwise the rebel agents will soon find it out and ruin your credit.

(c) **Individual oral propaganda:** This is the more efficient form of propaganda, because in public meetings the villagers will not dare reveal their feelings and thoughts as long as the village has not been purged. It must be conducted as follows: assemble every morning the unit occupying the village; explain the topic for the day, which is related to a recent local event; deploy the various teams in their respective sections of the village; have them hail passers-by and explain the topic to them, abruptly if necessary; the team leader will note the name of the villager, the length of the talk, and his reaction. This last bit of information will soon enable us to form an idea of the feelings of the villagers.

3. **Everybody takes part in propaganda work,** including the villagers, who will be ordered to affix and maintain the posters on their houses; the village militia will be employed during the day in posting the newspaper on the panels, and in painting slogans on the walls (it is not necessary for this that they be literate). In the course of public meetings, ask some of the villagers who visited the post to repeat the contents of the panels read to them.

4. The two **key themes** used with the **population** are:

(a) Our cause is good, the rebels' is bad; the situation is favorable to us, bad for the rebels.

(b) The population must choose between the rebels and us. To our friends, all the benefits that France can grant; to the uncommitted, nothing; to our enemies, the full brunt of the troubles we can make.

Concrete examples having a considerable value, take advantage of all the events related to these themes that have happened in the village or in neighboring locales; do not hesitate to bring in and display the people involved, such as the first volunteer among the villagers, a captured rebel (hence the necessity for making prisoners), the young girls from the nearby school, etc.

5. During this period the efforts of the *sous-quartier* commanders and their subordinates must be **supported by the higher units**, in particular by moving in specialized teams from the loudspeaker and pamphlet companies, by visits of psychological warfare experts, by sending exhibits of captured rebel weapons and documents, and the like.

6. The aim of **propaganda directed at the rebels** will be to dissociate the leaders from the followers, as in the preceding period, but more aggressively than before. Thus we should not hesitate to release some rebels unconditionally, but we must first bring them back on a visit to their village. We are strong enough to be able to afford such minor risks.

7. Next, our **psychological action on the youth** must take the form of organizing sports and games, fixing up a sports field, launching a program of civic education, and initiating various minor efforts for the benefit of the village.

8. **Psychological action** must also be used **on the women** through medical care and visits by female social workers. Direct references to politics and events are to be avoided.

Destruction of the Rebel Cells

1. The rebels' strength derives from the support they are able to exact from the population through the local political cells. These cells, moreover, are the instruments that rebuild any bands that, by chance, have been destroyed or expelled. Pacification is therefore impossible as long as the cells themselves have not been destroyed.

2. The technique for their destruction which is offered here has already been put to the test and is based on two facts that are obvious to everyone who has worked, however briefly, on pacification in Algeria:

(a) The population fears the rebels more than it fears us. It is futile, consequently, to expect that persuasion and reason will loosen the tongues.

(b) The entire population, willingly or by force, and to varying degrees, participates in the rebellion. Everyone therefore knows the members of the political cell in his village; and everyone has his share of guilt toward us.

3. Under these conditions, the purge can be undertaken as soon as three to five suspects have been spotted.

4. Arrest the suspects, who must be kept isolated from each other. Interrogate them firmly. But at the same time encourage them to talk, on the one hand by guaranteeing complete discretion, on the other hand by pretending to see in them minor culprits who were forced to act by the rebels and to whom we are prepared to be generous. If we are lucky enough that no cell leader is among the group of suspects, they will talk readily within ten days at most.

5. Once their statements check—and this is why it takes at least three suspects—we will then have the names of the cell members plus a list of accomplices. As the classical tendency of suspects is to accuse well-known rebels who have already disappeared, we must not be satisfied with that. It is also very important to attempt to find out through these interrogations who are the villagers hostile to the rebellion.

6. We are now in a position to throw out our net. However, if we do not have the means to occupy the interested village, it is better to do nothing. For, if the village were left unoccupied, the rebel remnants would soon recreate another cell and the whole task would have to be redone. Do not hesitate to take risks in occupying the village (experience shows that the risks are small, anyway); if necessary, assign to the village a unit smaller than a platoon.

7. Arrest now the people who have been denounced and interrogate them, beginning with the "soft" ones. When things have been sorted out, you will have found two to four leaders, the "tough" ones, who will have to be punished, having failed to make a full and sincere con-

fession. As for the others, they must be released if they promise, on the one hand, to behave well, and, on the other hand, to accept the responsibility of informing us on every suspicious activity in the village; otherwise they face detention in a camp. This deal must, of course, be offered not to the group as a whole, but individually and discreetly to each prisoner.

8. Provided that the operation has been conducted decently, with no unnecessary harshness and no personal animosity, the released prisoners will harbor no ill feeling toward us because of their arrest; they will be only too happy to get off so lightly when rebel propaganda has told them to expect the worst from us. This is why it is imperative that this operation be conducted from beginning till end by trustworthy and intelligent cadres.

9. Propaganda during this step:

(a) **To cadres and soldiers:** explain the necessity for acting in this manner; stress the nefarious role of the cells; point out that, although this police-type of activity is unpleasant, it liberates the population in the manner of a surgical operation and causes less damage than ordinary military operations.

(b) **To the population:**
— from the time of the arrests until the release of the prisoners: we are only after the leaders, the others have nothing to fear from us; in any case, the population has been given the choice whether to be with us or against us. (Authorize a few visits to the "soft" prisoners.)
— after the release: as was promised, the leaders have been punished and the others freed, a treatment which is our policy toward the armed rebels as well. The village, now occupied, has nothing to fear from the rebels any more; consequently, fence-sitting and a wait-and-see attitude will no longer be tolerated.

(c) **To the rebels:** their cause has suffered another setback; the population, free now of their terror, will work in peaceful construction. It is still time to join. We have proved our generosity and our firmness.

Installation of Provisional Elected Officials

1. The municipal reform now underway in Algeria is an excellent thing in itself. Implementing it before the purge is completed, unfortunately, amounts to placing the cart before the horse. Where this happened, we found during the purge that the president of the local special delegation, and many of the delegates, had been selected by the leader of the rebel cell.

2. Whether a special delegation exists or not, one must be set up as soon as the purge is over. The *sous-quartier* commander must not interfere in the choice of the members; he must, on the contrary, leave the entire responsibility to the population; were he to influence the elections in the slightest way, he would find himself in a bad position for getting rid later of any elected members who proved worthless. In any case there is little to worry about, for after the purge the population understands very well what kind of leaders ought to be elected.

3. There are no objections to the candidacy of people who were compromised during the purge. They can be expected, on the contrary, to be transformed into models of co-operation.

4. Propaganda on the population during this step will stress the following points:

- the importance of the elections and of the careful choice of delegates; the better the choice, the better the population will be served; delegates are not merely agents between us and the population, they are also the population's advocates vis-à-vis the authorities.
- the provisional nature of the elections; final elections will have to wait until peace has been restored in all Algeria. Meanwhile the provisional delegates and the population will start their apprenticeship in democracy under the guidance of the authorities.

Search for Activists

1. Pacification now enters a constructive stage. We cannot govern in Algeria without the co-operation of the population. Co-operation is always the result of an active minority's influence on the masses. This is as true for the most democratic regime as for the most totalitarian. The problem, therefore, is to identify and set up in power the activists who are for us. As long as we have not done so, all that we have accomplished up to that point remains useless.

2. All the measures taken during this step are aimed at this goal. It is the more urgent to do so since the government has offered to hold elections three months after a ceasefire; were the rebels to accept that offer today, we would risk losing Algeria because we have not yet found and set up in time the activists in our favor.

3. We will probably have no time to develop activists, but time only to discover the existing ones and to test them before the elections. We can be more ambitious if we win the elections.

4. There is only one way to discover the activists, and there is nothing mysterious about the process: it is to set tasks to a group of people and see who does them best, with the most spirit and good will. This is why the municipal reform, considered not as an end in itself but as a means, is very useful. By giving immediate responsibilities and an active role to the elected delegates, it allows us to assess them rapidly; the same thing is true for the self-defense organizations, the best members of which will be selected later for the *harka*.

5. An activist is moved by passion, by reason, and by self-interest. Given the long subversive effort of the rebels, who have always insisted on the racial aspect of the Algerian problem, we cannot count on passion; indeed, it will generally militate against us. We are thus left with the appeal to reason, and our principal points are that we are the stronger, that the rebels' cause is lost, and that the example of having given independence to Tunisia and Morocco, far from inciting us to grant it to Algeria too, has opened our eyes and persuaded us to stay in Algeria. We are left also and above all with the appeal to self-interest: having on our side might, administration, and money, we can do all for those

who side with us, on condition, naturally, that these powerful assets not be wasted by granting our favors and beneficences to all with no discrimination. If roads and schools are to be built, we will build them in those pacified areas where the population works hand in hand with us, and only there; social welfare funds, visas for France, etc. also will be distributed there. In other words, we must reward the good people and reward still more the better ones. These rewards will not be given on the basis of promises or words, but solely on the basis of concrete actions: this mayor, who has led the population of his village into disobeying FLN strike orders, must receive a reward; that one, who has done nothing, will be replaced and thus will lose his salary.

6. While the stick was our main instrument in the preceding stages, the carrot will become the principal one from now on. This is not to say that we must no longer show the stick. The weapons (authorizations, passes, privileges, etc.) and the money are not lacking. But the higher echelons, whether civilian or military, must understand the necessity of supporting promptly and to the utmost the cadres who work directly with the population. An unkept promise is a disaster, delayed appropriations ruin weeks of propaganda, and a missed opportunity for a spectacular gesture will never be found again.

7. The municipal reform and the setting up of self-defense organizations are worthy of a separate discussion, which would, however, exceed the limits of this analysis.

8. Propaganda:

(a) **toward the population:** it must be designed to force the population out of its noncommittal attitude. Construction begins now; it will be pushed to the extent that the population cooperates. (Here is the place for a good bite of the carrot: initial appropriations for the new communes.)

(b) **toward the activist:** it must be designed to encourage them. Describe the new Algeria and the role of its cadres; for those who are not tempted, others will be who realize where their best interests lie.

Grouping and Educating the Activists

1. In the same way that the armed forces are the instrument of war, a political party is the instrument of politics. By definition a party unites the militant. It is futile to look for militant supporters if they are not to be so grouped, for without a party they will be poorly utilized or not utilized at all.

2. A party is built around a program. The government has defined its program in Algeria; it is enough to launch the party above partisan domestic quarrels.

3. Its creation, its role, and its constitution are problems for the government, and will not be discussed here.

4. When this absolutely essential step has been decided upon, the pacification cadres' duty will be to recruit followers, to educate them according to government instructions, and to control them if such are the instructions.

5. The mission of the armed forces will then have ended for all practical purposes. With the armed forces and an active political party, the fate of the remaining rebels will have been sealed.

III.

A Few Concluding Remarks

1. Better a bad plan than no plan at all. The one offered here has the merit of existing.

2. A better plan will certainly be found, but only if one draws on the experience of all the cadres who, whatever their position, were confronted with the various problems raised by pacification in Algeria. They are groping now. One has the right to grope, but not forever. For instance, one can imagine ten methods to make a census, but there is surely one better than the others; this is the one that must be chosen, widely applied, and generally imposed.

3. The best way to assess a plan is to test it in the field. Its imperfections will then appear. It is only thereafter, when the plan has been revised, that one has the right to apply it everywhere. For the experience to be profitable, it must be conducted, not only with the leaders in charge of implementing the plan in the test area, but also with a crowd of observers, who will follow the experiment from A to Z, will take part in its final critique, and will subsequently move elsewhere, not to implement it directly themselves but to instruct and control the local cadres.

March 21, 1957
Captain D. Galula
Colonial Infantry
45th B.I.C.
S.P. 86-836 AFN